Home Decorating and Design

**Edited by
Barbara Chandler**

TREASURE PRESS

Contents

First published in Great Britain by Octopus Books Ltd
and distributed by Marks & Spencer Ltd

This edition published by Treasure Press
59 Grosvenor Street
London W1

© 1977 Hennerwood Publications Ltd

ISBN 0 907407 87 0

Printed in Hong Kong

Written by Barbara Chandler
and
Tony Byers, Carolyn Chapman,
Emmy Hettener, Jose Manser,
Doug Marshall

1. Understanding Your Home

Home for most people is the centre of their lives. It is their greatest capital asset, something they will want to maintain in good condition and to make look attractive. Even where property is rented the occupier will naturally want to take pride in its state and appearance. Regular maintenance and decoration add to a property not only value but deeply satisfying pleasure and enjoyment.

But whether we live in old homes or new homes, detached, semi-detached, terraced houses, chalets, bungalows or flats – or any other type of property – it is helpful to have some idea of its age, construction and special qualities before embarking on any project – whether to alter or decorate.

Below we look at some of the many varieties of home which you will find around the country, with an analysis of their special qualities. In each case we describe a furnishing and decoration scheme that suits that type of home. These examples are just that – examples – and are only one way of doing things. The reader will find many detailed alternatives presented later in the book.

THE GEORGIAN ARTISAN'S COTTAGE
These are small houses, probably with two rooms downstairs and two upstairs. Staircases have coarse banisters and the window bars are thicker than in a grander Georgian house, but they share the elegance which goes with that period. The rooms, though small, are of a good shape, the windows well-proportioned and there are no unnecessary embellishments to the outside. These are therefore simple houses to decorate, both inside and out. The original small iron fireplaces are probably still intact and the inevitable kitchen extension tacked onto the back of the ground-floor will be sympathetic to the straightforward architecture of the original. A bathroom may already have been made in one of the upper rooms. If not, this is a splendid opportunity to make a spacious dressing/bathroom with fitted carpet and clothes cupboards (thus leaving plenty of space in the bedroom). Small and light looking furniture looks good in this type of house. The currently fashionable stripped pine (the best of which dates from the Georgian period) would suit it well. To avoid swamping the delicate charm of this little house, curtaining and carpets could be light and pretty rather than rich and sumptuous.

THE GEORGIAN OR EARLY VICTORIAN TERRACED HOUSE
These are large houses originally built for prosperous merchants or professional men. Nowadays many of them are split into flats, but the quality remains – large, shapely rooms with high ceilings on the ground and first floors, tall sash windows with fine glazing bars, an elegant staircase, often approached through an arched hallway and, in the main rooms, simple marble fireplaces. These houses are a delight to the eye. There are, however, some drawbacks. Large rooms, particularly those with high ceilings, are expensive to heat; boarded floors need carpet; the areas to be decorated are vast and often include ornamental cornices and large panelled doors. Small modern furniture would look overwhelmed in such a setting. Decoration, both inside and out, should be simple, preferably in the white and pale pastel shades loved by the Georgians. Heavy patterned wall coverings should be

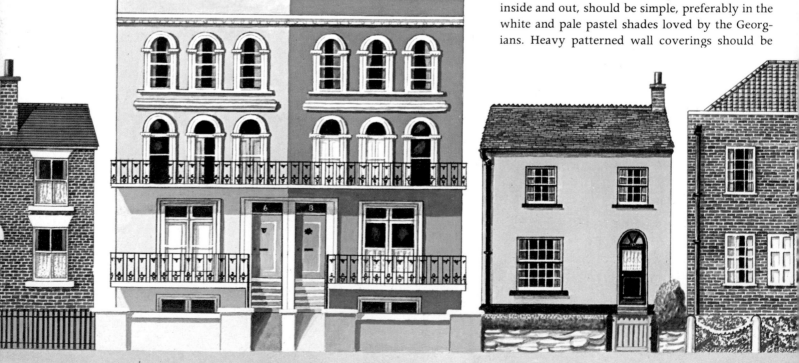

avoided although deep warmly coloured walls would also be very suitable. Try and spend as much as you can afford on heavy curtains and fitted carpets which will retain warmth as well as giving the house an immediate 'furnished' appearance, and then as money permits acquire the best quality modern and second-hand furniture. This combination will give the grandeur and style such a house deserves. The same principles apply even if you have only a flat in such a house.

THE VICTORIAN TERRACED VILLA
These were built in large numbers in and around industrial centres. They vary in size, some being back-to-back, some large with long gardens. But they all share a solidity and respectability reminiscent of the Victorian age. Modernized and well cared for, they can be pleasant places in which to live. Unrendered brick construction can make decoration simple as only the window frames need be painted. They may look better if neighbours could agree to paint them in a uniform pattern, rather than break the rhythm of the terrace with discordant colour schemes. Inside, they are larger than they appear, with two rooms opening off a narrow hallway which then leads to a kitchen at the rear. Rooms are a manageable size to furnish and to heat but sometimes difficult to clean as they have mouldings at ceiling level and around the central light fittings. Originally there was no fixed bath but one of the three or four bedrooms can be converted into a sizeable modern bathroom, or a simpler alternative, if you do not want to sacrifice a bedroom, is to add a bathroom to the back of the house. The kitchen is usually large enough to become a pleasant family kitchen/breakfast room. Often there is an outside lavatory. This type of house can look attractive if, as was done in Victorian times, the walls are lined with warm-coloured patterned wallpapers (which will conceal

uneven plastering) and furnished with buttoned sofas, thick rugs and velvet curtains. It also looks good with walls in white, or plain bright colours, and simple, inexpensive modern furniture.

THE EDWARDIAN SEMI-DETACHED HOUSE
The reign of Edward VII was a prosperous era. Rooms and staircases were spacious and building was of a good quality; yet many of these houses are not too large for the modern family. Doors are wide and heavy, skirtings are deep, hallways are tiled and often there is an inner front door to keep out draughts. The exterior with elaborate eaves, loggias and porches may not be easy to decorate, but there may well be a large front garden and possibly a conservatory, both of which were fashionable at the time. The kitchen may be dark (Edwardian ladies only visited the kitchen, they did not actually work in it!) in which there will be an alcove, formerly occupied by the range and now ready to take the modern cooker, and probably a scullery which can become a laundry room. One of these houses, with walls painted cream throughout, dark stained woodwork, inexpensive fitted cord carpeting everywhere and medium sized modern furniture, complemented by brightly coloured window blinds would combine the advantages of Edwardian quality with modern simplicity and comfort.

THE 1930s SEMI-DETACHED HOUSE
Half-timbering, tile hanging, leaded lights, glass front doors with sun-ray glazing bars and green roof-tiles are all featured, sometimes in the same pair of houses. Do not let this discourage you, however. These houses have a great deal to offer. If the outsides are decorated, perhaps in pairs if neighbours are co-operative, using soft colours to play down any discordant features, the effect can be very pleasing. There are usually large gardens with room for a garage to be built if required. Rooms are spacious by present-day standards. Kitchens became smaller as the decade advanced and most

It helps when you are planning a decorating scheme to understand the character of your home or flat. Here we illustrate some of the many types of home found in Britain today. From left to right: Victorian terraced villa, early Victorian terraced house, Georgian artisan's cottage, modern mock-Georgian house, local authority estate house, 1930s semi-detached house and a typical high-rise block of modern flats.

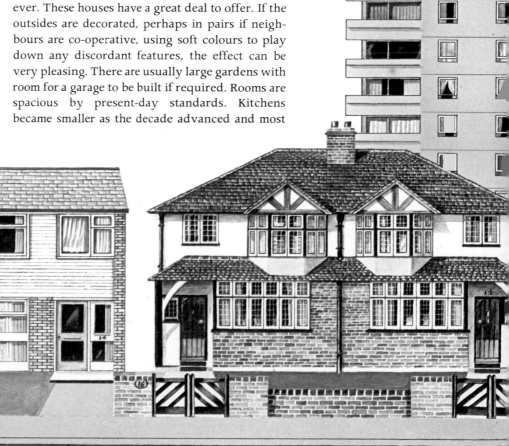

THE POST-1945 SEMI-DETACHED HOUSE

Exteriors are simpler now, though often the builder has applied horizontal boarding which if painted can be tiresome to maintain. Most houses will have a garage, sometimes reached from the house by a covered way. Because of their simplicity they can take strong colour treatment outside, and indeed often benefit from it. Rooms are likely to be smaller than those of a prewar equivalent but on the ground floor there is probably a vinyl tiled or wood block floor, both bathroom and kitchen will be fitted and require little if any extra treatment, and many houses will have central heating and bedroom cupboards. These houses are easy to clean, with flush doors, no picture rails, windows of a manageable size and, with new smooth plaster board on the walls, easy to decorate. Sometimes hardwood window frames which need no decorating make things even simpler. Furniture can be small and modern, but not of the hard, sharp-edged variety. Upholstered furniture can be soft and squashy, tables circular, with edges curved. Rugs may be soft and long-haired in bright, warm colours, with curtains in small but strong prints.

THE TERRACED TOWN HOUSE

These houses tend to be over-bright on the exterior often clad in coloured plastic panels or hard red tiles. Because this cladding needs no decorating and because the windows are often in narrow horizontal bands across the façade, they (the windows) are easy to paint, most of the work is capable of being done from inside. The guttering and drain-pipes are often plastic and this can obviate the need to decorate them. Often of three-storeys with integral garage and laundry room on the ground floor, many have open-tread staircases (which need no carpet) and a semi-open-plan living room and kitchen on the first floor. With fitted bedroom cupboards, fitted kitchens, sometimes two bathrooms, central heating and tiled floors, these houses are easy to run and furnish. A young couple setting up home could manage with little more than a bed and two or three floor cushions for the start of their married life. 'Serious' furnishing could consist of comfortable unit seating – the main room is often big enough to take a large L-shaped arrangement. You may need window blinds, as these houses can be overwhelmingly bright on occasions. Do not think that just because you live in a modern house, you have to stick to modern furniture. You could use a solid, round, second-hand table and chairs in the dining area with, perhaps, a large, richly patterned rug on the floor, to give an unexpected atmosphere to the room.

THE MOCK GEORGIAN HOUSE

These come in all shapes and sizes and some are better copies of the originals than others. All have proved very popular. Usually they are built of red

Older Victorian and Edwardian houses have many attractive period features which can be exploited cleverly for furnishing and decorating schemes. Here, the original wooden fireplace has been meticulously stripped of old paint and varnish to reveal the beauty of the natural wood. Original picture rails and ceiling cornices have been left intact. Making the most of the original features of a house can save you money for the cost of renovation and minor restoration is usually less than that of wholesale replacement.

had coke-fired boilers, but they can easily be updated with standard kitchen units. There is always a bathroom, usually with a separate wc. Windows are a reasonable size so that they are not too expensive to curtain; but floors are mainly boarding, with wood blocks in the hall of better quality. Fireplaces are ornate brick or tiles, often over-large for the room size. It might be an idea to replace them with a simple hole-in-the-wall. Nowadays, with central heating, many back and front rooms have been made into one large sitting/dining room which can look stylish if inexpensive modern furniture is mixed with, for example, Edwardian inlaid pieces. These latter are small enough to fit into such a house and give it a quality it is inclined to lack. Both the ubiquitous French windows leading to the garden and the waist-high bay windows should have floor-to-ceiling curtains across the whole wall and not the curious chopped-off arrangements which are too often seen. Bedrooms will seem more spacious if fitted with built-in cupboards and a dressing table across the obsolete chimney breast.

or brown brick. This type of house looks particularly smart with white paintwork. Black or dark green or some other dignified and unobtrusive colour would suit the front door. Inside are all the comforts the Georgians never knew – central heating, fully fitted kitchen, often two bathrooms, and usually a large sitting room and small dining room. Fireplaces vary; some are attractive pine reproductions; bedroom cupboards often have mouldings and decorative knobs to evoke the Georgian period; and windows are usually of the tall sash variety. Georgian walls were pale and the furniture simple and elegant; this should be one's aim, avoiding heavy patterns and strong colours. Curtains can be in silky materials, carpets plain and short haired and reproduction furniture kept in period. It would be interesting, though, to have uncluttered modern furniture of good proportions.

THE TOWER BLOCK FLAT
The exterior decoration will not be the concern of the occupant, but he will enjoy the splendid views and will probably have a balcony with plants which he can enjoy from his armchair. Windows will probably be large and pivoted so that they can easily be cleaned from inside. The flat will have a tight plan, that is with no space wasted on unnecessary corridors and hallways. There will probably be vinyl tiled floors, a well-fitted bathroom and kitchen with plenty of cupboards throughout. Of course there will be no fireplace but good central heating. Housework should therefore be minimal and this may compensate for some of the disadvantages – for example, the somewhat characterless, box-like rooms. These could be enlivened by distinctive decoration. Bright colours are required – or even a mural. Zany furniture can help. Prints for the walls and house plants in tubs and hanging baskets will make up for the absence of a garden.

THE LOCAL AUTHORITY ESTATE HOUSE
Many of these are extremely well designed. The floor-plan is expertly worked out to give maximum usable space in the minimum area. Usually there will be a separate cupboard for dustbins, a place for the pram in the hall and a kitchen which both looks and functions well. There will invariably be insulation to conserve heat. Houses built during the affluent sixties will be particularly spacious and well equipped. Outside there will often be a lavish planting of trees, plants and lawns around the estate. Inside, the simply-shaped rooms with tiled or wooden floors, the fitted bathroom and kitchen offer a choice of decorative options.

Owning a modern style of house does not necessarily preclude a traditional style of decoration and furnishing, if this is the style you prefer. In this modern house a traditional look has been achieved by the arched wall-storage units and the effect is heightened by the choice of antique and reproduction furniture. The most important thing about your home is that you should like the style you choose; our pictures and text are merely intended as suggestions and a starting point.

11

ABOVE *You can create your own Victorian or Edwardian stained glass effects with translucent coloured glass paints and self-adhesive leaded strips.*

BELOW *The floorboards have been sanded and sealed to protect the newly-revealed natural wood. This is a simple and inexpensive floor treatment.*

Construction

The way in which your house is constructed will directly affect the kind of cladding or decorative treatment you can give it. So be sure to find out exactly how it is built.

● *Floors:* These are likely to be of concrete or timber construction. The former – generally found at ground level in houses built before 1930 and at all levels in blocks of flats – gives you complete freedom for any type of surface finish as concrete does not deflect under a heavy weight.

A suspended timber floor of joists and boards, chipboard or plywood, which is common in most modern houses, has greater limitations since it tends to deflect under a heavy weight. Stone, quarry tiles and similar materials should not therefore be used but all the lighter coverings are acceptable although old boards may require a hardboard lining.

● *Walls:* External walls are usually of brick or block construction. After plastering they can be decorated internally in almost any manner, from tiling or tongued and grooved panelling to wallpaper or hessian. Or they may simply be left unplastered and sealed, or sealed and painted. They are strong enough to support any type of fitting, for example wall-hung cupboards, in almost any position. Internal walls, if they are not structural (i.e. providing support for the rest of the house) are either lath and plaster in the case of older houses, or of timber stud construction if built within the last fifty years. Here again any type of decoration is possible, including tiling, as long as the plaster surface is relatively even and sound. Wall cupboards can also be fitted, but the fixing must be to the studs (timber uprights) with long screws. It is no good trying to make fixings in the plaster void between the studs – the whole lot will probably collapse! Find the studs, which will generally be 400mm apart, by tapping the surface. Occasionally, however, one will come across an internal wall of about 50mm blockwork. Avoid hanging *anything* heavy on this.

● *Ceilings:* In newer houses these are of plasterboard; in older houses they are of plaster. There will be concrete or timber joists above. Light fittings will be inserted between the joists, but if it is planned to hang something weighty – a basket of plants, a hanging wicker chair or a chandelier – then make sure it is suspended from a joist and not from the gap between, or disaster will follow!

● *Roofs:* Pitched roofs are covered in tiles, shingles or slates or sometimes, where the pitch is shallow, in sheet metal such as copper or lead. Flat roofs may be covered in felt or asbestos tiles. Never – as one might be tempted to do in the case of a flat-roofed extension – put heavy earth-filled plant tubs or furniture on them without first checking with an expert that the roof can bear the weight.

Glossary

Manufacturers and builders and even shop assistants use words for products or architectural features whose meaning is perfectly obvious to them but which can seem like a foreign language to many people. The following is a useful list:

Airbrick: perforated block built into wall to ventilate room or underside of wooden floor.

Architrave: collective name for the various mouldings covering the joint between frame and wall surface around a door or windows.

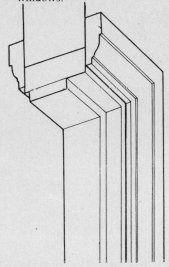

Balusters or banisters: upright sections that support the handrail of a staircase.

Balustrade: row of balusters.

Batten: strip of wood used for example for fixing slates, tiles, cupboards, panelling etc. to a wall.

Beading: semi-circular moulding used to cover a joint.

Blocks: hollow or solid blocks of materials such as clay, gypsum or concrete, which are used like bricks, but are larger, cheaper and quicker to lay.

Carpentry: structural woodwork, i.e. joists, beams.

Casement window: one which is hinged to open along its vertical edge.

Cavity wall: a wall consisting of two leaves or layers of brickwork with a gap between.

Chasing: groove cut into wall or floor to take pipes or cables.

Chipboard: man-made wood-like boards made from compressed waste wood and resin.

Cladding: any material fixed as a non-load bearing covering to structure of building.

Clapboarding: overlapping boards of wood used as cladding.

Conduit: metal or plastic tube for encasing cables.

Cornice: an ornamental moulding running round the wall at ceiling level.

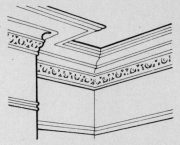

Course: continuous horizontal layer of bricks or blocks in a wall.

Coving: concave surface which bridges the join between floor and wall or between ceiling and wall.

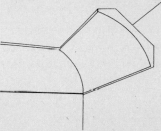

Dado: panelling above the skirting on lower half of wall.

Damp-proof course: layer of material such as slate, polythene or copper, which is impervious to moisture, laid in wall to prevent rising damp.

Dormer window: one which projects vertically from a sloping roof.

Downpipe: pipe carrying rainwater from gutter to a drain in the ground.

Drian cock: tap fixed at lowest point of water or heating system through which water can be drained.

Dry or wet rot: timber decay caused by fungi.

Eaves: horizontal overhang of a roof projecting beyond wall of the house.

Facing brick: good quality brick used for visible part of wall.

Fair-faced brickwork: good quality brickwork with neat pointing, left unpainted.

Flashing: watertight metal seal (used for example around joint between chimney and roof).

Flush door: door faced in hardboard or plywood, with no moulding or panel.

Footings: wall foundations.

Frieze: that part of the wall between the cornice and picture rail; in modern terms it can refer to any decorative strip, usually paint or paper, applied round the walls of a room.

Gable: triangular upper part of wall at end of pitched roof.

Georgian wired glass: thick glass embedded with square mesh wire for safety reasons.

Glazing bar: wood or metal bar holding panes of glass in a window.

Grout: thin mortar used to finish joints between wall or floor tiles.

Jamb: the vertical side of an archway, doorway or window.

Joinery: finished woodwork, i.e. doors, shelves, etc.

Joist: beams supporting floor or ceiling (usually timber).

Key: roughening of a surface so plaster, mortar, adhesive or paint can grip.

Lagging: insulation round pipes and water tanks.

Laminated: made of thin layers stuck together.

Laths: narrow, flat strips of wood used as the backing for plaster.

Lattice window: one with small diamond shaped panes set in lead.

Lining paper: thin, plain paper (usually white or cream) used on top of plaster as base for wallpaper.

Lintel: beam over door or window structurally essential to bear weight of wall above.

Load-bearing wall: part of basic structure of house which cannot be removed without insertion of a joist.

Matchboarding: boards laid side by side and used as cladding.

Mortar: mixture of cement, sand and water used for bricklaying.

Moulding: applied decorative beading (as on architrave).

Oriel window: one which is in a projecting bay supported on brackets.

Party wall: wall separating two houses or flats.

Pebbledash: exterior finish consisting of small stones embedded in rendering.

Pediment: a low pitched gable over a door or window.

Pointing: facing mortar between joints of brickwork.

Primer: sealer used on exposed metal, wood, plaster, etc., before painting.

Rafters: sloping timbers which support the roof.

Rendering: covering of cement or plaster on external wall, so that brick or stone is not visible.

Reveal: the return face of wall inside a window or door opening.

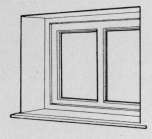

Riser: vertical piece in a staircase, connecting two treads.

Rising butts: hinges which lift a door as it opens to clear carpet.

RSJ: rolled steel joist, inserted as an essential support after the removal of a structural wall.

Sash windows: vertically sliding windows.

Screed: the layer of plaster or concrete which finishes a floor surface.

Shingle: wooden roofing tile.

Skirting board: wooden board fixed to foot of wall to prevent scuffing.

Size: liquid seal applied to walls before papering.

Soil pipe: vertical pipe carrying sewage from house to drain.

String course: moulding or narrow projecting course running horizontally in exterior wall of building.

Structural: all parts of building which carry weight.

Stucco: smooth exterior plaster.

Stud wall: non-structural internal wall made of timber posts and cross-bracing, lined on either side with plasterboard.

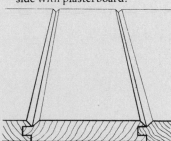

Tongue-and-groove: joint made where tongue on one edge of board fits into groove on another.

Tread: surface of a step on which the foot is placed.

Wainscoting: wood panelling up to dado height.

Winder: triangular or wedge-shaped tread forming bend in stairs.

2. The Potential of Space

It is possible to go into two identical houses, even next-door neighbours, and for one of them to seem spacious and airy, the other cramped and claustrophobic. And the reason is simply that, by design or otherwise, one family has used space to the best advantage, while the other has squandered it. Space is a precious commodity and the struggle to conserve, extend and exploit it should be planned like a military campaign.

First, make a list of your needs, and this particularly applies when looking for a new home. While listing them, try to reassess them, to get away from any preconceived notions. Think about the life your family *really* leads now or will lead in the next few years, and not about the life it would like to lead, or likes to pretend that it leads, or used to lead at some earlier time.

For example, if you eat all meals in the kitchen except for Christmas dinner and two children's parties a year, why have a table and six chairs taking up the space of one whole room which is not used for anything else? If the children have no playroom and their toys clutter the sitting room,

the hall and the stairs, turn the dining room into a playroom, at least until they are older when you can think again. The table can go and the chairs be redistributed to lead useful lives elsewhere in the house; for special events borrow or make a trestle table. Meanwhile your house will have recovered from the tide of large toys which once engulfed it.

So get that list going in a really objective and realistic way. For example, it could start as follows:

1. How often do we entertain friends?
2. At what time of day do we have tea, Sunday lunch, evening drinks, etc?
3. Is the kitchen used as a family room or just a place for cooking and washing up?
4. Is the bathroom overworked? Why not have an extra washbasin, wc or even a small shower-cubicle in another part of the house?
5. Is there any room which is over-used, e.g. kitchen, sitting room?
6. Are bedrooms used only for sleeping at present despite the fact that they may be centrally heated throughout the day?

Once real needs are determined, set about trying to satisfy them as suggested above. Rooms which are little used can be converted to another purpose to ease the pressure elsewhere. A small, seldom used guest room, for instance, can become a bathroom if there is at present a large family clamouring at the door of a single bathroom each morning and evening. A warm bedroom can have a sewing area fitted up for dressmaking, thus clearing at least one corner of a crowded family sitting room.

BELOW *Removing interior walls, as in this two-up and two-down 19th century cottage, creates a feeling of spaciousness. Remember, however, that you may lose some privacy and that it would be necessary to heat the whole area in winter. You might also be left with a series of alcoves and chimney breasts which would require the kind of unified treatment shown in order to be successful.*

RIGHT *Modern mirror panels have been cleverly fixed above the radiator to make the room seem larger. You can also find attractive mirrors, such as the one on the left, in second-hand shops.*

BELOW RIGHT *Cleverly designed furniture can help to make the best use of limited floor space. The seating units shown are raised on a simple wooden platform which conceals pull-out beds.*

And a room too small to be used as a bedroom can perhaps become a laundry room for the family whose kitchen is used as a place for eating and talking as well as cooking, where there really is not sufficient room for such items as a washing machine, clothes dryer, ironing board and extra sink.

Fitted furniture can be used to make more space in your house. There are various ranges on the market, some free standing, some wall-hung on battens, and some with wooden panels which fix to battens and give the appearance of an attractive wood panelled wall. Prices vary as much as the designs but if you have only a little money it is generally possible to start off with a small unit and add cupboards and shelves as you can afford them. A range of such units built across one wall of the sitting room, filling in the alcoves on either side of the fireplace, will immediately provide a tidy home for all those things which previously littered the room and dispense with the need for odd little tables and cupboards elsewhere, giving the room a much more spacious appearance. The tiniest dining room or dining area, where there is barely room for a table and chairs and which is ludicrously cramped with the addition of a sideboard or serving table, will often happily take useful wall-hung shelving. There are some excellent designs of this type with various veneers, including black stained ash; they make a neat and unobtrusive storage and serving arrangement without using up precious floor space.

Heavy, dark furniture looks splendid in a large, high-ceilinged room, but if your rooms are of normal modern proportions, aim for small furniture with simple, uncluttered lines. Avoid overblown, bulky upholstery as this will give your room the appearance of bursting at the seams – and, anyway, small curvaceous armchairs and sofas are just as comfortable. Try to have furniture on light looking legs rather than coming down in solid panels to the floor. A room looks much larger if all the floor area can be seen and much of it is not obscured by solid bulk.

DECORATION

Solid, deep colours appear to pull in walls and lower ceilings quite markedly. So, too, will large, aggressive patterns on walls, carpets, curtains and upholstery. Keep to soft or pale colours and small, restrained patterns. If you are close carpeting, the same background colour carried right through the house will give a pleasant impression of continuing space. Chopping and changing colours from one room to another is discordant and emphasizes the smallness of each individual area.

Mirrors are great deceivers and they can be cunningly exploited to create an illusion of space. Try lining one bathroom wall with a mirror to double its apparent size; or put a mirror into an alcove to give a room an appearance of greater depth than

actually exists; or bring an outside view into a room by placing a mirror on the wall near a window so that it captures the view in its entirety; or butt a strip of mirror against the angle where two walls meet to make it look as though the room goes on – this is particularly effective if there is a horizontal stripe on the wall, a painted dado perhaps, to emphasize the illusion. The possibilities are endless, the cost relatively low in comparison with the effect achieved. Most local glass shops give an excellent service of cutting, drilling screw holes and delivery. Just be sure that your measurements are accurate and fix sturdy battens or wall plugs ready to receive the mirror when it is delivered.

It may be simple to think up grand schemes for alterations in this way. It is not so simple to be sure that they will work. Can this item be slotted into that space? Will there then be room to walk between it and the new sofa we were going to buy? The answer is – make plans. First, measure up using a steel tape. Then make a rough plan and fill in all your measurements on it. Rather than experimenting with expensive graph paper, buy a pad of tracing paper complete with a sheet of squared graph paper. Lay a sheet of tracing paper over the graph paper and then draw your house as it is, empty of furniture. Make an overall plan of each floor first, using a 1mm to 50mm scale, and follow this with a plan of each room including doors, windows, radiators and other important features. Use the largest convenient scale for this, probably 1mm to 25mm. Try out your new arrangements on paper, first in the individual rooms, then as an overall scheme.

You should be able to see whether space is being used to its best advantage without too much heaving and pushing about of furniture – or too many expensive mistakes. Include existing light and power points, as the positioning of lamps, television, hi-fi and so on is as important as everything else.

So far it has been assumed that your house is basically big enough for your needs, merely requiring some rearrangement. It may be, however, that after your efforts with sheets of tracing and graph paper, you reach the painful conclusion that you need more space, that what you have at present is just not enough. If you like your house and neighbourhood and do not want the expense of moving, consider alterations within the existing framework of the house or, more drastically, an extension of some kind.

INTERNAL CONVERSIONS

These can be quite minor. They might consist merely of inserting a serving hatch between dining room and kitchen. If the kitchen is tiny and needs to be made larger, consider removing the conventional hinged door which takes up a great deal of space when open, and replacing with a door which

16

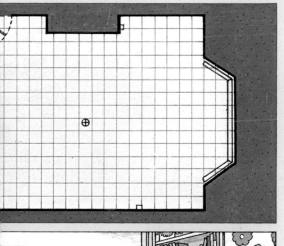

FAR LEFT *Partitioning the children's room is one solution to a space problem. You could give each child his or her own sleeping area, using a shelf unit or headboard as a room divider.*

LEFT *In older houses, taller rooms allow the building of platforms to create more room for living. You can use your platform for sleeping, leaving the space below free for a study area (as illustrated) or for storage or for a sitting or dining room. Alternatively, use your platform for high-level storage.*

BELOW LEFT *Whether you are moving in or only contemplating rearranging a room, it is best to start by making plans. The four illustrations show the stages in planning a room. The first step is to measure up (obviously it is easier to do so if the room is bare). Transfer the measurements onto a piece of graph paper (a scale of 1 to 25 is convenient). Make a note on the plan of all fixtures, such as sockets, light fittings, radiators and so on. Remember to include the sweep of the door. Experiment with arrangements on your plan. Here, planning shows that a sitting room cum dining room cum study can successfully be accommodated in the original room.*

folds back on itself. Bought ready to fit, and available in a variety of colours, they are relatively inexpensive. Consider also two-leaf swing doors, as in cowboy saloons; these are easy to construct for oneself with two ready made narrow doors bought from the local do-it-yourself shop and hung to the door frame on hinges. A sliding door is a space-saver too, but tends to be more expensive, especially the kind which disappears into its own framework. Sometimes a door can be removed entirely, especially if the house is centrally heated – for example between a kitchen and dining room (make sure there is a good extractor fan or food smells will permeate the entire house), or between a bedroom and its en suite bathroom, or between a tiny dining room and the hall. It is not sufficient merely to lift the door off its hinges and leave it at that. Widen the opening or turn it into an archway so that the rooms flow into one another and the eye is deceived into thinking there is actually more space when open, and replacing with a door which must be removed, the plaster made good and the opening decorated.

By erecting partitions two rooms can be made where previously there was only one. This is a useful device when there are too many children for too few bedrooms. Shapes and proportions are important. Never slice a room in half regardless of windows and ceilings so one is left with two gaunt spaces, much too tall for their size, each dimly lit by the chopped off half of a window.

Here is an example of a splendid partition built across the bedroom of two boys who had reached the age when they hated sharing. Their father made the partition himself. It is timber framed, lined with chipboard and then painted, with an individual writing desk fixed to each side. There are shelves for their books, fluorescent tubes fixed beneath the shelves to light the writing area, and lots of pin-up board on which they can fix post-cards, posters and other oddments. But the out-standing feature of this screen is that it only reaches to head height (about 1400mm) so that although the boys have a feeling of privacy, the pleasant shape of the room is preserved. The view on entering the room encompasses the whole ceiling and includes a complete window on each side of the partition.

A dining area can be carved out of a large kitchen by building a waist-high screen of kitchen units (also useful as a serving top) with a blind above from ceiling to cupboard top to be pulled down when the cooking stops and the eating starts. Or a study area could be made at one end of a long family sitting room by building a floor-to-ceiling partition (from timber framing lined with plaster-board) across half the room, and decorating it so that it looks like a real alcove wall. The student is then tucked away in his private area, screened from view and partially screened also from the noise of the family at the other end of the room.

Try also to bring into play some of the space which most of us forget. The cupboard under the stairs, for example, can, with the addition of a wash basin, a few pegs and a shoe rack, become a downstairs cloakroom instead of being a repository for old newspapers and the vacuum cleaner. If it is large enough it can have a lavatory too. Indeed, if you live in one of the Edwardian houses mentioned in the first chapter of this book there may be room for a shower as well. The smallest useful shower tray is only 700mm by 700mm and about the same amount of space again is needed to step out. Or remove the door under the stairs, and the space, with a comfortable seat and a shelf, could be a place for telephoning; or with rows of shelves and colourful plastic boxes on the floor it could be a capacious toy store; or it could even double as an occasional guest room if it were fitted up with a comfortable mattress disguised during the day by a suitable cover and large colourful cushions to remove the bedroom appearance.

Similarly a large landing cupboard could be turned into a small shower room for children if the household plumbing is reasonably close. The deep recesses on either side of a chimney breast often found in older houses tend to be so much wasted space if only filled with a couple of small pieces of furniture. In a bedroom, for example, why not incorporate them into a storage wall of cupboards,

ABOVE LEFT *Some buildings (this one was built in a Victorian Gothic style) can be gutted completely and the space inside reorganized.*

LEFT *In family homes, it is very pleasant to have a living area opening out from the kitchen, although separated from it. A waist-high division – either part of the original dividing wall, as here, or created with storage or kitchen units – works well.*

ABOVE *An extra room can be created by converting your loft. Such rooms, with their distinctive sloping ceilings often have great decorative character.*

RIGHT *The area under the stairs can provide a great deal of storage space.*

dressing table and shower. A 700mm square shower would certainly not overtax the space in a large old-fashioned bedroom. Landings were once icy areas to be crossed at speed. In a centrally heated house they deserve better treatment. A small study area could be made from a row of wall shelves with one slightly wider at desk-top level, a comfortable chair and perhaps a screen to give a certain amount of privacy. Owners of lofty Victorian rooms could make better use of those heights – which take their share of heating. If the room is 3.5m or more high, build a bed platform reached by a ladder, with storage, sitting space or a desk and shelving underneath. Or run a bookshelf round two or three walls of the room above door height: accessible from a library ladder (a simple home-made affair), this would leave the lower walls free for other furniture and pictures.

Until now we have talked mainly about adding something in order to gain space. A more drastic method is to knock down. Once you decide to embark on work of that nature it is always essential to consult a reputable builder or surveyor to ensure that what is being removed is not structural. If it is, the project will entail inserting new structural steel or concrete beams to support weight. *Never* neglect to take professional advice about this type of undertaking. Space can be created by removing a wall between hall and living room, especially if a covered porch is added to the house to act as a draught lobby, or by removing a wall between kitchen and dining room if your life style favours cooking, eating and entertaining in a single room. If you have abandoned open fires for ever (certainly so far as bedrooms are concerned) you can bring more space to a small room by removing the chimney breast. Here again some form of alternative support is often necessary for the weight above, so consult a professional before removing even one brick.

If there are two lavatories, consider combining one with the bathroom, if adjacent, making a room spacious enough to house additional storage units thus giving more room elsewhere in the house.

Radical alterations such as these are, however, more than just a simple matter of knocking down. They involve making good afterwards – matching up cornices, replastering and considerable redecoration. And consider, too, the amount of privacy which is lost immediately a wall is removed.

BUILDING AN EXTENSION

This is an even more radical step, but if your space needs are too great, it may prove to be the only alternative to moving! Again, professional advice is essential. You may know how much extra space is required but a professional will best tell you how to achieve it.

He will advise you whether your extension comes within the bounds of permitted develop-

ment· without planning permission or whether planning permission is necessary. This is essential (*a*) if the proposed extension exceeds one-tenth of the floor area of the existing house or 50 cubic metres whichever is the greater, subject to a maximum of 115 cubic metres; (*b*) if you intend extending upwards so that your house will be higher; (*c*) if you intend to extend the face of the house fronting a road. If planning permission is to be obtained drawings must be submitted to the local authority. *Every* extension, however small, must conform to the Building Regulations and, in London, to the London Building Acts. Your local authority will advise. They may require rough plans of proposed alterations together with specifications of work to be carried out. A professional, e.g. an architect or a builder, may be able to relieve you of some of these legal and administrative responsibilities.

An extension must not only be well built, it must also work well and look good. Does the design allow the most efficient and comfortable use of the extension for your particular requirements? Will the windows line up neatly on the facade? Will the rooms be well proportioned, i.e. not too long for

the width? Does the extension connect smoothly with the house? Again the professionals can help you, but the more you involve yourself (discussing, supervising, controlling) the more likely you are to get what you want.

An extension can also be gained by using one of the proprietary dry-construction (ready-to-erect) rooms which are widely advertised. Some are not insulated and are little more than sun rooms – and that may be exactly what you want. Others are fully lined and insulated with various types of external cladding, such as wood, textured concrete or acrylic coated fibre board. They are delivered in post and panel form, with windows already glazed and need only to be erected by you or a local builder on a 100mm concrete base set on hardcore. These packaged extensions are a quick, clean and inexpensive means of adding an extra room or two to your house.

Do not forget the space in or on the roof. Attics will normally be in use anyway, their sloping ceilings contributing character to even the smallest room. But an otherwise neglected loft space is often large enough to be put to better use than the storage of household junk. Reached by a folding stair or, more attractively and comfortably, by a spiral staircase if the landing is large enough to contain it (and both items can be bought ready-made), the loft should be insulated, lined with plasterboard or hardboard, and windows inserted in the slope of the roof. These can be simple pivoted affairs bringing in the requisite amount of light; or a whole section of the roof can be cut away and with a balcony and plate glass sliding windows your lumber room can be made into something like a penthouse. Whether you decide on anything so ambitious will depend on the state of your pocket, the extent of your requirements and of course the view from the balcony when finished. An architect is essential for these tasks. And you must use his services if you intend to remove the roof entirely and to add a whole new floor level. This is a major and very expensive operation, which *must* have planning permission and which would change the whole scale and character of your house. There are, however, some occasions when it would be preferable to the option of moving.

There is another area of many houses where space potential is often neglected. Basements can be dark, unattractive places where electric light burns nearly all day and rooms have a dinginess which no amount of imaginative decoration will dispel. Many basement rooms, however, open on to a garden or yard at the back of the house. If an existing small casement window is replaced by large, plate-glass sliding doors, the whole underground feeling is minimized and light floods into the room.

Space-saving, once you begin to think about it properly, can bring about a whole new way of life.

3. Colour, Pattern and Texture

Adding colour, pattern and texture is one of the most exciting parts of home decoration and design. But because the results are so obviously there for anyone to see who enters our home, perhaps we worry unduly about making the right choice. The following pages will give you the confidence to go ahead and create just the kind of furnishing scheme that suits you and your family.

Colour

It is worth while taking both time and trouble to understand how colour can work for you in your home, for choosing colour schemes can be one of the most enjoyable aspects of home decorating. Through colour you can express your personality, and make a home uniquely yours. Although the products you may be using will almost certainly be mass produced, such as paints, floor covering, wallpapers and so on, the way you put them together will create rooms with an individual character and a total home which is different from any other. In an age of standardization and mass-production, this is surely much to be valued.

It is a pity that so many people worry so much about choosing colours, for worry takes the pleasure out of furnishing and decorating. The result is that they tend to lack confidence. Furnishings and decorations are expensive; hence few people can afford to make mistakes. Choosing the wrong colour for the walls is far more disastrous than choosing the wrong colour for a new tie or blouse!

The secret is to obtain as much experience as you can before actually buying anything. You could call it 'getting your eye in'. Start looking at other people's homes and see if you like what they have chosen – but remember to keep your criticisms to yourself if you want to keep your friends! Study the rooms you see pictured in colour magazines and advertising brochures; look critically at the room sets on your colour television; look, too, at the window and room displays in the big stores and in the manufacturers' showrooms. All these places give an invaluable opportunity to see how colours and patterns work together. They can provide you with the necessary experience and so help to build up your confidence before you actually spend any money. Moreover, they cut down on the risk of your making expensive mistakes.

Remember that it is what you like and what you dislike which is important – not what your neighbours have or what is the latest fashion. This is your home and there are no right and wrong ways to choose colours and patterns. The notes outlined below are here for your guidance, to help you towards a more confident and certain attitude. In no way should they be interpreted as a set of 'musts' to be followed at all costs. You may feel like going ahead and doing just the opposite from what is suggested – that's fine, if that's what you want.

COLOUR WHEEL
A good starting point is what is known as the colour wheel, illustrated on this page. You will see that it consists merely of the colours of the spectrum, or the rainbow, arranged in a circular fashion. This simple chart can be used to illustrate the main relationships of colour. An understanding of these relationships can be very helpful when choosing furnishings, wallcoverings, paints, and other materials.

The primary colours each appear about a third of the way around the wheel: red, yellow and blue. Between the primary colours lie the secondary colours, all of which can be made up of combinations of two of the basic primary colours. Thus, green, falling between blue and yellow, is made from combining these two colours. Violet is made

BELOW *A colour wheel is a good starting point to understanding colour and its effects. How to use it is explained in the text.*

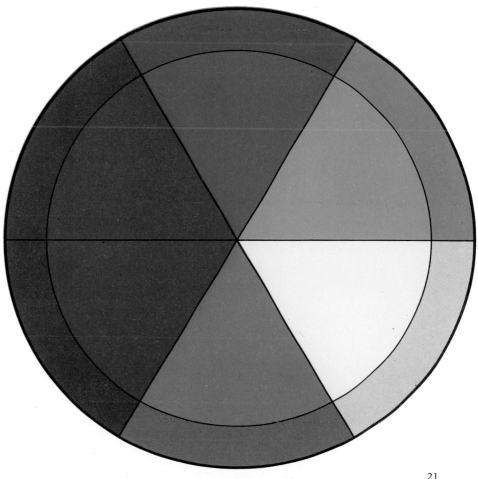

from combining red and blue and therefore lies between them on the wheel. In the same way, the secondary shade of orange is made from combining red and yellow and falls between these two colours on the chart.

Of course, this is only a diagram and therefore a very great simplification of the colour scene. As you go around the wheel, there are innumerable shades which occur, according to which of the primary colours dominates the colour mixture. For example, on one side of the secondary shade of violet there is red violet, adjacent to the primary of red with red dominating. And on the other side there is blue violet, adjacent to the primary of blue and with blue dominating. If we were seeing a greater degree of accuracy, there would be an enormous number of shades for this violet section alone; but for the purpose of this diagram, they have been simplified to those shown on the wheel.

Using this colour diagram, various principles can be applied to help you in colour selection for home furnishing and decoration.

COLOUR HARMONY AND TONE

Firstly, there is the principle of colour harmony. Colours which harmonize – which go together, to put it simply – lie adjacent to each other on the wheel. Generally speaking, colours harmonize which have a common basic element. Blue, for example, is a basic element of the various shades of green and the various shades of violet; it is this common element which makes for a harmonious effect when these colours are used together.

And so, too, with the colours which contain the basic primary shade of yellow – these will be on either side of yellow on the wheel. Again, all the colours with red in them will harmonize, and these will be on either side of the red area on the wheel.

One must repeat that the wheel as shown greatly simplifies the complexities of colour. For one thing it does not take into account the important matter of tone. For within each of the sections on the diagram of the colour wheel there are many different tones, ranging from light to dark. For example, in the orange section, the different tones would include all colours from the palest apricot shades through the various tones of orange itself to the deeper tans and browns. The same range of tones will be present in each of the colour segments on the wheel.

Within one single section of the colour wheel it is possible to build up a very pleasing colour scheme merely using different tones of this one main colour. This is sometimes called a 'tone-on-tone' scheme.

You should always bear in mind this question of tone when planning the colours for a room. For even if you do not intend to use colours from the same colour group, you should try and vary the tones within a room to prevent all the colours

attempting to strike with the same impact. A sound rule is to adhere to the order of tones which are to be found outside in nature. Thus deeper tones are appropriate for the floor, with medium tones for the walls and lighter tones for the ceiling. This is a good general rule and it has the practical advantage of the darker colours being where they are needed to disguise dirt and staining.

Of course, there are people with a sense of colour adventure who will reverse this tonal order. They use, for example, an off-white carpet for the floor and a dark dramatic colour for the ceiling. This is precisely why the effect *is* dramatic – the natural order of tones has been reversed.

COLOUR CONTRAST

The colour wheel can also help in the planning of colour schemes by illustrating the possibilities of colour contrast. Sometimes too many harmonious elements in a scheme may seem monotonous and one is looking for just the right colour to offset the others and so, as it were, bring the scheme to life. On the wheel, contrasting colours are found directly opposite each other. A contrasting colour is sometimes called its complementary. The contrast or complement to red is green; the contrast or complement to blue is orange, and the contrast or complement to yellow is violet. This idea of contrast is represented here in a crude fashion; in practice it is modified a great deal by variations of tone. For example, blue and orange in their brightest versions, as shown on the colour wheel, do not seem good partners for a happy colour mar-

ABOVE *This kitchen corner demonstrates well the principles of colour contrast. The green-painted whitewood sink unit has designs in contrasting red. The patterns are achieved with stencils (see pages 128–130). Note the use of simple open storage and the pine panelling to take hooks and nails for suspending saucepans and other kitchen utensils.*

riage. If however orange is deepened to rust and blue is lightened to a powder blue then a very pleasing combination is beginning to show. So, too, green and red do not appear to be happy combinations in the crude way in which they are opposed on the simplified colour wheel; but if we think perhaps of deeper olives with a touch of scarlet, we can begin to see how colour contrasts can be made to work for us.

Sometimes a pleasing contrast cannot be found from the colour immediately opposite on the wheel. In this case try taking the opposite colour and then move a little round the wheel in either direction to see if there is a colour which you like better. For example, you are looking for a contrast for navy blue and do not like the direct contrasting opposite of orange. Moving round the wheel in one direction you have yellow: buttercup yellow can look delightful with navy. Moving round in the opposite direction you find red: why not consider shocking pink as your accent?

When using the principle of contrasts or complementaries in decoration, it is important not to use these contrasts in equal amounts in a scheme. They should be used in small quantities – in the odd cushion or lampshade or tablecloth. Indeed, colour contrasts should often be incorporated last of all into a scheme in the form of easily added small accessories. The object is to offset the main colours – if the contrast is used in equal quantities, the two colours may begin to conflict.

There is a very simple formula which many people find helpful in creating colour schemes.

Choose a main colour which pleases you and use this for a dominant furnishing item, for example the curtains (and the settee, too, if you like). Then choose an accent colour from the opposite side of the wheel as a complement or contrast. Link these two together with any neutral colour which you find pleasing: off-white, cream, grey, beige, fawn are all possibilities. Of course, you can use your three basic elements of main, contrast and neutral colours in as many different tones as you wish – you may even find that your chosen neutral is one of the palest tones of your main colour.

Different colours can create different moods, and it is helpful here to look once again at the colour wheel. Draw a line down the middle, so that red, orange and yellow are on one side with green, blue and violet on the other. The first group of colours we call the warm colours, and the second group we call the cool colours. These names describe the 'visual temperature' created by these groups. Once again, it is important to stress, we are talking in generalizations, for colour means different things to different people. Colour is always a very personal matter. One person may find reds lively; another may think them threatening. Personal associations sometimes have their influence. One person may find pale greens elegant; another, who has, for example, spent some time in a pale green hospital ward, may find them sickly.

Generally, colours create moods in rooms as follows.

● *Reds* are the colour of fire, associated therefore with warmth and liveliness. Reds have a rich,

ABOVE *Blue is the dominant colour motif in this room, repeating itself harmoniously in the settee, the carpet, the cushions and the painting. Plants work particularly well in this room as blue is a basic element of green. While blue creates a feeling of spaciousness, it can be over cool unless set off by a warm touch, here by the pink cushion and the flowers.*

ABOVE *The four pictures demonstrate the moods created with different colours. In their simplest form, these effects can be yours for the price of a couple of large cans of emulsion paint. Most manufacturers now have some deeper tones even in standard ranges.*

The red *hall and passage way is well suited for this colour, giving a warm and welcoming feeling. However, red can make small rooms seem even smaller.*

The yellow *dining room has the sunny, happy quality achieved with the deeper tones of this colour.*

The blue *bedroom shows the soothing restful feeling this colour can create.*

The green *living room uses the colour somewhat daringly, but successfully.*

welcoming quality, but they can be over-aggressive unless treated with care. Pinks, a paler version of red, retain warmth, but are delicate and dainty and less overpowering.

● *Blues* are the colours of sky and water, creating a cool, spacious, restful feeling. Tranquil blues can be used to calm things down – for example in a kitchen, study or bedroom. They may, however, need odd contrasting 'warm' touches to prevent an over chilly feeling.

● *Orange, tan and golden brown* are all warm cosy colours and hence their deserved popularity for sitting rooms. Deeper browns may, however, need offsetting with brighter colours to avoid a drab effect. Bright orange, while admirable for colour accents, can be tiring if surfaces are large.

● *Yellows,* the colour of sunlight and spring flowers, bring brightness and lightness to the home. They have good light reflecting qualities and can be used effectively to brighten dingy rooms.

● *Greens,* perhaps of all the colours, are regarded as nature's own. They are cool spacious colours except when they veer towards the yellow shades, when they become warmer.

● *Plums and purples* have a formal, almost regal association which sometimes makes them a little difficult to use in home decoration. Their paler version, the mauves, can be deliciously delicate.

It is important to understand the question of warm colours and cool colours when considering the aspect of a room. This simply means finding out which way the windows face for this will govern the amount and type of light. Rooms facing south receive lots of light and therefore seem warm to the eye. Rooms facing west are touched by the sun at the end of the day and therefore seem fairly warm in the afternoon, but could feel chilly in the mornings. Rooms facing east have the sun in the morning only, and may seem rather cold for the rest of the day. North facing rooms rarely have any direct sunlight, and therefore seem rather cold. We are of course talking here about the 'visual temperature' of the room created by the quality of the light it receives. This has nothing to do with actual physical temperature, created by the level of heating.

Once you have determined the aspect of the room, you can see whether you wish either to emphasize or counterbalance the qualities of the natural light with your colour choice. The 'warm' colours (such as reds, pinks, yellows, golds, oranges, rusts, tans and golden browns) can be used to 'warm up' rooms which for the greater part of the day have a cold aspect – rooms facing north, north-east, or east. Where, however, the natural light is of a warm quality (in rooms facing south or south-west) cool colours can be used to good advantage, choosing schemes with blue, grey, slate, turquoise, navy, royal, olive and emerald – to name but a few of the range of blue/green colours.

It is important also to think about the time of day when the room will be most used. Bear in mind that the normal (tungsten electric) light switched on in most homes in the evening emphasizes the warm colours (reds, browns, etc.) and makes them look warmer still by imparting a rosy glow. On the other hand, electric light usually makes the cool colours (blues, greys, greens) seem cooler still, so that what is pleasingly tranquil by day can suddenly seem somewhat chilly and severe by night.

If a room is to be used only during the evenings (perhaps because everyone is out at work or school during the day) it may mean that the room is flooded with sunlight during the morning or afternoon when no one is at home to benefit. Be careful. Choosing a cool scheme to exploit this daytime natural light may be disastrous; for when the room is used with artificial light during the evening a cool scheme will seem definitely cold. With such a room, it is better to choose warm colours to fit in with the normal time when the room is most used – the evening.

Pale cool colours have, too, what are technically called 'recessive qualities'. That is to say they make surfaces look further away than they actually are – a useful point to bear in mind when treating, for example, a low ceiling. In the same kind of way, warm colours can make surfaces appear closer than they really are – hence warm reds or reddy browns can diminish the spacious effect of a room. Tall ceilings painted red make them seem closer to the eye. A warm shade at the end of a corridor or long narrow room is a good decorating trick, making the wall appear closer and removing the narrow effect.

Natural materials like wood, quarry tiles, slate and so on (frequently used in rooms for floors or architectural features such as fireplaces), have a colour of their own which must be taken into consideration when planning a scheme. Just because these are natural materials it does not mean that they will blend harmoniously with any colours. Consider, for example, the wood commonly used for the popular tongued and grooved boarding which can act as a good disguise for imperfect walls. Pine is yellow/brown in colour and is very warm in tone. Are you going to continue this warm element through the colour scheme, playing up its qualities with warm browns and perhaps a little orange, or do you propose to use the warmth of the wood as a contrast for, say, a cooler scheme based on blues or the cooler shades of green? In either case the colour of the wood must be taken into account. The same principle applies to all fixed features in a room – determine their colour and take this into account when planning.

COLOUR REFERENCES

Try and assemble colour references for all these unchangeable elements. You may even be able to produce a small sample of the material itself – a tiny offcut from the carpet or a little snippet from the upholstery. Perhaps you have a spare tile or little piece of the boarding. These will be invaluable for the rest of your colour matching. It pays dividends to keep samples of this kind, even when you have finished furnishing a room: if you want to make some changes later these little samples will be really useful.

But if it is impossible to have an actual sample of any material (for example you have a carpet that was down in the house when you arrived) try and find a piece of coloured paper or fabric which matches the colour as closely as possible, so that you can use this for reference when you are building up your planned colour picture for the room – and, too, when going shopping for the new elements you need.

It is almost impossible to remember exact shades of colour in one's head: there are so many different

BELOW *Schemes that are created around varying tones of the same colours, or from those that closely harmonize, are more restful than schemes which rely extensively on colour contrast (although most rooms require a small amount of contrast to set them off). Note also the differing effects of warm and cool colours. Below, tones of pink have been used to create a bedroom with a warm, harmonious atmosphere. Bottom, lilac and grey are cooler colours, but the effect is equally harmonious.*

BELOW *Three views of the same kitchen corner, but notice the different looks achieved by varying the decoration.*
The top kitchen has a crisp, cool look which comes from the blue-checked wall covering and the blue and white tiles. In the centre kitchen, the flowery paper and the pretty café curtains create a softer feeling.
In the bottom kitchen, a bold use of orange gives a lively, warm atmosphere which is particularly effective at night.

shades and tones of any one colour. Professionals never take risks of this kind but always work from samples or from the real thing itself; if not they refer to a colour chart which is as near to it as possible.

While you are making a list of the things in the room which are fixed, you should also make yourself a plan of your room (see page 16). This will be invaluable for estimating quantities of materials and replanning furniture arrangements, lighting effects and other matters.

Consider the aspect of the room, as already mentioned, taking into account the amount of light during that time of the day when the room is most used. Consider the mood you want to create for the room, and that of course means analyzing what the purpose of the room is – a bedroom for rest and relaxation or a study bedroom, where keeping

awake for at least part of the time is essential! Or is it a living room used mainly for sophisticated entertaining – or for the rough and tumble of family life with young children? Think carefully about the uses of your room before making any decisions about colours or materials.

Now you can decide whether you want to try and build up a cool colour or a warm colour scheme, whether the mood is to be calm and tranquil or lively and stimulating. For example, consider a room with a pretty blue carpet, and with little direct light during the day, as the windows face north; it is a sitting room and it is intended to use it throughout the day, not just at night time. You may decide to use your area of blue as your contrast area, and to look for wallcovering and upholstery materials in complementary colours, such as warm tones of brown, tan or rust. If on the other hand the room were flooded with light during the greater part of the day, giving it a very warm feel, then you might emphasize your blue carpet with a tone-on-tone scheme of blues, or a scheme based on blues and greens using the principle of colour harmony (see page 22).

It is only after you have taken these general decisions as to the kind of colour mood and emphasis you want for your room, that it is time to go shopping for new materials. Avoid the temptation of starting to shop before you have done your colour homework. If you do you may be lured into buying a gorgeous product simply for its own sake, and then find that it fails completely to fit in with the total effect you had planned. Take with you all the little samples or colour references you have collected. Keep a special file or envelope for these, a room file, which you can also use to keep furniture and lighting brochures, paint swatches and so on, and of course your basic floor plan.

In the shop itself, delay making an instant decision on your new materials, whether wall coverings, fabrics or paint. Take a sample home and consider it in the room for which it is intended. View it in that room both by natural light and by artificial light. Whenever possible view your samples from the angle from which they will finally be seen – laying the piece of carpet on the floor, the upholstery swatch across the sofa, and bunch your curtaining samples to get some idea of drape. Try also to hang your sample wall covering in order to get an idea of its effect.

Pattern

Introducing pattern into a room is one of the most enjoyable parts of decorating. There are many beguiling patterns now available for most of the things we use in our homes. Proceed with caution, however, or you could end up with a mass of designs each of which is lovely on its own, but disastrous when competing with others for your attention.

In many cases, patterns can serve the practical purpose of disguising dirt and stains; patterned floorings, wall coverings and upholstery fabrics can all help to conceal the natural effects of wear and tear.

People who are uncertain in their use of colour can often successfully base their room scheme on a pattern. Choose the pattern you like for your wall-paper, fabric or carpet, and then base the colours for the rest of the room on this pattern, applying the colour principles of harmony and/or contrast as discussed. The patterns from all leading wall-paper and fabric makers represent the work of skilled and trained colourists and designers. Take advantage of their expertise and use their ideas as a starting point for your own schemes.

Of course, patterns create moods just as colours do. Bear these moods in mind when choosing furnishings for the rest of the room. Simple stark geometrics, for example, can go well with the rather more severe style of modern furniture and fitments; but unrestrained, floral, chintzy patterns might call for a rather more comfortable style. The types of patterns available are widely varied and include geometrics, abstracts, florals, pictorials and so on.

When choosing a pattern, remember the various points already made about colour. A wallpaper pattern, for example, will often appear in a pattern book in several colourways. Notice how the same pattern in the cool blues will be very different in the warm browns.

With wall coverings, it is essential, particularly with large pattern repeats, to see the pattern over a

BELOW *Here expert pattern mixing relies on close colour matching for its effect. Notice how well the curtains, bedspread and valance and cushions work together. You can find ranges of co-ordinated papers and fabrics specially designed to create mixed pattern effects in some decorating shops. The bed may look expensive, but a clever needleworker could create the same effect with home-made curtains and valances.*

larger area than just the page sample in the book; the pattern can look completely different. The manufacturer's pictures of room settings give you some idea, but you may also be able to see a display panel in the shop or showroom. So, too, when choosing fabrics, always look at a draped length of the design before making up your mind.

The scale of a pattern is very important. It has been very fashionable over the past few years to have large patterns with enormous repeats. On the other hand, there has also been a trend towards the tiniest of mini-prints. Both these extremes have their decorative uses. The large scale patterns naturally look attractive over large areas, such as a staircase wall, or a bedhead wall, where the pattern can be displayed to full effect. These large patterns however can also look good in small rooms, particularly where the colours are the cool, receding blues, and where the background is pale. The effect here is to take the eye out of the room and make it seem larger.

·Little miniprints on the other hand, are at their worst when used over large surfaces – they can have a measly or spotted effect. This type of design however looks attractive in smaller rooms, particularly where there are lots of surfaces at different planes and angles. Thus in an attic room a mini-design can be used to cover all surfaces, including the ceiling, to great effect.

Today there is an increasing trend towards mixing patterns in decoration. Caution is, however, necessary.· Study the newer coordinated wallpaper/fabric collections which have taken the agony out of mixing and matching. Often a curvy, floral design, is teamed with a restrained and formal geometric (for example, a stripe or trellis pattern) in the same colours and the effect can be striking. Use this method yourself for your own pattern teaming a neat geometric in the same colourways as a curvy floral. But get your eye in by studying the patternbooks first!

Patterns of the same type and same colourings can be mixed very successfully in small areas. For example, the cushions on a settee can all be made from miniprints in different patterns but in the same basic colourings. This is the same reason that patchwork bedspreads work so well, where the patterns are linked strongly by their colours. This idea does not however extend very successfully to large patterns on a larger scale.

A relatively new idea for coordinating patterns is to provide a choice of the same basic design but in two different scales, a large and a small version. This idea is easy to use and looks most sophisticated. Other coordinating patterns take a single design element from a pattern (a small flower perhaps) and present that as an alternative on its own. Again these patterns are made so specifically to match each other that sophisticated mixed pattern effects can be achieved without difficulty.

ABOVE *One of the easiest and most traditional ways of mixing pattern is to build up designs for cushions, tablecloths or even curtains from patchwork. Collect a good selection of fabric pieces – some stores sell mixed bags of remnant pieces – before starting the work.*

RIGHT *Large, modern geometric patterns can look stunning used flat over a large area as a roller blind or even as a wallhanging.*

Texture

Another important element in a decorative scheme is texture. Texture is essentially something which one feels. It gives surfaces an interest which is nothing to do with pattern (although some rough textures almost make a pattern in their own right). The dictionary definition of texture is 'the quality conveyed by touching'. Of course this does not mean that one must go around touching everything the whole time, but many materials have qualities which can almost be felt as well as seen. This is the correct meaning of texture: roughness, smoothness, silkiness, shininess, glossyness and so on.

Everything in the home has a texture of one kind or another – even a flat emulsion painted wall with a smooth texture. However it is the uneven surfaces which we usually describe as textured, whether they are hard like a rough cast plaster wall, or soft like a knubby upholstery tweed.

Texture can add life to rooms which if considered merely in terms of their colours, might be rather uninteresting. Thus rooms schemed around the 'tone-on-tone' colour principles can often be rather bland: there may be nothing to offend, but there is also nothing to excite. When one starts to vary the textures in the room, for example by contrasting a hessian wallcovering with a silky curtain fabric or a slate fireplace with a twisted wool pile carpet, the room takes on an extra quality through associations of touch.

ABOVE *Many surfaces rely for their decorative effect not on pattern but on texture – like the attractive rustic, rough-textured look of the exposed brickwork in this living room.*

LEFT *A room schemed around one colour only could be a little boring, unless you diversify the effect by using different textures. Notice how the smooth upholstery contrasts with the shaggy carpet and the plastic surfaces.*

4. A Guide to Materials

Before you can implement your ideas for home design and decoration, it is advisable to get to know the materials available. Indeed, sometimes exploration of the materials will suggest a particular idea. The aim of this section is to introduce you to some of the main groups of materials found in the home for decorative and functional surfaces and finishes.

Later on in the chapters dealing with walls, ceilings, floors, windows, doors and furniture you will find specific materials suggested for particular functions, together with further details. This introductory list is merely intended to show you how vast the scope, how exciting the possibilities within even the simplest of decorating schemes, for nowadays the sophisticated developments of modern technology and the enterprise of modern trade make possible a veritable treasure trove of materials for use in the home.

BRICK

One of the most basic and oldest of building materials, bricks, today are made from various kinds of clay (including hard mudstone, shales, marls, and even some of the softer varieties of slate), fired to very high temperatures in excess of 900°C. Different materials may be added to produce the enormous varieties of colourings available, for example lime or chalk may be added to make yellow or buff bricks. Bricks today may also be made from calcium silicate, which is a mixture of silica sand, lime and water. The estimated 1,500 to 2,000 different shades of brick available fall into colour groups such as Reds, Yellows, Browns, Whites, Blues, Greys, Blacks and Multis. Traditionally, various brick colours are associated with the different kinds of clay found in different parts of the country, but today a wide choice of brick colours is available in all parts of the U.K.

Commons, as their name suggests, are used for general work, usually covered with rendering or plaster. Facing bricks have a special finish which can be applied sand or other textured material on at least three sides to be used on the outside of work. Some projects may require bricks which are faced on all six sides. Engineering bricks are particularly hard and durable, being impervious to water. Handmade bricks may be entirely produced by hand, or with varying degrees of mechanical assistance. They differ from machine-made bricks in

their particularly attractive surface texture, and in some cases in their irregular sizes and shapes.

Newer metric British Standard size is 215mm by 65mm by 102mm, replacing, but almost exactly the same as, the old imperial size of $8\frac{5}{8}$in by $2\frac{5}{8}$in by $4\frac{1}{8}$in. If new bricks are used to repair old brickwork, the thickness of the mortar joints can be adjusted to compensate for any discrepancies. Good quality bricks, unplastered, can make a handsome internal wall. You can use bricks attractively for uprights between shelves and cupboards, also for hearths, fireplaces, or even working surfaces if well sealed. Bricks for floors create an unusual and hard-wearing surface; make sure your bricks are suitable for this purpose. Special paving bricks called paviors are available. They can be laid in a variety of patterns including traditional herringbone and fan shapes. Building blocks moulded from lightweight concrete or clay are now used instead of bricks in much modern construction work.

CERAMICS

Clay-based fired ceramic materials have numerous uses in the home. In addition to everyday chinaware, you will find that sinks, washbasins, lavatories, bidets and shower trays are traditionally made of ceramic with a vitreous (glazed) surface and are harder wearing in some respects than the newer acrylic and glass fibre versions. Wall and floor tiles, both glazed and unglazed, are made in ceramic and come in a multitude of colours, qualities, shapes and patterns. They also look good used on working surfaces, for instance on a bathroom vanitory unit or in the kitchen. You could protect vulnerable edges with a wooden lipping. Flush ceramic panels with electric heating elements concealed beneath are a fairly recent development in electric cooking.

CORK

Manufactured from the bark of the cork tree, cork has unique qualities that make it a very useful asset in decorating a home. It is resilient, attractive in colour and appearance, yet wears well for floors and walls. Cork floor tiles can have a thin plastic coating on them, so that they are relatively impervious and easy to clean. Untreated cork floor tiles must be sealed after laying. There are also tiles or panels varying in size and thickness to cover walls; these give very good sound and heat insulation. Some are of wafer-thin cork with a paper backing which can be hung in the same way as wallpaper. Colours vary from the almost black to pale honey, and there are numerous different designs. There is at least one range of fitted living room furniture which has cork-covered door panels, and you can use sealed cork tiles for desk or table tops.

BELOW *Good quality bricks on an internal wall.*

BOTTOM *Sisal, a natural fibre.*

ABOVE *Ceramics.*

BELOW *Cork.*

BOTTOM *Nylon.*

GLASS

Widely used, of course, for different kinds of table and kitchen wear and other decorative small objects, glass can also play a larger part in decorative schemes. Float glass, which is perfectly flat and free from all distortions, is commonly used for windows in sheets 4mm thick. For larger windows the thickness should be increased to 6mm. Tinted Antisun float glass can be used for wall units, table tops, doors and screens, and is available in thicknesses up to 12mm, in bronze or grey shades. Patterned glass has a textured surface in a choice of modern and traditional designs, available in colours such as blues, greens and ambers. A new kind of Chameleon patterned glass has the design actually within the body of the glass, leaving both surfaces completely smooth. Colours in the glass change as the viewing angle and light intensity changes. It can be used for doors, screens, partitions, and table tops. Armourplate toughened glass, either clear or tinted, is up to five times stronger than ordinary glass, and breaks into granules rather than jagged splinters. It can be used for safety reasons as doors, partitions, shower screens, and table tops. Alternatively, wired glass contains embedded wire mesh – this is sometimes call 'Georgian wired'. Available clear or frosted, the mesh holds the glass together if the pane is broken. Antique-type glass such as that used in mullioned windows, and small expensive stained glass panels, are available for restoration purposes or to add a period flavour to modern projects. Mirror glass, in addition to its use in looking-glasses, can be used to enhance and visually enlarge interiors.

FIBRES

NATURAL

Natural fibres are still widely available for use in the home. As demand increases, however, natural fibres are becoming scarcer. Nowadays, even traditionally inexpensive fibres like cotton are rapidly rising in price. As a result, many natural fibres are now mixed with man-made fibres in an attempt to keep prices stable. In fact, often the resultant blends are in at least some respects improvements, giving the best of both worlds: the attractive look and feel of the natural fibre, combined with extra durability and easy care qualities. Here are some of the main fibres still found for home products.

Wool is warm, resilient hard wearing, does not burn easily and dyes into lovely colours, to give carpets and upholstery fabrics a beautiful rich quality and long wearing properties. Wool lends itself to interesting textured effects for fabrics, such as bouclés (with a looped pile) and slubs (with yarn that varies from thick to thin). The international wool mark is a guarantee of quality for all-wool products. But these are becoming increasingly ex-

pensive, and wool blended with man-made fibres such as nylon or viscose may be cheaper and just as durable.

Cotton is still used on its own for furnishing fabrics, although increasingly in cotton/viscose or cotton/polyester blends. Printed cotton fabrics in a wide choice of plains and patterns make attractive curtains, table cloths, bed covers etc. which are easy to wash and iron. Cotton denims and ducks can be used on upholstery, as can some tougher cotton pile fabrics, such as corduroy. Cotton in its pure form for sheets has virtually disappeared on the mass market, being replaced by blends of cotton with man-made fibres, such as polyesters and viscose.

Flax (linen) has virtually priced itself out of the market; printed cottons or cotton/man-made blends are now used for table 'linens'. Linen sheets are definitely in the luxury class. Linen 'union', a blend of linen and other fibres is available as very attractive hard-wearing fabrics for loose covers. Silk always was a luxury fibre, and today this applies more than ever. Paper-backed silks are available as wall coverings, but pure silk for upholstery or curtains has on the whole been replaced by the wide range of very effective man-made silk imitations.

Coir is the name given to the thick fibres around the inner shell of the coconut. It is used for low cost matting now available in more expensive rubber-backed versions. These mattings are in attractive natural colours, and a limited range of dyed shades, but are very coarse to the touch. Sisal is also used for coarse, hard-wearing cord carpeting, available in a wider range of colours than coir. However, although it was once inexpensive, recent world shortages have pushed up the price. Jute is used to make hessian, a less expensive fabric of coarse texture available in natural browns and a range of colours, including prints. It can be used for curtaining, and it also comes paper-backed for use on walls. Rush was once popular for chair seats, but it is now rather expensive and difficult to obtain, even for replacement purposes. Seagrass in the form of a rough kind of string is now widely used in its place. Rush, however, is still used for matting sold in squares which can be sewn together to any size. It used to be a relatively inexpensive floor covering, but now like so many other products based on natural fibres, prices have risen.

MAN-MADE

New developments in man-made fibres are taking place all the time, and the great variety can be confusing. Man-made fibres can be divided into different families or generic groups and each fibre group has different properties. There are different brand names within the same group for fibres which are basically the same, and the existence of

31

foreign brand names confuses the situation still further. Under recent EEC regulations, all fabrics and carpets are now required by law to carry a label stating their fibre content in generic terms (i.e. the fibre family or families from which the fabric or carpet is made). However, some fibres are more commonly known by their brand name rather than their generic names, so these labels are not always as helpful to the general public as they might be. Some manufacturers and retailers are in fact adding the fibre brand name to the generic name in order to help the consumer.

Here we list under their generic names some of the most common man-made fibres used for decorative products around the home. These are the names you will find on the labels. We also indicate in brackets some of the more common brand names by which these fibres may be known. Some of the most satisfactory carpets and textiles are clever blends of different man-mades or man-mades and natural fibres, combining the qualities and advantages of different fibres in one end product.

Viscose, formerly known as Rayon, (Evlan, Evlan M, Sarille, Scandair). Viscose was one of the first of the man-made fibres, and is still widely used. It can be used on its own for curtaining, and is also sometimes used on its own for cheap carpeting, but has poor resistance to soiling and tends to flatten, However, viscose blends well with other fibres, to produce more hard-wearing carpets, which at the same time are reasonably priced. Increasingly, viscose is being used for a wide variety of upholstery cloths, including interesting tweedy and bouclé effects.

Acetate (Dicel). You will find acetate used in the home for curtaining with the look of slubbed silk, at a realistic price. This fibre may be blended with viscose.

Triacetate (Tricel). In some furnishings, this fibre may be used for 'spring-tuft' fabrics, such as bedspreads and bathroom sets with a candlewick effect.

Modal (Vincel). A newer fibre development, this has a high wet strength, and a good resistance to shrinkage. It blends well with cotton for easy-care hardwearing curtainings and sheetings.

Acrylic (Acrilan, Courtelle, Orlon, Dralon, Cielle). This fibre family has sometimes been called the 'wool substitute' for it is possible to produce acrylics which resemble wool closely in feel and handle. But acrylics are very versatile and can alter their appearance according to their function. Acrylics are used for luxury cut-pile carpets, where they may be blended with other fibres, such as nylon and rayon. Acrylics are also used for a wide range of fabrics, including tapestry-style curtaining, open-weave sheers, and upholstery fabrics which include luxurious-looking velvets in rich glowing colours. Acrylics are used effectively for long-pile rugs in a choice of colours, lacy-style blankets and

a wide variety of bedspreads.

Modacrylics (Teklan). A new fibre development, with inherent flame-resisting qualities, which makes it particularly safe whether in the home or in public buildings. Some long-pile rugs are now being made in modacrylic, and the fibre is being developed for contract curtaining and carpets.

Nylon (Bri-Nylon, Enkalon, Timbrelle, Celon, Du Pont, Antron). Nylon, the tough fibre, is often blended with other fibres, such as wool, where added strength is required. Nylon is also being used increasingly on its own for new developments in carpets. Older types of nylon had a tendency to attract dirt, but were easy to clean. Some also had a rather unpleasant glittery appearance. Newer nylon fibres are overcoming to some extent nylon's traditional disadvantages and some, such as Timbrelle, have good soil-hiding properties and a soft, warm feel. Nylon is appearing in a wide range of attractive carpets which include plush pile effects, printed loop and cut-piles, and silky-looking shag-pile carpets made from fine-denier nylons. Nylon is used for attractive curtainings, including velvet or brushed effects, and for ranges of stretch upholstery covers for example in tweeds and prints, which are becoming increasingly sophisticated.

Polyester (Terylene, Dacron, Lirelle). This fibre is used in the home for an attractive, reasonably priced range of net and other curtainings which are easy to look after and will not shrink. Polyesters mix well with other fibres such as man-mades like viscose, and modal. You will also find polyesters blended with natural fibres such as cotton and linen, where it helps to stabilize costs and improve wear and easy-care properties. Polyester/cotton mixtures, for example, are used extensively for sheeting, to produce fabrics which can take a more sophisticated range of colours and prints than all-cotton fabrics could.

Polypropylene (Meraklon, Ulstron). Used in home furnishings for some upholstery fabrics and for several ranges of carpets, both cut and loop pile, which have good stain-resistant properties.

Glass-fibre was used extensively for cheaper printed curtains, but has recently become more expensive.

Non-Woven Fabrics. Many man-made fibres are now used for the production of new types of non-woven fabrics. The term non-woven takes in all the new ways of making fabrics other than by weaving or knitting. Bonded fabrics, for example, are made by bonding a web or mass of man-made fibres together with a chemical agent, and then compressing this into a flat sheet. Melded fabrics are made by heat-bonding man-made fibres into strong fabrics which have a pleasant feel. Cambrelle is one brand name for this particular process, rather than (as is often thought) the brand name of a particular fibre. Stitch-bonded fabrics have a

ABOVE *Leather makes an attractive upholstery cover.*

BELOW *Plastics have many uses, from plates to furniture.*

mass of man-made fibres stitched together into a fabric by high-speed needles.

HIDES AND SKINS

Leather, although expensive, is still deservedly popular as an upholstery covering, with various thicknesses available in a wide range of beautiful colours. Leather 'patchwork' using up scraps is an attractive and cheaper version of real leather covering for upholstery and cushions. Leather always feels pleasant to the touch and wears well, although vinyl imitations are becoming increasingly difficult to distinguish from the real thing. Small areas of leather can also be used most effectively for desk and table tops, or even for door panelling.

Skins from various animals are used for floor rugs. You can buy quite cheaply small woolly irregularly-shaped sheepskins, treated to make them washable, in shades of cream, brown and white. Goatskins have a longer, silkier pile, and are available in a range of standard sizes in white and shades of brown. Be warned, however, because they always moult, and the long hairs get transferred to people and other furnishings. More exotic animal skins are available for rugs, but these are becoming very expensive. In any event it seems a shame to diminish the world's wildlife for the sake of a rug, when so many other alternatives are available.

METALS

Many different kinds of metals are used around the home, often cleverly combining a decorative appearance with a functional requirement. Steel is used for radiators, baths, cookers, furniture frames, and a multitude of small fittings, but it will rust unless protected, by, for example, metal primer plus paint film. Chromium plating adds a shiny glossy silver-coloured finish which is particularly attractive on tubular-framed furniture. It is also used widely as a trim for cookers, light fittings and so on. There are several possible types of finish for steel; vitreous enamel, for example, may be used as a surface for steel where wear is great, such as cooker hobs or baths. A glass coating is baked onto the steel at a very high temperature until the two fuse together to form an exceptionally durable finish. Stove enamelling is a very hard wearing type of painted finish, which has been sprayed onto the metal and baked at a high temperature. It is available in white or other colours for cookers, fridges and other metal surfaces subject to heavy wear. Alternatively, steel can be given a hard-wearing colourful epoxy resin painted finish, which also goes through a baking process to make it extra durable. Stainless steel is an alloy of steel, with a small amount of nickel and chromium added to produce a metal which is resistant to rust or other corrosion. You will find it used around the home for cutlery, sinks and

draining boards, cooker trims, expensive working surfaces and tiles, and occasionally as a decorative trimming on modern furniture and lamps. Cast iron is still used for baths. also with a vitreous enamel finish, whilst wrought iron makes balusters, screens, gates, and a variety of smaller objects, all of which need to be finished to prevent rusting. Aluminium will not rust or corrode, because the surface becomes coated with a layer of protective aluminium oxide when exposed to the atmosphere. However, anodizing gives aluminium extra protection, and improves its appearance. You will find aluminium all over the home, for window frames which never need painting, saucepans, door furniture and furniture trims. Copper is used for plumbing pipes, fire and extractor hoods, and kitchen utensils. Brass, although expensive, is still used for attractive door furniture and curtain fittings, and sometimes as a trim for furniture and light fittings.

PAINT

Two basic types of paint are available: gloss for a shiny finish or matt for a dull finish. Gloss paints are usually oil-based, and matt paints usually water-based, (emulsions), but glossy emulsions and matt oil-paints are also on the market. For further details see pages 70–71.

PAPER

Decorative printed paper for hanging on plastered walls is a time-honoured fashion which still has a great deal of potential for modern homes. An enormous range of designs is now available from traditional to ultra-modern. For further details see pages 74–77.

PLASTICS

There are innumerable different types of plastics with widely varying properties. Plastics look good when used in their own right, as the material for a brightly coloured washing-up bowl or draining rack, or a moulded plastic chair. Here they are not pretending to be anything else. They can achieve a density of colour and glossiness of surface which would be impossible with any other materials. Plastics, too, can be moulded into shapes in a way that no other material can. They are also made in a wide variety of imitations of ·natural materials, such as leather and wood, and if the imitation is good enough, these imitations can be quite acceptable in the home, particularly where the cost of the real thing puts it well beyond your financial reach. There are, for example, plastic wood veneers which are so cleverly printed and embossed that they are almost impossible to distinguish from real wood. Plastic upholstery fabrics also very cleverly simulate leather. Materials of this kind often have the added advantage of being easier to look after than the material they imitate.

33

Clear plastic coatings of melamine, polyurethane or polyester, for example, are often used to protect another more vulnerable surface such as wood or cork. Here you are getting the best of both worlds: the individual beauty of the real thing, plus the durability of plastic. Melamines may also be used for white or patterned (e.g. imitation wood-grain) surfaces for materials such as chip-board, used for furniture and shelving. Some tableware, too, is made from melamine. Polyurethanes are used for the newest kind of upholstery fabrics which imitate leather. They have a soft, fine feel, and the wear problems which occurred when these fabrics were first developed have now been overcome. Plastic laminates, used to protect and enhance flat and upright surfaces on tables, kitchen units, and other furniture, come in a huge choice of colours, in plains and patterns, some which imitate natural materials such as wood, marble, fabrics and so on. Some are textured to add to the effect. Plastic laminates are also available for facing doors and walls. Acrylics, available in an exciting range of translucent colours, and also in opaque form, are used for baths and other bathroom fittings, furniture and numerous other small items around the home. A.b.s. is used for the casing for domestic appliances, and for moulded plastic furniture, including chairs, tables, and small storage units. Plastic furniture should however be bought with caution as, if badly designed, it tends to show early signs of stress and wear. Polypropylene is used for chair shells (either on its own or with a top layer of upholstery) for parts of domestic appliances and for small kitchen accessories such as washing-up bowls and bread bins. Polyethylene is also used for small domestic items of this type. Vinyls are used in flexible form for wallcoverings, for pvc upholstery fabrics, floor tiles and sheets, and as a component for paints to add extra durability. Expanded vinyl upholstery fabrics have a thin foamy top layer, with a knitted cloth backing. In rigid form, vinyls are used for pipes and other fittings and for roofing sheet. Nylon is used for hardwearing fittings, such as curtain rails. P.t.f.e. is used for non-stick coating inside kitchen pans.

STONE

Cut natural rocks include sandstone, yorkstone, granite, and limestone. Or more cheaply, cast stone can be made from chippings mixed with cement. Stone can be used as a primary building material but except in the areas where it is quarried is normally too expensive, and is therefore used only in small quantities in the average home. A stone floor, which needs a solid under-floor for support, is expensive, though it is virtually indestructible. More feasible would be a stone hearth, perhaps extended to form a wide seating shelf across the room, or a stone fireplace. Both might be rather overpowering in a small room. Slate is available in a

wide colour variation according to the quarry, from dark blue or green to heather colours. It makes a very expensive flooring, but you could use small amounts for a fireplace, table top or window-sill. Marble is a special kind of stone formed from limestone and can be polished to a smooth finish. It is immensely hard wearing but also very expensive so that, although it makes magnificent floors and even wall coverings with a great variety of patterns and colours available, it is rarely used in a domestic context. But some homes can enjoy a touch of luxury with a piece of marble set into the kitchen work surface for pastry making, a marble-topped coffee table, a slab of marble cantilevered on the dining room wall to form a serving table, or a marble top to a bathroom vanitory unit.

WOOD

Wood and wood-based products are among the most attractive and easily available products for improving your home. The charm of real wood is that each piece is unique – no two pieces of wood are ever exactly the same, even if they come from the same tree.

Botanists divide timber into two main groups: softwoods and hardwoods. These terms are also used in the timber trade – you have probably come across them in your local DIY shop or timber yard. But beware, because they can be misleading. They are not always an accurate assessment of the physical hardness or softness of the wood. Some softwoods, for example, are in fact very tough to work with e.g. Parana Pine.

In strict botanical terms, softwoods are the wood from the coniferous or cone-bearing (usually ever-green) trees. They grow more quickly than hard-woods, and therefore tend to be cheaper. Pine is the softwood with which most people are familiar, and the different types available include: Red Baltic pine, is also known as Scots pine, or red deal. You will usually get this wood when you ask simply for pine in a timber shop. It is used widely for joinery in houses – for floor boards, frames, joists and so on. Douglas Fir is often called knotty pine, because of the attractive markings caused by the grains and knots; the colour is a pinky yellow, with knots in dark brown. It looks particularly nice as pine furniture, and as wood tongued-and-grooved panelling. Parana Pine is less widely used as the timber often warps and twists as it dries. Norway Spruce is sometimes called 'white deal' or 'white-wood' because of its even pale colour. It is used for whitewood furniture and is stained and/or sealed or painted. Western Red Cedar is used out-side as cladding for sheds, houses and so on. Unlike the other softwoods, it contains natural oils which make it more resistant to rot.

Softwoods are in general used for structural work around the house, such as roof timbers, floor joists and boards, skirting, door and window

ABOVE *(clockwise):* *mahogany, chipboard, pine and oak.*

BELOW *Wood is one of the most basic products used in home furnishing.*

frames (available ready-made in standard sizes), battening, frameworks for built-in structures, shelving and so on. Where a decorative finish is required, softwoods can be stained and/or sealed, or painted, using knotting, primer, one or more undercoats and a top coat.

Hardwoods are usually much denser and harder to work with than softwoods. Taking much longer to mature, they are usually more expensive than softwoods. They come from the broad-leafed (and in temperate zones usually deciduous) trees like the oak, elm and beech of Europe, and the teak and mahogany of the tropical countries. They can vary enormously in colour and graining.

Teak comes from India and Burma. It has a distinctive mid-brown colour with a yellow tinge. An oily wood, it is resistant to rot and decay. It is used outside, e.g. for garden furniture, because of its durability, and inside in solid or veneer form for furniture which has steadily continued to be popular since the Scandinavians first pioneered the trend, around twenty years ago. Afrormosia and iroko both resemble teak, and being cheaper are often used instead of or combined with teak. Mahogany, one of the best known hardwoods, is mostly used in veneer form although you can still find beautiful second-hand furniture in the solid wood. There are various types which include Sapele and Utile. It has a reddish-brown colour and fine graining. Beech is a popular wood for furniture, with a straight close grain, and pale colour. It is good for children's toys because it does not splinter easily. Beech responds well to 'turning' to make plain round shapes for chair legs etc, or more intricate shapes for the spindles now available at DIY shops. Oak is very expensive, so is used mainly in veneer form. The colour of oak starts as a palish yellow, and then gradually darkens with age. Rosewood is used in veneer form for expensive table tops, and panelled walls and cupboards. It has a beautiful reddish-brown colour, sometimes with a tinge of purple, with blackish intricate graining.

Hardwoods are used mainly for furniture (either in solid or veneer form, see below) and for some external woodwork such as doors and window-sills; also for decorative wall panelling and floorings in strip form or as parquet panels. Hardwoods are usually left unpainted to show the beauty of the wood, but will generally need protection in the form of a preservative, sealer or polish.

A veneer is a thin slice of wood stuck down to another wood or (more commonly these days) to a wood-based material such as chipboard or plywood. Many of the more exotic and beautiful woods are very expensive; veneers bring the attractive appearance of these woods within reach of the average pocket. Veneers are used extensively for furniture and for wood panelling. You can buy chipboard wood-veneered panels in a choice of various timber finishes for your own furniture and shelving projects. Modern production methods and adhesives have ensured that veneers are adequately hard-wearing on most of the surfaces for which they are commonly used. Veneered boards are more stable than solid wood; they will not warp or twist in centrally heated houses.

WOOD-BASED PRODUCTS

Chipboard (sometimes known as particle board) is made by bonding together small chips of wood (or flax or hemp) with resins under heat and pressure. It has no grain-direction, and is relatively stable (i.e. will not warp or shrink); but its screw holding power is low. You can use screws in chipboard by first inserting a plug, or by using special double-threaded chipboard screws. Chipboard is available unfinished, and can be satisfactorily painted, or stained a bright colour and sealed. Or you can buy chipboard with wood veneer, or with a facing of plastic laminate. You can use chipboard for all kinds of furniture, shelving and built-in projects. Special grades are available for flooring. Usual sheet size is 2440mm by 1220mm, and thicknesses range from 4mm to 25mm. Smaller standard sizes are available veneered or plastic-coated for furniture and shelving – check sizes before planning a project. Plywood is made by bonding together (usually with synthetic resins) three or more veneers of hardwood or softwood, or a combination of both. The grains of the different veneers or 'plies' run at right-angles to each other, which makes plywood very stable, and resistant to splitting. Plywood is used for furniture and flooring; it can be painted, or stained and sealed. Thicknesses available range from 3mm to 32mm, and the usual sheet size is 2440mm by 1220mm. Blockboard consists of strips of wood up to 25mm wide, sandwiched between ply sheets of one, or sometimes two, veneers, placed so that their grain runs at right-angles to the grain of the strips. Available in thickness from 12.5mm in sheets of 2440mm by 1220mm, and used for doors, panelling, partitioning, shelves and furniture projects. It is resistant to warping, and holds screws satisfactorily. Hardboard is made by pressing out woodpulp into thin sheets 3.2mm or 6.4mm thick. Although flexible, hardboard is reasonably strong when well supported and can be used for cladding frameworks in built-in constructions. Hardboard can also be used for covering floors. One side is a smooth shiny brown, the other has a dull textured 'mesh' finish. The smooth side can be painted or sealed. Special panels with decorative finishes are available for walls, screens etc. Hardboard panels cut out with a decorative fretted design are particularly attractive. Perforated hardboard (known as pegboard) is useful for lining walls and cupboards, to take pegs or clips for hanging up tools or utensils in kitchens or workshops etc. Sheet size is commonly 2440mm by 1220mm.

5. Lighting and Heating

It is easy to think of lighting as a means of getting rid of darkness, more difficult to treat it as a method of decoration. Yet a room can be transformed by good lighting. It can add immeasurably to the pleasure we take in our homes and the cost of installing and using lighting is small in relation to the benefits.

There is a bewildering choice of light fittings in department stores and electrical shops: up lights, down lights, bowl lights, globe lights and wall-mounted fittings, with, of course, the ever popular standard and table lamps – something for every room and every position. The trouble is that homes are never built with enough electrical points. Usually each room has no more than a connection in the centre of the ceiling with, perhaps, two connections in the living room for wall lights. Socket outlets are expected to provide for standard and table lamps and only the light for the hall and stairs will be wired for two-way switching. There are simple methods of improving such lighting without undertaking a complete rewiring.

How much light and how many lighting points are needed depends on the purpose of the light. Look at each room in turn and first aim at providing a general level of lighting possibly with a lighting dimmer so you can alter the amount. Next look where you need to give extra concentrated light such as at a worktop or desk or at a bedhead: and, last, look for objects or places which would benefit or be made more decorative with extra light. Mark the light positions on a rough plan of the room (see page 16) and then examine your existing wiring to see how far you can meet these within the limitations of your present connections.

It is essential to obtain professional help for re-wiring or for any scheme to improve lighting. Be wary of odd-job electricians without adequate qualifications. Choose someone on the list of the National Inspection Council for Electrical Installation Contracting. This list is to be found at the local Electricity Board office or in the public library.

Standards for home wiring are established but prices are not. Get competitive quotations. All recognized electrical contractors must comply with the wiring regulations drawn up by the Institute of Electrical Engineers. If you think you can cope reference libraries carry a copy of these regulations to which you can refer.

Wiring

Houses are wired in two ways to provide lighting. First there are lighting circuits, which are normally protected by a 5-amp fuse. This means twelve 100-watt lamps or twenty 60-watt lamps can all be used at the same time on that circuit.

The lighting cable travels from the main fuse unit to the meter and thence to the lighting points. As it has also to connect to the switch which turns the lamp on and off, it must do this in such a way that the individual switch, unless purposely designed, does not affect the operation of other lights. This is the reason why there are sometimes as many as five or six connecting cables behind the ceiling rose and the switch. An electrician can usually expand the number of outlets or alter their position.

point and it will switch on with the ceiling light or a pull cord switch fitted behind the curtain.

A single point ceiling rose can be replaced by a multi-outlet ceiling plate, so that a group of pendants can be hung in a bunch at different lengths or the flex carried by ceiling loops to other points in the room. This method, although very simple and inexpensive, needs care as flex is never sightly.

Fitting a rise and fall pendant in place of a ceiling rose can be done without even disturbing the decorations. A pendant light can have its height adjusted at a touch.

Many fittings, such as adjustable spotlights and surface mounted and recessed downlights, come with their own ceiling rose; an electrician will connect the wires so that the existing connections in the rose are maintained.

When planning lighting, position fittings so that bulbs are easily changed. Remember that you will need a stepladder to change bulbs at ceiling level.

Many light fittings, especially those of continental manufacture, have screw holders for the lamps instead of the British bayonet (BC) fitting. The wiring is identical – just ask for a bulb with a screw cap, called ES (Edison Screw) in the trade.

Lighting cable is not decorative and needs to be disguised; the PVC cable cover must also be protected from damage. There are many ways of hiding wiring and an electrician will advise you. For example, you can buy skirting, cornice and architrave, made in a tough plastic, to conceal cable and plastic can be painted to match the woodwork.

The second method of providing electricity for lighting is from the ring circuit either by a 13 amp plug (with 3 amp cartridge fuse) into one of the sockets such as you would use for table and standard lamps; alternatively light points can be connected direct to the ring via a 'fused spur'. This is a single section of cable which can be taken from almost any point on the 30 amp ring circuit and protected by a small cartridge fuse. The fuse fits into a square plate the same size as a single socket but without the three rectangular holes. Lighting for a garage or under the worktop in the kitchen is often wired in this way.

The difficulty in extending and improving lighting lies not so much in the electric wiring itself as in disturbance to the decorations, particularly where separate switching is required. Moving a lighting point is simple *for an electrician* where there is access to floor and ceiling, particularly if the new point can be sited within the same space as the existing point. Two or more lights where there was only one can be operated from the same switch or from a dimmer switch. A dimmer allows you to alter the amount of light which a lamp or lamps will give out and there are various types for different wattages. There are also dimmers for table lamps, some which fit bulbs and lamp holders, some which fit between socket and plug, and some of a special type for fluorescent lighting.

It is also possible to have two or three switches on the same switch plate – and modern switches are of the rocker pattern which need only a light touch to operate. Switching a light from more than one point (two-way switching) needs an extra switch wire, but this is a simple matter for an electrician to do when rewiring.

As far as possible try to make use of existing points even if they have to be moved to another position. Very often a light in a curtain pelmet which 'washes' the curtain with light (a fluorescent tube is best) can be connected from the ceiling

The design and range of choice of light fittings has improved enormously in the last five years. It is now possible to buy both modern and traditional styles of fittings relatively inexpensively. From left to right around this spread we show: a small traditional-style wall light (it looks best if the wiring can be concealed within the wall); a neat little spotlight which would fit unobstrusively anywhere; a rise-and-fall pendant fitting ideal for over dining tables; a traditionally-styled pendant to suit antique or reproduction furnishings; a ceiling spotlight that can be fitted to a track; an elegant modern metal pendant; a simple cylindrical downlight; and finally a choice of three tablelamps ranging from traditional to modern.

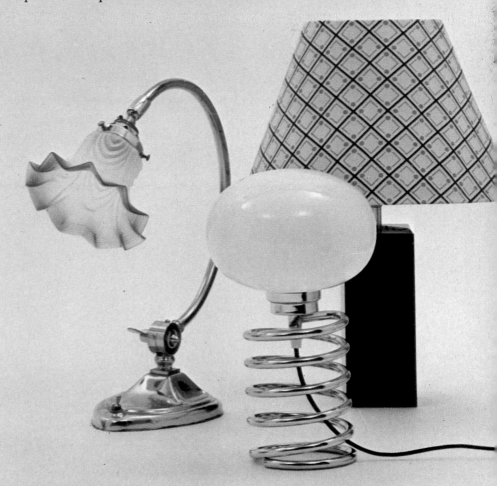

Lighting from the ring circuit to the back of a socket or to a 30-amp junction box (the fused spur) is the method electricians use most often for providing lights in an alcove or on a wall. An electrician can convert a single into a double socket. This is a better, safer method than using an adaptor for connecting table and standard lamps.

Track lighting can be fitted to almost any lighting point. The metal and plastic channel carries continuous live, neutral and earth conductor strips and the lights are mounted on special adaptors which can be plugged anywhere along the length of the track.

LIGHTS AND LAMPS

For reasons which are rather obscure, the source of light which most of us like to call a bulb is called by the trade a lamp and the fitting which we like to call a lamp is called a light or light fitting.

The terminology in the catalogues may also be confusing. The table of different lamps may help but the basics are simple. Most lamps are GLS which stands for general lighting service and this covers all the popular ordinary lamps with a filament which gives a high proportion of its output as heat rather than as light. Except for the long life type, a GLS lamp has a life of about 1,000 hours and its running cost can be calculated on the basis that 100 watt lamps will burn for ten hours at the cost of one unit of electricity.

The second most popular lamp used in the home is the fluorescent tube (MCF in the catalogues) which comes in various lengths and three diameters, 16mm, 26mm and 38mm (except circular types which are 34mm). Fluorescent tubes are much more efficient in converting more of electricity to light rather than heat – about 35 lumens for every watt compared with an average of 12 for most GLS lights. The average kitchen can obtain excellent general lighting from a 1500mm fluorescent tube at the same running cost as a 100W lamp and it will provide four times as much light. Wattage is dictated by length. Much of the light from fluorescents however depends on reflection from light surfaces so that it is never easy to give a precise guide.

Although fluorescents cost more, they are not only cheaper to run but have a lamp life almost eight times that of most GLS lamps. Light is produced by an electrical discharge in a gas in the tube and this involves some complicated electrics. The colour of the light can be rather hard, cold and unflattering from fluorescents but tubes can be coated to give it warmth. We are so accustomed to the yellow light from the GLS lamps, that it is probably best to get a tube which matches it.

Some professional decorators prefer natural as a fluorescent tube colour for curtain pelmets, for lighting china and glass and for make-up mirrors and porches, as the colour is close to daylight. Do not use it in the kitchen – you will feel that you want to wear a warm sweater!

Fluorescents of small diameter are perfect for decorative lighting. They are small enough to be fitted into Terry clips along the back edge of a shelf. The control gear for several tubes can be fitted in a convenient space nearby or a tube together with the controls can be bought as one compact unit. These slim tubes can create a beautiful effect for ornaments and alcoves.

Three other types of lamp deserve a brief explanation. The Crown Silvered (CS) lamp has the front dome silvered so all the light is reflected back. Fitted into a parabolic reflector, the light is skilfully concentrated into a beam without creating glare in one's eyes.

The Internally Silvered lamp (ISL) does the same thing but the other way round. It has a long neck with a reflective lining so that light is directed in a beam from the front. There is a glare if you have to look towards it from the front but it needs no reflector fitting and it can fit into the simplest and cheapest of spotlights usually by means of an ES

TYPE	APPLICATIONS
Pendant	For general and decorative effects; can be hung singly or groups of anything up to five at various heights
Spotlight	For throwing a concentrated beam of light at an angle typically between 15 and 35 degrees
Wall light	Best used for decorative effect. Must be shaded to prevent glare
Cylinder Downlighter	For concentrated lighting. Can be recessed wholly or partly into ceiling or mounted on it. *Best if dimmer controlled.* Some types will angle light against wall.
Surface mounted	Background general lighting. Suitable for dimmer control. Also good for porch and patio
Suspended, Rise and Fall	Adjustable height, suitable for background lighting and for bowl pendant for dinner table lighting. Suitable also for dimmer control
Table	Concentrated local area lighting. Minimum height from table to bottom of shade 300 mm (12 in). Low candle-type lamps also suitable for dinner table if well shaded
Standard	Concentrated, local area lighting. Minimum from floor to top of shade 1·5 m (5 ft)
Straight Fluorescent	General lighting but should have a diffuser to conceal tube
Circular Fluorescent	General lighting for centre ceiling use with choice of various covers to conceal tube

screw—a ceiling rose, a pivot and a narrow sleeve containing a lampholder. It also fits into spherical and eyeball fittings where its round dome complements the shape of the fitting.

Finally there is the Parabolic Aluminized Reflector (PAR 38) made from a tough Pyrex glass manufactured to withstand the heat it creates. It must be used in a fitting made to cope with the heat and the light intensity. The advantages are its long life – about 1,500 hours, the high intensity of light output (about 1000 lux from a 100W, 1,800 from a 150W), and it can be used outdoors with a special weather-proof fitting.

LIVING ROOM

Central lights and standard and table lamps are the choice of most people for the living room, but while they can create the feeling of cosiness they are neither imaginative nor practical. There must be concentrated light for studying and sewing. There should also be some decorative lighting and, when visitors arrive and the television is switched off, there needs to be a good level of general lighting.

The lighting in the ceiling does not have to shine down: it can be directional, using spotlights. If these seem to be too modern in appearance, consider recessed eyeball spotlights which can illuminate a wall or a picture or the curtains. Consider also putting a light inside a curtain pelmet, or using fluorescent or tubular lights where they can illuminate shelves – perhaps in particular where there is the hi-fi.

Pictures can be lighted with tubular fittings set out from the wall so that they throw their light on to the canvas; or spotlights can be set above them in the ceiling or on an adjacent wall to aim their beam at the picture. Glass-covered pictures need care: the light should be placed so it flows downwards. Framing spotlights can be obtained to match exactly the size of the picture but they are expensive.

For watching television there should be just enough light to prevent the picture becoming too glaring and the room should be light enough to see the shape of the set and the surrounding furniture. Any table or standard lamp must be placed to avoid its reflection on the screen.

Height and shape and shade of the table or standard lamp is also important. When buying a shade judge its capacity to match the decorations when unlit as well as when lit.

ABOVE *Exciting shapes give modern light fittings an arresting sculptural appearance. When choosing always consider the appearance of decorative fittings both lit and unlit; ask the shop to demonstrate. Consider screening windows with a poor view to let in light but shut out an unattractive exterior.*

LEFT *As genuine traditional fittings become more scarce, manufacturers are producing a range of reproduction styles, such as this pretty decorative pendant.*

pendant with a glass crystal drop as a better accompaniment to your décor. A rise and fall unit may be bought independently of the fitting, but the weight of the fitting must match the capacity of the spring in the unit; details are usually shown on the packing.

The dining-table light can be supplemented by wall and/or floor lights, depending on the size of the room. You may need an additional light for a serving hatch or sideboard. Be careful of spotlights in a dining room. Unless they are positioned very carefully they can dazzle a diner when he looks up from his plate.

HALL AND STAIRS
The hall should be well lit but not too brightly as eyes need time to adjust from the outside darkness.

Stairs always need good light. Pendant lights in groups, cylinder lights (including the recessed type), or even spotlights can be used. There must however be light from the top to make a clear distinction between stair treads in light and risers in shadow. Take care that there is no glare into the eyes at any point on the stairs.

KITCHEN
The kitchen can be conveniently lit by a fluorescent lamp fitted with a diffuser parallel to and above the front edge of the sink. A larger kitchen may need a second lamp in line with the opposite wall or at right angles to the first. A circular fluorescent fitting with a diffuser is a suitable alternative for smaller kitchens. Small fluorescent or double cap tubular filaments can also be used fitted neatly under wall cupboards or light work surfaces. The lamp can be concealed by a wooden strip fitted to the front base of the wall cupboard.

ABOVE *In kitchens especially, it is vital to see what you are doing. Fit good lights over sinks, hobs and work tops. You can use spotlights or, as pictured here, strip lights fitted to the underside of kitchen units.*

RIGHT *In this bedroom, functional requirements have been cleverly combined with a soft and attractive decorative effect.*

DINING ROOM
The dining table needs good lighting with, perhaps, an inverted bowl pendant fitting centred above it or a chandelier placed not to interfere with the view across the table or to dazzle the diners. A pendant on a rise and fall cord so that its height can be easily adjusted, and the amount of light controlled by a dimmer switch, is a good idea, or consider a

Lighting can produce a wide range of moods and effects. Here we show how four different ways of lighting alter quite dramatically the look of a room.

ABOVE RIGHT *General overhead lighting produces a bright room with a minimum of shadows.*

ABOVE FAR RIGHT *A shaded floor or table lamp gives a subdued, mellow light.*

RIGHT *A strong downlighter illuminates the table, but casts very strong shadows in the rest of the room.*

FAR RIGHT *A standard spotlight is useful to pick out a decorative feature, in this case the flowers.*

Ceiling-mounted spotlights can also be used in the kitchen but they need more regular cleaning than fluorescents. Pendants are ideal over a breakfast bar; or try cylinder downlighters, if there is space, recessed within the ceiling. The larger types give out considerable heat as well as light, so that it is wise not to exceed a 100 watt lamp.

BEDROOM

Here the main ceiling light should ideally be two-way switched – one at the door and one by the bed. A two-way dimmer, even though expensive, is a desirable refinement. Bedside lights are probably best fixed to the bedhead or wall or suspended from the ceiling; table lamps can easily be broken and they take up room on the bedside table. A bedside light should always be set at eye level or slightly above and preferably should be capable of being set at different angles. A headboard or wall fitting with a pull-cord switch is simple to find in the dark.

Good light is needed for a dressing table. Try a pair of pendant lights hanging from the ceiling on either side of the mirror just above head height.

Cupboards and wardrobes can be fitted with lights for added convenience. Small pushbutton switches on the inside edge of a door can make a light operate automatically when the door is opened and closed.

BATHROOM

Fittings should be made from plastic or from plastic and glass; metal will be affected by steam. Enclosed fittings flush to the ceiling or the wall are best and there are inexpensive textured glass styles which give a sparkling mottled-light effect on white surfaces. Switches must be pull-cord or fitted outside the bathroom.

An enclosed fluorescent light with a shaver socket (together in one fitment) is ideal in the bathroom, but it must have an isolation transformer designed for bathroom use.

THE EXTERIOR

A front door needs a good light if only to illuminate the number or name of the house. It should be placed so as not to throw glare into the eyes of anyone coming up the path but to light the door and step. If the house has two doors, light is also needed at the rear and side passages; a patio, too, should not be in the dark. The simplest and cheapest form of illumination is the light 'brick', a cube of translucent material containing a GLS lamp and screwed to the wall.

A garden, too, can be lighted. This is not merely to discourage prowlers – a switch in the bedroom is a good idea in lonely areas – but lighting can enhance trees and plants as it does with decorations indoors.

Heating

This section does not aim to give advice on the merits, performance and costs of the various types of heating systems, although all these should be investigated carefully before deciding on the appropriate one for your particular needs. However, the ways in which heating appliances affect the design of a room *are* our concern. A badly designed fireplace or a misplaced radiator can ruin the appearance of an otherwise pleasant room. It is important, therefore, that the choice of heating system should be given as much thought in terms of design as every other piece of furniture and equipment in the house.

● *Open fires* are enjoying a huge revival in popularity with people opening blocked flues in order to enjoy the glow of a real fire again.

In an older house may may well find that the existing fireplace will form an attractive feature in its own right. You may have to clean old stone, marble or slate, or even strip off layers of old paint. Wooden fireplaces can be stripped back to the natural wood or repainted. An attractive fireplace for a small, modern room is one which provides a simple, unobtrusive complement to the fire itself. A plain hole in the wall with a chrome trim and a slate, brick or stone hearth beneath is nearly always successful. If something more substantial is required, a neat brick or stone surround, perhaps spanning the whole wall, with a hearth extending into a seating shelf below, would be attractive. Traditional and reproduction fireplace surrounds are available from specialist shops. Remember, however, that niches, ledges and other such decorative additions collect dust and could detract from the spacious lines of the grate and the glow of the fire.

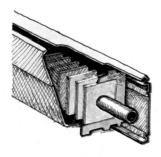

Bear in mind the following safety points with open fires: regular chimney sweeping is essential and fireguards are always desirable, indeed are essential for families with young children.

● *Stoves* can be used in the same manner as an open fire. They convect as well as radiate heat, and many of them are designed to heat the domestic hot water and to run seven or eight radiators. Some, particularly those in which modern lines are combined with traditional materials such as cast iron enamelled in soft browns or blues, are extremely attractive and would fit into a wide range of colour schemes. Less successful are the stoves in which chrome, wood veneer and brightly enamelled iron have been incorporated to give an unfortunately restless appearance. However, for a stylish touch you could install a stove of modern design. These are simple and elegant and are available in colours such as peat brown, caramel, beige or poppy red. Or you could fit a tubular iron stove available in

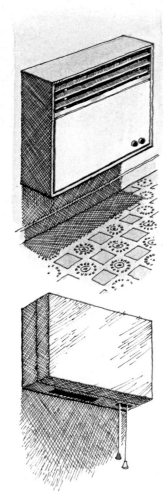

stainless steel or black stove enamel, which have been on the market nearly a hundred years and, gently updated, are still among the best stoves available.

● *Gas and electric fires* may have developed technically over the years, but it is still difficult, though not impossible, to find truly modern designs. An over-lavish use of chrome and wood veneer finishes can make them both obtrusive and awkward-looking. Gas and electric fires are often installed into an existing fireplace surround where they tend to dominate a room. A more attractive alternative could be a fire set into a simply decorated wall with no surround. Electric 'coal' or 'log' fires look as ersatz today as ever they did, but a recent addition to the British market, gas 'logs', do work successfully. These, mounted on a simple cradle designed to fit any fireplace, with the gas flames flickering realistically around them, have much of the appeal of a real log fire.

● *Radiators* have evolved considerably from the days when they were hulking, dirt-collecting monsters, large enough to sit on. The best of the present-day slim panels have no dirt-trapping crevices and come in shapes and sizes to suit any room. When planning the installation of radiators be sure that they are placed so as to make furniture arrangement easy.

Radiators can be decorated in colours to merge with the walls behind them or, more interesting but more difficult to do, in colours to provide a glowing contrast for instance a bright red radiator in a beige and white hallway or a bright green one set against green and yellow and white floral wallpaper in a bedroom. In certain positions, for instance, in a window recess, or set into a wall of fitted cupboards, or in an alcove, radiators must be boxed in behind screens of a perforated material so that their presence is barely discernible.

● *Skirting panels* (radiators which run around the skirting) can be purchased in sizes to fit any room shape and can be treated in much the same way as radiators. In a really large Victorian room with high ceilings they could be decorated in a brilliant colour to produce a stunning effect complemented perhaps by a streak of the same colour painted all around the room at cornice height.

● *Convector heaters* can be run from gas or solid fuel boilers, or by electricity. They generally take up less room than normal radiators and are therefore particularly suitable for the small house. Unfortunately their boxy presences tend to obtrude into a room. Constructions of wood veneer, glossy stove enamel, anodized aluminium, simulated leather and the like, make these heaters difficult to decorate to make them disappear into their backgrounds. So purchase one which will best fit in with existing furnishings. Do not, for instance, buy teak veneered units if the rest of the furniture is pine or vice versa.

● *Night storage heaters* take electricity at night at the cheap off-peak rate and gradually give off heat during the following day. They come in a variety of finishes, usually wood or plain neutral paint. They can be painted to match the rest of. your colour-scheme as long as you use special heat-resisting aluminium paint. Another decorative possibility is to add a shelf above the top using wrought-iron brackets; a wooden shelf should have the bottom surface lined with hardboard to prevent warping, but a glass one does not require this treatment, and could make an attractive base for a collection of house plants.

● *Warm air* is one of the most discreet forms of heating. It is carried via concealed ducts to every room and then expelled through simple grilles.

This form of heating is not easy to install satisfactorily in an old building; although a good architect can often exploit the necessary ducting to form lowered ceiling levels, raised seating shelves and wall columns (or vice-versa).

● *Boilers*, which operate many types of heating, are often far better designed than the outlets, and it is comparatively easy to find a slim, oblong box to fit gracefully into the kitchen, cellar or cupboard or even into a more public part of the house. They can be painted to fit into a decorative scheme.

● *Electric underfloor or ceiling* heating is totally invisible. It consists of elements concealed beneath the floor or above the ceiling surface. This kind of heating eliminates the problems of co-ordinating a heating system and a decorative scheme.

ABOVE *In older houses with chimney breasts consider opening up the fireplace. Take care, however, that all safety precautions are taken.*

LEFT *Different forms of heating: (a) reproduction cast iron stove (b) a cutaway of a skirting panel (c) a wall-mounted convector heater and (d) a combined wall light/fan heater.*

6. Room-by-Room Guide

So far we have been concerned with the overall main principles of interior design and decoration. Now is the time to look at each individual room, assess specific problems and explore potentials.

Living rooms

Living rooms compete with kitchens and bathrooms for the title of the most used room in the home. Careful planning is vital; moreover, the smaller the room, the more vital is the planning required. Read through carefully the section on making a floor plan on page 16.

Before you decorate and furnish a living room in a new home, or make any changes to your existing arrangements, it is a sound idea to make a careful list of the activities which take place in the family living room. Every family, of course, is different; indeed, the needs and activities of the same family vary as its members get older. The list might include communal, often noisy, activities such as television watching, talking together, entertaining, playing board or card games, playing rowdy games at floor level (with younger children), watching slides or home movies, and so on. The list might also feature more individual, personal activities, such as reading, studying, sewing and knitting, writing letters and paying bills, solving crossword puzzles, pursuing a hobby like stamp-collecting or model-making, listening to music, doing yoga, catching a quick nap, and many other things.

It is obvious that any family living room is going to be hard put to cope with all the kinds of activities suggested above. Perhaps some of these can be diverted to other parts of the house. Can the bedrooms be put to fuller use? (see the section on bedrooms). Can the television set be taken out of the living room and placed in a small cosy back room or spare bedroom, which can be equipped with comfortable chairs for the grown-ups and possibly with 'sag-bags' or floor cushions for the children? This would considerably relieve the pressure on the living room and would make it much easier to entertain visitors without interrupting somebody's favourite programme.

When you have pruned activities down to essentials, you can consider the furnishing plan. The way furniture is arranged is crucial as this will

determine the way your room is used. If you are having your room or house rewired, try and arrange your furniture plan beforehand so that, for example, your socket outlets are fixed at exactly the places required for lighting and for electrical leisure equipment such as hi-fi and television sets.

Upholstered furniture costs a lot of money and takes up a lot of space. Do not automatically think in terms of a three-piece suite. Some other combination may suit better, for example a pair of two seater settees, or a corner arrangement with unit seating. In smaller rooms, you will need to group seating along the walls to ensure sufficient central floor space for free movement, but in a large room a right-angled arrangement of seating units can be a good way of breaking up the space.

Cut out the shapes of the upholstered furniture you intend to buy drawn to the same scale as your room plan; then move the shapes around to find the best arrangement. If you are concerned whether a large chair will take up too much room, cut out its actual shape from a newspaper, and place it on the floor in the intended position. Let it stay there for a few days and see how the family cope with moving around it.

You will find that the upholstery of your choice is certain to be available in a wide range of covering fabrics. Loose covers which detach completely for cleaning are invaluable for families with young children. But do not expect sleek tailored lines with loose covers.

Make sure you see the manufacturers' full ranges of fabrics in their pattern books before making any final decision, and read carefully their notes on cleaning, wear properties and other qualities. Ask for a small sample of the fabric, so that you can see how it fits in with the rest of your scheme. Such a sample may have to be ordered specially for you, but it is well worth a wait to avoid an expensive mistake.

Buy the best wearing fabric that you can afford; it will not necessarily be the most expensive. You will need to seek the retailer's advice, for the complexity of modern fibres and fabric constructions make selection a specialist affair. A laboratory 'rub' test, for example, will show how a fabric resists abrasion – a tough cloth will be able to withstand around 50,000 to 70,000 rubs. There are however, other factors to consider when assessing wear properties – such as fraying and resistance to soiling. Matching arm or back 'caps' or 'sleeves' can often be ordered to protect furniture at its most vulnerable points. It is important to brush or vacuum upholstered furniture regularly to prevent

LEFT *The many uses to which living rooms are put need not detract from a smart and welcoming look. Floral print ranges of upholstery are now available with loose covers for easy cleaning.*

excess wear from embedded dirt and grit.

If you cannot afford upholstered furniture at the outset there are several low cost ways of providing seating while you save. Build in seating platforms and use them with foam cushions and bolsters – the space in a bay window is ideal for this. Foam blocks, or large floor cushions can also be used. Look, too, at the ranges in garden furniture departments; comfortable chairs are often sold here at low prices. This kind of inexpensive portable furniture can be transferred to other rooms (perhaps for the children) when you become more affluent.

If you have chosen to keep your television in your main family living room, make sure that everyone has somewhere comfortable to sit from which to view the screen. If you like eating while watching, make sure you have enough surfaces for plates, cups, etc. A shelf running behind a sofa at the same height as its back makes a useful place for these. Tables at either end of a sofa of the same height as the arms are both useful and smart.

Storage furniture is very important in family living rooms. At its simplest and cheapest this consists of shelving – shelves of varying widths supplemented perhaps with boxes, bins or baskets. The cheapest material for shelving consists of old planks

LEFT AND ABOVE *Planning is essential in creating a room that is both comfortable and practical. The plan has shown that it was feasible to create a study/office area in the far corner of this living room.*

46

or floorboards; the enterprising have been known to salvage these from builders' skips! Ask permission first. Also available cheaply is thick 19mm chipboard. This requires supporting every 900mm or even every 500mm if shelves are to carry heavy items like books. A wide range of veneered boards including those with a plain white melamine finish can be obtained from D.I.Y. shops. These come in various standard widths including 150mm, 200 mm, 305mm, 380mm, 460mm and 610mm. Other materials for shelving include 12mm plywood or 19mm blockboard. Natural timber (softwood) can be used, 19mm thick for light items, and 25mm for heavy objects. For longer spans between 610mm up to 1020mm increase the thickness of the timber to 30mm.

The cheapest form of shelving support consists of second-hand stacked bricks – about three or four bricks between each shelf, and painted to taste. This method is not recommended for stacks of more than four shelves as the whole structure could topple over. Why not combine bricks with old floorboards, well sanded and sealed and have almost free shelving?

If the room has alcoves the walls on either side (the return walls) can be used for shelving fixings. Drill, plug and screw battens to support the shelves – an extra batten along the back will provide extra support for very heavy loads. Use simple angle brackets to fix shelves to the wall – they do not look unattractive if shelf, wall and bracket are all painted the same colour. Heavy duty brackets are available for a shelf which will be used for a television set, or as a writing desk. Alternatively, you can use one of the many systems on the market with slotted uprights into which are clipped brackets in various sizes to suit shelves of different widths. Once the uprights are level and fixed the height of the shelves can be adjusted at any later time, as and when the storage needs changing.

It is important to remember that with all types of wall fixed shelving firm fixings are essential, so that time and trouble should be taken to make sure that shelving is securely fixed. If the fixing is inadequate and the shelves come away from the wall, members of the family might suffer a dangerous accident, and many of your valued possessions might be broken. Use screws of sufficient size and length fixed firmly into wallplugs or wall-filling compound. If you doubt your D.I.Y. abilities, have your shelving fixed professionally.

Add doors (and possibly ends) to a set of shelves, and you have the makings of a built-in cupboard. If you cannot afford doors, or as a convenient alternative, use roller blinds to pull down over a set of shelves in an alcove, to hide untidiness from view, and keep out at least some dust.

The assortment of speakers, turntables, tape-decks and so on that make up a stereo system can be accommodated very satisfactorily on adjustable

LEFT AND ABOVE *There are shelving units to suit most decorative schemes and budgets.*
RIGHT *Simple box units with covered foam slabs make inexpensive seating.*

wall fixed shelving. Each piece of equipment should be placed at exactly the right height for both its function and your convenience. This has the added advantage that the record player will not be affected by vibrations from the floor. With some systems, wiring can be concealed in the wall channels, and lighting can be fixed at strategic points around the room.

If more money is available, you may be able to afford free-standing storage furniture. Try making a list of everything you want to store, in order to find a system that meets your needs. Beware of mail order advertisements. Check measurements very carefully; some systems look deceptively large in the attractive photographs!

There are many small extra touches which can add to the comfort of a family living room without much extra cost. Are there plenty of cushions, for example? Is there small-scale storage for the inevitable family clutter – mugs for pens and pencils, small bowls or baskets for such items as odd buttons, coins and beads? Larger baskets with lids or even small linen baskets are very useful as they allow the quick clearance of sewing or knitting or scattered toys. Consider the provision of one more electrical point than you think you need, so that you really do get the lighting where you want it. And what about an extra small table so that everybody can eat in comfort.

Flooring for living rooms must be hard-wearing and easy to clean; if you have small children or pets choose a darkish colour, preferably with a texture or pattern to disguise staining. If you are buying pile carpeting, which looks and feels lovely, do

buy the best you can afford; otherwise choose a good quality cord and add rugs. Living rooms can look delightful with wood floors but they may be a little noisy when a lot of people move about the room at the same time; as an alternative consider cork tiles or even one of the more sophisticated vinyls either in sheet or tile form.

Dining rooms

RIGHT *Dining rooms are useful but they can also be pleasing. A table carefully laid with pretty china, napkins and glass is well worth the trouble taken.*

BELOW *Hang a low light over a dining table to create a warm, intimate atmosphere.*

A separate dining room is an old fashioned idea but it makes a lot of good sense for modern families. Most people like to have some facilities for eating in the kitchen, where food can be quickly and easily served for everyday meals. However, unless the kitchen is very large, and can provide space for some form of partitioning or screening, it is very difficult to divorce the eating from the cooking. On special occasions such as Christmas, anniversaries, birthdays, entertaining or even the weekly Sunday lunch, it is pleasant to be able to provide a meal in a separate room, with special table settings and the best tableware. Sometimes it will be convenient to feed the children in the kitchen, while the adults eat in the dining room.

It is important to have the dining room close to the kitchen, to avoid long journeys with food. Where possible, arrange for a door to open between the dining room and the kitchen or at least provide a serving hatch. Make sure your hatch space is large enough – small hatches can be very frustrating in use. An area of about 500mm wide by 460mm high will give plenty of room for passing large dishes and tall bottles. Double or sliding doors help to shut out kitchen noise and smells.

Choose dining furniture with care. Furniture designers are not always perfect and it is a good idea to spend a while in the furniture shop sitting at the dining set you have in mind. When matching chairs to tables look for at least 255mm of knee room between chair and table. Test this out for yourself if you can and be particularly careful when matching old chairs to a modern table. If you are buying chairs with arms (sometimes called carvers), make sure that they will tuck away tidily under the table. Check that there is enough space at the table for the number of people likely to be seated. A dining table for four persons needs to be about 900mm square. In the same space, a round table of 900mm diameter could take five persons. A dining table for six will measure around 1500mm by 900mm. Larger sizes are available for eight or ten persons. The best value here, if there is space, is probably a second-hand table but this may be too big for the average home. Alternatively, try a table for four or six which extends either from the middle or from the end. Check on the seating comfort of the extra persons by testing the extension, which should work easily and smoothly.

Sideboards are often available to match tables. They provide useful storage in the dining room for sets of cutlery and china kept for best and away from the rough and tumble of daily kitchen use.

However, there is more storage space in a modern wall unit system than in a sideboard. Cupboards with doors in glass, wood or plastic are best for storing china or glass. If furnishing on a strict budget, try a set of wall-mounted shelves, with a shelf 450mm deep at a height of about 900mm for use as a serving surface.

Choose a floor covering which is easy to clean but not noisy when chairs scrape back. Vinyl tiles or sheet, cork tiles, or carpet tiles with synthetic pile are all suitable.

Make sure the colours and patterns selected provide a pleasant background for eating – reds, browns, and purples can be warm and cosy. Avoid strident patterns and harsh contrasts.

When the room is not in use for meals, it can provide a quiet area of reading or study. You will need to provide a comfortable chair and a protective covering if the tabletop is to be used for hobbies or study. Make sure that there is extra storage space in the room to take books, half completed models and other things when the time comes to clear up for a meal.

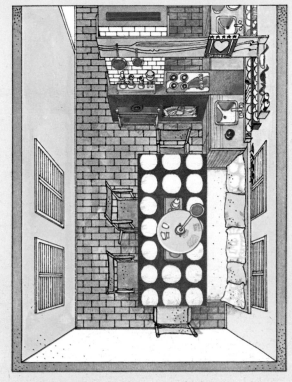

FAR LEFT *A practical idea is to create a dining area opening out from the kitchen. Here a sophisticated look is created with built-in box seating and tube and cane chairs in classic shapes.*

LEFT AND ABOVE *The plan view shows that a large enough kitchen can be easily divided by means of a counter and storage units to create a comfortable dining room. Note how the built-in seating saves space. The rise-and-fall pendant provides ideal lighting and the tablecloth makes a splash of colour.*

Kitchens

With most families the kitchen is the heart of the home. Apart from the obvious functions of food preparation and storage, and washing-up, most families use the kitchen for at least some, if not all, meals. Younger children like to be close to their mothers and may play in the kitchen and older children quite often do their homework there. People tend to congregate in kitchens to chat. The kitchen is also often used for washing clothes, although it is not the ideal place for this.

A well-planned kitchen does not have to have wall to wall glossy cupboards and expensive coloured tiles. On the contrary, if a kitchen is to have any character and individual appeal, it will probably have the minimum of such things. What is important is that the actual work flow arrangement of preparation and cooking is planned sensibly, that the surface treatments of walls, floors, worktops, etc., are hard wearing and easily cleaned, that there is enough, but not too much, storage space, and that the whole room is attractive and welcoming – in short, a place where the family likes to be.

Remember that some of the most successful kitchens have, by dint of good design, been made in unpromising spaces (too small, too big or ill-shaped) and not in the lavish areas usually depicted in advertisers' kitchens.

PLANNING

This is a question of making the best possible use of the space available whether large or small. A useful guide is the work flow recommendation of the Parker Morris Report, which has been a bible for post-war housing. This states that in a kitchen, the work sequence should be in the following order: work surface / cooker / work surface / sink / work surface; and there should be no gap or obstruction between sink and cooker. This flow does not have to be along one wall; in fact it is probably better if it is not. It can be along two adjoining walls (L-shaped) or, in a small room, along three walls (U-shaped). It does not have to be along a wall at all, for it is possible to build a sink or hob into a peninsula unit jutting out into a room The most travelled route in your kitchen is from sink to cooker and this should not be disturbed by any through circulation – for example people walking through the kitchen to get to the back door. Your sink, cooker and fridge will form a basic work-triangle. To avoid on the one hand cramped working conditions and on the other unnecessary walking, it is recommended that the total extent of the work triangle should be between 1800mm and 3600mm.

An important aspect of kitchen planning often

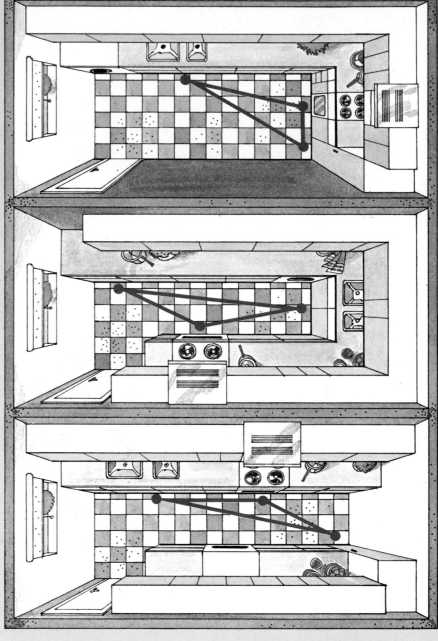

ignored is the correct height of the work surface. This is vital unless the cook is to work in perpetual discomfort. Recommendations for persons of average height include the following:

Work surface (including hobs)	850mm–1000mm
Sink top	900mm–1050mm
Bottom of wall units above worktop	1350mm
Highest shelf for general use	1800mm

There must, of course, be some leeway as people vary in height. To test the working height which suits you best, set up a trial surface with a board and two supports, trying various heights until you reach your optimum level for working. When buying units, bear in mind this need for adaptability. Wall-hung, cantilevered units are no problem, and where floor units have a plinth, it is usually possible to reduce or increase their height.

ABOVE *One of the fundamental precepts of good kitchen planning is to create an unbroken working surface between cooker and sink. Sink and cooker (or hob unit) and working surfaces can be arranged in an L shape (top), a U shape (centre) or in a straight line (above). Try and ensure that the path between sink and cooker is not crossed by any through traffic.*

ABOVE *A pretty and well-planned kitchen with unbroken working surface between hob unit and sink. Tiles behind the cooker make for easy cleaning as does the quarry-tiled floor. The built-in shelving is a perfect way of saving space and providing adequate storage.*

LEFT *A built-in hob with storage space underneath is one way of dealing with cramped conditions.*

When work flow and the height at which it is to operate are settled, the next move is to make the best use of the space available. In a tiny kitchen this will involve little more than arranging the working area described with cupboards hanging on walls above, and perhaps a small counter shelf and stools for meals. In larger kitchens, however, it is worth trying to break down the space into three separate units: the preparation, working and cooking section; the eating area; and the laundry area if you have no separate laundry room. In a large square room this is no problem, and the space can be made easier to use by being divided into smaller areas with the aid of peninsula or island units. There is no need to tramp great distances between the sink, the fridge and cupboards and the cooker; they can all be grouped together, with the eating area separated from the work area by an island unit which provides storage space for cutlery and crockery as well as being a worktop and serving table. A long narrow kitchen, sometimes regarded as a problem shape, can be exploited similarly, with the work area arranged in the Parker Morris fashion around three wall surfaces at one end with the eating area separated off in the middle by two peninsula units, and the washing area, with its large separate sink, at the far end.

Any of these arrangements can, at some expense, be achieved by using new kitchen units. Do not imagine, however, that it is impossible to create an attractive and workable kitchen without a vast number of cupboards. Much can be done with the units you already have, arranged to make them function in the most effective way, and perhaps improved by one or two additions. The whole lot can be drawn together by a new work surface and perhaps a fresh coat of matching paint. The minimum of new units can be purchased – to house the sink, for example, and to provide the basic work surface – while the remaining storage and work surface can be in the form of a second-hand cupboard or chest and table with home-made open shelving.

EQUIPMENT

Think carefully about the needs of your family and do not be lured into buying equipment which will be largely unused. As well, investigate each item before you part with any money. The following are some ideas on how to incorporate equipment into your kitchen plan.

● *Cookers,* whether gas or electric, are free-standing but are usually designed to be sited against a wall. A split-level arrangement consists of hobs built in to the working surface with a separate oven. Both gas and electric models are available so it is possible to have a combination of fuels. However, split-level, built-in cookers tend to be expensive and sometimes take up more room than a simple cooker.

Do not site your cooker or hob unit in a corner as you will need room to stand comfortably in front. It is also useful to have a heat-resistant working surface on either side of you at the same height as the hob.

● *Refrigerators* are virtually essential for every family. Buy one slightly larger than you think you need, particularly in a small modern house with no larder. Smaller fridges will tuck under your working surface; but if you need a tall fridge or fridge/freezer it should be sited at the end of your run of working surface so as not to interrupt the work flow.

● *Freezers* are a boon to those with access to large quantities of fresh vegetables, fruit and meat. The Electricity Council advise a capacity of 55 litres for each member of the household, plus an additional 55 litres – though the size of your vegetable garden, orchard and pocket would seem to be equally important. The larger models, both the chest-type and front-opening type, should be kept in a garage, cellar or utility room and not consume space in the kitchen. For those with lesser needs the combination freezer/refrigerator with separate doors will fit into even a small kitchen. Manufacturers' leaflets give exact measurements which enable one to plan before purchasing.

● *Dishwashers* should be situated as closely as possible to the water supply and drainage as well as to the sink, so that plates may be rinsed before stacking. They can fit below or on top of the work surface, or be fixed to the wall at shoulder height, according to their size, type and make. The front loading type fitting below the sink is very convenient, but be sure there is sufficient space for

LEFT *As an alternative to sets of kitchen units, consider open shelving for storage. Placed over a cupboard unit, as here, it creates a dresser effect.*

ABOVE *In a larger kitchen, space can sometimes be broken up with an island unit. This one contains a sink and useful working surface.*

● *Extractor fans* can no longer be regarded as luxuries. One installed above a cooker with a wide hood whisks away food smells before they penetrate the whole house and make the atmosphere stale and unpleasant.

● *Sink grinders* (or waste disposal units) can also be invaluable in a household where there is much cooking, as they obviate the need for making messy little parcels of eggshells, vegetable peelings, and so on for consigning to the dustbin.

SURFACES AND DECORATION

Floor surfaces should be hard wearing, relatively impervious to water and grease spillages, and attractive in appearance. They should also be slip resistant. Busy cooks constantly on their feet will also appreciate a degree of resilience. Sheet and tile vinyl makes an excellent, reasonably priced floor covering both warm and quiet to tread, as do cork tiles, which are particularly satisfactory in a kitchen if bought with a thin plastic film already applied. Despite the claims of manufacturers, it seems doubtful whether soft floor coverings, like the special kitchen carpetings or tiles, are a practical proposition in a kitchen. Their designs are uniformly bad. The very hard floorings, such as quarry and ceramic tiles are exceptionally durable but can be hard on the feet. Further suggestions for flooring can be found on pages 92–108.

Wall surfaces can be painted in an easy-to-wash gloss or eggshell oil-based paint or more conveniently with a vinyl emulsion. Add tiling around the sink and cooker areas for extra protection against food splashes. Vinyl (or a washable) wallpaper, again perhaps with tiles as a splashback, is inexpensive and can be extremely attractive. If plaster is old and damaged, tongued-and-grooved-boarding, sealed with polyurethane varnish, makes an attractive cover-up, but do not use more than two wall coverings in any one room. Try wood around the eating area, with gloss paint elsewhere; or plastic-coated wallpaper throughout with a tile splashback; or have vinyl in the cooking area and tiles in the laundry area.

Work surfaces can be covered in easily cleaned, laminated plastic which come in some good plain colours though the patterns tend to be dull and mere copies of natural materials. Post formed laminates make curved edges to work surfaces and these can be ordered from many manufacturers along with their ranges of kitchen units, though it is also possible to have them made to order to suit special requirements. Surfaces can also be made of hardwood, which is expensive, or of ceramic or quarry tiles which as well as being expensive tend to crack and must be carefully laid so that no dirt-collecting gaps appear. It is also useful to have small insets of different materials for particular uses: a square of wood inset as a chopping board, marble for cool pastry making and stainless steel

the door to be let down, especially if you have a narrow galley kitchen or a central island unit.

● *Washing machines*, a necessity rather than a luxury for many families, should ideally be situated in a separate laundry room or in a separate area of the kitchen. The largest washing machines are twin tub models. These are less expensive than automatic machines but they tend to take a smaller load, perhaps up to 3kg dry weight. The only hand work required is in the transfer of clothes from the washing tub to the spin dryer. Automatic machines, when plumbed in, need no manual attention and can take up to 5kg dry weight. They are expensive, especially if they include a built-in tumbler dryer, but they take the hard work out of washing. Several makes have complementary tumbler dryers which fit on top or stand alongside. Both should be fitted on an external wall so that steam from the machine can easily be expelled.

ABOVE *Pine panelling and painted brick gives this kitchen a country look. The peninsular units break up the kitchen as well as providing several working surfaces. Clever storage ideas include the overhead cupboard which opens from both sides, open shelving and a suspended framework from which to hang kitchen utensils.*

near the cooker where hot pans can be set down.

Decoration involves the selection of colours and patterns for everything in the kitchen. The first aim should be simplicity as has been indicated above. Too many colours, materials and designs can be discordant, so plan for two or three colours and two or three materials. The following are a few suggested schemes.

If you like the idea of a country kitchen (even if you live in the heart of a big city) why not choose pine kitchen cupboards, new or second-hand? These look good with a deep red quarry tiled floor (or a vinyl imitating quarry tiles if neither your purse nor your floor structure will allow for quarry), with plain white gloss walls, multi-coloured floral curtains at the windows and pale green plastic work surfaces.

If, on the other hand, you want a family kitchen which hides the wear it tends to get, you might choose kitchen cupboards in a plain dark green with a pale green patterned laminate surface, easy-to-wash cork floors in pale gold, and a green, gold

and white patterned vinyl wallpaper with plain white fringed blinds at the window.

Alternatively, a sunny room could have cupboards faced in the new plastic which looks like blue denim, with plain pale blue surfaces, blue and white patterned paper on the walls, a deep blue vinyl floor, bright yellow curtains and plastic chairs and a yellow and white table cover.

If you like smart surroundings and have no children, you could choose a black and white scheme – white or black and white vinyl floor, black stained cupboard doors, white tiled work surfaces and splash-back, with white painted walls and boldly patterned red and white blind and table covering.

If you plan along these lines, adding bright greenhouse plants, a few inexpensively framed prints and perhaps tablecloths, and napkins to match the curtains, or tea towels which pick up a colour in the wallpaper, you will have a charming and distinctive kitchen without that fatal over-crowded look.

Bathrooms

Shortage of space or money or both cause most people to make do more or less with the bathroom which they already have. In many homes the bathroom is small and possibly bleak as well.

If your bathroom is small, it may be out of the question for you to enlarge it without major building work. Consider relieving the pressure on it by duplicating some of its functions in other parts of the home.

For example, could you install a second wc elsewhere? A wc with a very small washbasin can usually be fitted into a space of about 800mm by 1630mm. Building regulations allow a wc opening off a bedroom, provided that there is another wc in the house or another entrance to the wc not through the bedroom.

Can a washbasin be fitted in any bedroom, thus relieving morning congestion? To install a washbasin and use it comfortably, you need a space of about 1000mm by 1100mm.

Is there anywhere in the house where you could install a separate shower unit? Shower trays are from 700mm to 915mm square, and you will need a clear space in front of your shower of around 700mm by 900mm for undressing and drying. Overall height averages about 1800mm. Prefabricated shower enclosures are available as complete units.

If your bathroom is bleak, the remedy is usually simple – i.e. add physical warmth with better heat-ing. Heated towel rails can be connected to domestic hot water rather than the central heating circuit so that they provide warmth through the summer as well. Safety is the prime consideration with any form of electrical heating. Never use any portable electric appliances in the bathroom, apart from shavers plugged into their own special sockets. Never use portable electric fires, record players or electric hairdryers, or even washing machines. As an alternative form of heating, consider an oil-filled thermostatically controlled radiator, or an electrically heated towel rail, installed by a competent electrician and connected to a point outside the bathroom.

You can also add visual warmth with the use of warm colours, such as brown, red and orange. The high ceilings you find in some bathrooms in old houses can look particularly attractive when painted orange or scarlet, and this also helps to reduce the apparent height. Modern vinyl emulsions stand up well to steamy bathroom conditions. Vinyl wall coverings are also suitable for bathrooms; many of them have pleasantly textured surfaces which also make them warm to the touch. Wood can be a pleasant decorative finish; well sealed tongued-and-grooved pine panelling, for example, provides a wall covering which both looks and feels warm and which can often be used to conceal ugly pipework. One of the most pleasant ways of adding colour is to use brightly coloured towels. This need not involve the expense of buying new towels; deep-dye those which you already have. Use cold water dye for colour fastness.

The floor, of course, is mostly used by bare and

BELOW LEFT *Bathrooms need not be boring, although they all too often come last on the list of decorating priorities. In fact, the bathroom is an ideal place for decorative experiments, such as wall murals.*

BOTTOM *Larger bathrooms give you the chance to put in extra storage or equipment, a shower or a bidet, perhaps. Here storage is provided by an old-fashioned chest of drawers which fits in well with the cottage mood of the room.*

often wet feet. It is essential that it feels warm. Altering floor covering from, say, chilly lino to bathroom carpeting is one of the most pleasant of changes. Make sure that any carpeting you choose is suitable for bathrooms; rubber-backed carpets with synthetic piles stand up best, and it is possible to buy washable bathroom carpeting which you can cut to shape yourself with a sharp pair of scissors. Vinyl is a practical waterproof floor covering. The cushioned versions are the most attractive but vinyl, like ceramic tiles, is slippery when wet. Cork tiles are ideal as they both look and feel warm, but they must be well sealed against the inevitable moisture. With all these floor coverings, even the fitted carpet, it is important to provide an absorbent bath mat to take up as much moisture as possible when a person gets out of the bath.

Besides warming up the temperature and the colour-scheme, and changing the flooring, there are other small and inexpensive improvements which can be made to the average bathroom. For example, most bathrooms are very short on storage. Add lots of extra storage in the simple form of open shelving. Bathroom shelves can be as narrow as 100mm and still serve a useful purpose for bottles, aerosols, jars, spare packs of soap and toilet paper, and a host of other items. It is essential to provide a separate locked cabinet for the medicines. This does not have to be sited in the bathroom, and being locked will eliminate the risk of accidental poisoning to small children.

Plenty of large dry towels make a great deal of difference to bathroom comfort. If you cannot afford to install a heated towel rail, at least make sure that you have adequate rails on which towels can dry. It is often possible to fit extra towel rings in odd spaces too small for full length rails. Make sure that rails are firmly fixed, as they tend to be used as hand grips especially by children.

Installing a new bathroom, or dramatically altering the layout of that which you have already, is a matter for the experts; you should consult an architect, surveyor or qualified builder on the legality and practicality of what you have in mind. Building work, other than of a repair or maintenance character, requires the approval of the local authority, which will check that the proposed alterations conform to the building regulations and bye-laws. If you are installing a bathroom in a house previously without a bathroom ask your local authority about the possibility of getting a government grant. You should not start any work until your grant has been approved.

EQUIPMENT

If you are involved in choosing new bathroom equipment, there are some useful guides. With all equipment, make sure that you have adequate floor space for comfortable usage – do not, for example, install wc or basins too close to a return wall. The

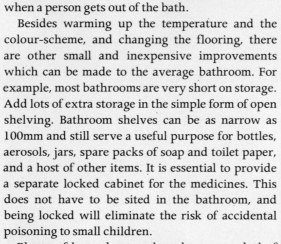

TOP RIGHT Plants thrive in the humid conditions of a bathroom. Use them to add warmth and to impart elegance to your bathroom.

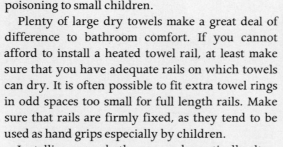

ABOVE RIGHT Ceramic tiles and pine cladding give a bathroom a clean and attractive appearance as well as being most practical. Make sure, however, that wood panelling is adequately varnished.

RIGHT A shower unit is a perfect solution to the problem of a cramped bathroom. Decorate in pale colours to increase the feeling of space.

to repair. Common basin sizes are 635mm by 455mm and 560mm by 405mm. Many other sizes are available, however, from mini to luxury. Basins can be mounted on pedestals, which conceal the pipework, or fixed to the wall (the recommended height is 785mm). In all cases do make sure the fixings are secure. Vanitory units are convenient with the basin inset into a cupboard top or long

cheapest fittings are white, but you can add your own glamorous colours with the rest of the decoration.

● *Baths.* Make sure that you choose a bath long enough for the comfort of the tallest member of the family. Metric lengths available are 1500, 1600, 1700, and 1800mm, and baths are still being made in imperial lengths of 60in (1525mm), 66in (1675mm) and 72in (1830mm). Widths of baths vary between 700mm and 800mm, and matching end and side panels are available for most modern designs. If panelling the bath yourself, make sure that you have a removable section for access to the plumbing. Baths are commonly made from cast iron, pressed steel, or acrylic plastics. Metal baths have enamel coatings which can chip. Plastic baths are much lighter and can be moulded into more exciting shapes. The colour goes right through the material which is, however, vulnerable to scratching and can be scarred by lighted cigarettes thus making them difficult to clean.

● *Washbasins* for homes are usually made from vitreous china – a ceramic base with a tough outside coating of glass-like enamel. Take care of your basin, as cracks and chips are virtually impossible

shelf which provides a handy area adjacent to the basin, for the use of anything from cosmetics and hair rollers to changing the baby!

● *Wc pans* are usually made of vitreous china, normally about 400mm high, with cisterns of the same material or of plastic. Wc pans are usually free-standing. Close-coupled wcs are, however, increasingly popular, the cistern fitting directly to the back of the pan to reduce the overall height. Slim-line panel cisterns are available where space is restricted. Wall-fixed wcs are available for use with concealed flushing cisterns. There is a choice between a washdown flushing action which is cheap, noisy but efficient, or various forms of syphonic action which are quieter but more expensive.

● *Bidets* are still a novelty in this country but most people who have used them abroad will appreciate their value for personal hygiene. Unfortunately, limited space often prevents the inclusion of a bidet in a bathroom plan. Bidets are designed in vitreous china either to fit close to the wall or to be free standing. Consult your local authority about the strict water regulations which govern their installation.

Bedrooms

The focal point of the bedroom is the bed itself. Whether or not you make use of the bedrooms in your home during the daytime as suggested below, it is of paramount importance that your bedrooms provide a good night's sleep to revitalize you for your daily activities. You may be unconscious but you are using your bedroom as much while asleep as at any other time – perhaps even more so. Make sure, therefore, that you site your more important bedrooms in the quiet positions in the house. For example, it may be more convenient to have a double bedroom in a smaller room at the back of the house if the large front room faces a noisy street. If you plan to double-glaze your windows to cut out excess sound, you will need a larger gap for sound insulation than for heat insulation – at least 100mm, preferably twice that amount.

The position of the bed is important. The head of the bed should not be placed under a window or between a window and a door because of draughts, although these can be minimized with foam self-adhesive strip and generously sized thick curtains. If you place the bed opposite a window, the early morning light may be disturbing, particularly if the window faces east (although this problem can be overcome with thick curtains or well fitting blinds). A double bed can often be conveniently sited against a chimney breast if the fireplace has been covered up. The alcoves on either side can be used for storage, and the breast wall can be made into a special feature – perhaps with a large-scale wallpaper design which, being behind you, will not distract you while resting.

Single beds can be lengthways along the wall, and so provide a good back rest for daytime lounging. But double beds need space on either side to avoid one partner having to clamber over the other, as well as to facilitate bed-making. A space of at least 400mm is required around a bed for bed-making with 550mm at its foot.

Select a good quality comfortable bed – the right choice should last at least ten years. It is most important to choose a bed which is large enough for you; a small bed is a false economy. Don't hesitate to lie on beds in the shop while making a selection – a timid prod is useless. Lie flat on the bed with your hands behind your head, and relax your elbows on the mattress. See that your elbows do not overlap the edge and make sure that the bed is at least 150mm longer than you are. Our table shows the standard sizes of beds available in shops, and the corresponding sizes of sheets, blankets and duvet covers.

Consider weight as well as size. Firmer beds are better for heavier people. A couple should shop together for a double bed so that both can try it out.

If there is a great inequality of weights, it is possible to buy two beds of different firmness which 'zip-and-link' together to make a double. This prevents the lighter person rolling into the middle and is also beneficial if one person is a restless sleeper.

Open, individual coil springs represent the most common type of mattress construction. Posture springing, the patented method of one particular manufacturer, is made from one continuous length of wire – the advantage claimed is that the stress imposed by the body is more evenly distributed over the surface of the whole bed. Pocketed springs, found in more expensive beds, are individual springs each sewn under tension into a separate calico pocket so that, it is claimed, each spring acts independently of the other and the mattress conforms to the shape and weight of the body. With both these types of sprung mattress, the more dense (i.e. the more numerous) the springs the better. Layers of insulating upholstery containing such materials as woollen mix, cotton felt, curled hair or foam, are placed over the springs to prevent the feel of the springs and to add warmth and some initial softness to the mattress. Foam mattresses are made from latex (natural or man-made rubber) or polyether (man-made plastic). These mattresses are often attractively slim-line; made in one piece, there are no springs which can possibly creak!

There are two main types of bed base. In a sprung edge base, the springs themselves form the edge of the base, standing up above the wooden frame, to give softness to the very edge of the bed. In a firm edge base, however, the wooden frame forms the edge; this makes the edge firmer and more suitable if people will be sitting a lot on the edge of the bed. It is important to use a mattress on the base for which it was designed; never attempt to put a new mattress on to a worn base. Some new designs of bed base have pull-out drawers for valuable extra storage. With this ottoman type of base, the mattress and top of the base lift up to provide storage for bulky items such as spare bedding.

Traditionally, storage has been provided by wardrobes, dressing tables and chests of drawers. Pieces from large old fashioned bedroom suites are still easy to find fairly cheaply in second-hand shops, so that if you have a large bedroom, you can provide a lot of storage at relatively low cost. With smaller rooms, however, careful planning and maximum use of fitted or built-in units makes a better use of space.

Take time and trouble to plan your clothes storage system. Each adult needs at least 900mm of hanging rail. Children up to about twelve years can manage with less, perhaps 600mm. A wide range of fitments is available to give the neat look and convenience of a custom built-in unit. You can install these systems yourself to cut costs, or you can use the fitting service provided by the shop. Units come in a choice of widths so that any length of

wall can be fitted to within a few millimetres. In many cases, the manufacturers merely provide the sides and front, leaving your own walls to form the back; this can save substantially on the cost of materials and labour. Top cupboards take the wardrobes to within a few inches of the ceiling, and a panel is then made to fill the gap. Doors can be sliding or hinged. Sliding doors take up less space in cramped bedrooms, but they make it difficult to find a particular garment as it is not possible to see everything inside the cupboard at a glance. One of the least expensive and most effective of these new built-in systems is the 'sliding wall' where large sliding panels are fitted in tracks along the floor and ceiling, partitioning off as much storage space as required.

Crucial to the efficiency of a storage system is the way the space is divided inside cupboards. The wardrobe part of the system will be around 1850mm high. With the top cupboards, best used for storing bulky items not in constant use (sports equipment, suitcases, spare bedding etc.), the total height will be about 2300mm. In the wardrobes, some full length hanging space will be needed for long dresses and coats. Blouses, suits, trousers and so on will, however, fit into a vertical space of

ABOVE *A well-planned bedroom will have plenty of storage to dispense with the clutter of discarded clothes. Duvets (or Continental quilts) with pretty covers make bedspreads unnecessary. Note how the bed, although simply furnished, provides an attractive focal point to the room.*

LEFT *If you need an extra bedroom and do not have the space, consider building a platform bed.*

about 1000mm and the space below can therefore be used for a second rail or for extra drawers or shelves. Adequate wardrobe depth is around 600mm, usually somewhat deeper than the average alcove on either side of a chimney breast. Wardrobes built-in to alcoves may therefore project into the room. Bridge the gap between them with narrower shelving; a shelf of about 750mm will serve as a dressing table. Alternatively, if the fireplace can be closed off, the space inside the chimney breast can usually be opened up without too much trouble to provide more cupboard space.

When space is very short, and it is necessary to provide hanging space in a shallow alcove, pull-out hanging fitments can be bought to fit to the underside of a shelf. Add a roller blind or a curtain to make a low cost wardrobe, which will serve while you are saving up for something more substantial. There are other ways of providing low cost clothes storage. Curtain off a length of wall and simply fit a rod behind with rod sockets; or use a shopfitter's dress stand, or paint or paper stout cardboard boxes, varnish them and add a hardboard lid to make cheap storage units.

You will need drawers, or pull-out racks, or even simple pigeon holes in which to keep all the items of clothing which cannot be put on clothes hangers. Shallow drawers, about 100mm deep are useful for small items such as stockings, handkerchiefs, belts and scarves. Deeper drawers, about 200mm deep are useful for underwear, tee shirts and so on. And drawers about 300mm deep are needed for bulky sweaters and similar garments. Some of this drawer storage can probably be provided behind the wardrobe doors. Extra sets of drawers can also be added to the system, possibly bridging a gap between two chests or between a chest and a wardrobe with a long work top. This can serve as a dressing table and, for a luxury touch, a washbasin might be fitted into this counter top, adjacent to an outside wall if possible to facilitate the plumbing.

You will need somewhere to put clothes at night – plenty of hooks and hangers are required. Alternatively, an old-fashioned chair with an upright tall wooden back or even an old-fashioned wooden towel rail can make a good resting place for suits, trousers, skirts and shirts.

Where a couple share a bedroom, it may be convenient for one of them to dress elsewhere – either to relieve early morning bedroom congestion, or to avoid disturbing the other person when they are catching up on sleep. If the bathroom is large enough, this can provide an alternative dressing room, and it may be convenient to have some storage of clothes near at hand, for example on a landing, if space permits. Many women prefer to keep their cosmetics in the bathroom, as it is more convenient to apply make-up where there is easy access to running water.

ABOVE *Fitting doors to built-in cupboards can be expensive. An alternative idea is to use roller blinds which are available in a variety of colours and patterns. The adjustable spotlight provides essential lighting.*

ADDITIONAL USES FOR BEDROOMS

Important as it is to get a good night's rest, a bedroom used only for sleeping effectively limits its use to six to eight hours plus the time it takes to dress and undress. As bedrooms take up at least one-third if not more of the space in a family home, remarkably little value is obtained from a room which is a bedroom and nothing else.

Spend a little time, therefore, thinking about the other uses to which a bedroom can be put, both during the day and the early evening. When planning the decorating and furnishing of a bedroom from scratch, think about these additional uses from the very beginning because they will involve extra furnishings or equipment. The following are some of the other uses for bedrooms.

● *Reading.* If you have a television set or rowdy children in the living room, it is very difficult to find a quiet place to curl up with a good book or catch up on the newspapers and magazines. Bedrooms provide the answer if they have adequate heating and, possibly, extra lighting. A comfortable chair is important, or if there is no room for this, have some cushions for use with the bed – bolster or wedge-shaped cushions against the wall are ideal. If there is enough wallspace, provide bookshelves with a wide shelf for magazines and papers. If space is limited, try fitting a bookshelf at the end of the bed or a simple rack to take magazines. For ideas on shelving, see the section on living rooms on page 47.

● *Studying.* This is really an extension of reading. Members of the family may need somewhere to study – including children at school, teenage students, and adults who are attending classes or following a correspondence course. In addition to the facilities for reading described above, there will have to be a suitable surface for writing. If space allows, this can be a small desk – possibly a junk-shop find. However, a wide shelf at least 460mm deep is perfectly adequate, fixed at about 700mm to 750mm from the floor. Use heavy-duty wall angle brackets, or incorporate this work-top shelf into a wall shelving system. In either case, make sure the fixings are really firm. Alternatively, a desk can be made by bridging the gap between two chests – whitewood chests or junk-shop finds are the cheapest. If there is room, the cheapest kind of desk top is a standard size flush door (1981mm by 762mm), but narrower widths are available. Shelving will also be needed for books, files, etc.

● *Hobbies.* Bedrooms can provide a welcome retreat to pursue a hobby (dressmaking, model making, stamp collecting and so on) away from the bustle of living room life. Work can be left in the various stages of completion without the continual need to clear up. There is also less danger of precious projects being sabotaged by pets or by younger members of the family. You will probably need to provide the same kind of extra facilities as for

studying, together with adequate heating and lighting.

● *Leisure activities.* It may suit to have a second television set in a bedroom to avoid bitter disputes about who watches what on which channel and when! Or the bedroom may be a convenient place to establish a listening centre for tapes or records. You will need the comfortable seating described for reading use with storage to accommodate your equipment, adequate power points, and effective heating. It may be necessary to consider providing extra sound insulation – carpeting and thick curtains will help deaden noise, and the walls could be lined with insulation cork.

● *Play activities for younger children.* Bedrooms, provided they are adequately heated, provide good places for children to play during the day – particularly older children who are not in need of constant supervision. For more details of bedroom/playrooms see the section on children's rooms on pages 62 to 63.

COLOUR SCHEMES
Colour schemes for bedrooms should be restful and harmonious. Most of the suggested extra bed-room uses also benefit from a peaceful background. Schemes based on shades of one colour (tone-on-tone) are always effective – blues and greys are particularly soothing. Pastel pinks, the bedroom cliché colour, can be cloying and over feminine unless they are sharpened, for example with touches of shocking pink or offset, perhaps, with grey. Other ideas are given in the section on colour scheming at the front of the book.

Bedroom flooring is important. It often comes into contact with bare feet so that something warm and welcoming is needed. Choose carpeting or carpet tiles – by all means select a cheaper grade as bedrooms do not receive the same concentrated wear as halls and living rooms. Money can be saved by carpeting only around the bed and not underneath it, especially if the bed base rests on the floor. Carpets help to deaden noise from bedrooms to floors below. As an alternative, cork tiles may be used to make a good bedroom floor; they are both warm and pleasant to the touch.

Before fitting any flooring make sure you have dealt with squeaky floorboards – they are particularly annoying in shared bedrooms! Further details on floorings can be found on pages 92 to 108.

ABOVE *This bedroom is given a traditional look by the patterned wallpaper, older style storage units (chest of drawers and wardrobe) and a lovely patchwork quilt with matching cushions which provides a splendid focal point to the room.*

Children's rooms

Most children's rooms are combined bedroom/playrooms. If on the other hand you are lucky enough to have a large house, you could consider giving the children a separate playroom of their own. This will considerably relieve the strain on the family living room and will be particularly appreciated by older children for entertaining their visitors.

SAFETY

Safety is the most important consideration to bear in mind at all times when planning children's rooms. They will be in their rooms unsupervised, possibly for hours at a time, and you will certainly want to minimize the possibility of accidents.

You will need heating – you cannot expect a child to play in a cold room. But make sure whatever method is chosen is completely safe. It is illegal to have an unguarded open fire. Radiators which get too hot to touch can frighten a child badly or even inflict a burn. Consider boxing in the radiators and covering the front with a decorative metal or hardboard grille. Never have any form of electric fire with exposed elements, even if these are protected by an open wire grid. Children might not realize the danger of poking or prodding. For the same reason, make sure that electrical sockets in children's rooms are of the shuttered type – that is, they will not open up until a plug is pushed in them. Consider also placing sockets halfway up the wall rather than in the skirting board at direct toddler reach. In all places in your home, take care not to have electrical equipment with loose connections or with frayed or long and trailing flexes. This is especially important in children's rooms.

Make sure that windows do not open in a way which would allow a child to fall out. Children are expert climbers. Secure the windows with safety catches or cover lower windows with louvre panels or perforated hardboard; or fit bars – vertically, not horizontally, as the children might be tempted

to climb them! Make sure that any large pieces of furniture or sets of shelving are completely stable; children have been known to topple over cupboards by climbing up the inside shelves or to use shelving units as a climbing frame. It is a simple matter to bracket a cupboard to the wall, and any sets of shelving should be fixed as firmly as possible. Roller blinds are probably safer than curtains; children sometimes try to swing on the curtains with the result that rail and curtain come crashing down. During the night children often need to seek parental comfort or go to the bathroom; make sure that they can see properly so that they do not trip over and hurt themselves. If a dimmer switch is fitted to the main light, leave the light on all night, turned down very low; or fit low wattage night-lights in the children's rooms and in the passageways. Bathroom pull-cords may need lengthening with a piece of string. Make sure that the main light switch in the children's room is low enough for them to turn on themselves. Try and have plenty of lightweight bins or boxes into which the children themselves can stow their smaller toys and other items – many minor playroom accidents are caused by tripping over, or stepping on or leaning on toys which have not been cleared away.

Children need firm beds to support their growing spines. After a child comes out of its cot, it is really not economical to buy anything other than a full-size bed for children grow amazingly quickly. As many people need to put two children into one room, bunk beds are deservedly popular, leaving extra floor space free for playing games. Choose the type which can be split into two single beds later on. Make sure that the top bunk has a full-length double safety rail and that the child is old enough to negotiate the top bunk with safety. The exact age for beds of this type depends on the child, but generally speaking, not before five years of age. Children who sleepwalk or are very restless in their sleep should not be put in a top bunk. Many accidents are caused by children falling out. Bunk beds are very difficult to make unless they have duvets and fitted bottom sheets. The child in the bottom bunk must have a reading light of his/her own for this area is very dark, even when the main room is brightly lit. Children like to have their friends to stay, and you can buy beds which conceal another folding bed underneath; or there are beds which turn into chairs or small tables when not in use.

Children love to draw and to paint, and for these and for all kinds of hobbies, they need a stable horizontal surface. This could be a sturdy second-hand table if there is space. The disadvantage is that younger children will have to sit on tall stools in order to reach, and it is all too easy to topple off these. Alternatively, you can sacrifice the table by cutting down its legs. Younger chil-

that, too – this kind of chair is often to be found in second-hand shops. Any surface provided for drawing or other hobbies should be well lit to avoid strain on young eyes – adjustable wall-mounted spotlights are invaluable.

Children need plenty of storage if they are fairly to be expected to obey adult commands to keep their rooms tidy! Provide plenty of hooks for dressing gowns, odd cardigans, jackets and so on. Hooks plus gaily coloured cloth or even carrier bags are an easy way of keeping different types of possessions separate so that they can be found quickly – one bag, for example, for brownie or cub uniform, another for sports or dancing clothes, and so on.

Do not buy fitments with small-size drawers or cupboards – children's clothes can be very bulky, and they soon grow out of small-size storage. It is better to have an adult-size cupboard well divided and with adjustable hanging racks, drawers and shelves. If drawers are labelled clearly, it helps both you and your children to keep clothes under control. Use all possible spaces for extra storage; for example, drawers on castors under the beds make good storage for toys or bulkier clothes. Bins for toys and games need not be expensive – paint large, sturdy cardboard boxes and fit them with rope handles. Or use brightly-coloured washing-up bowls which can be stacked neatly on open shelving.

Older children like occasionally to sit in their rooms and listen to records or read; make sure they have somewhere comfortable. Cover a second-hand chair with a bright fabric, softening any hard or lumpy spots with cushions. Or provide floor cushions or bolsters to turn the bed into a daytime sofa. In rooms for younger children, you will want a comfortable chair for yourself when reading stories and for sitting with the children if they are taken ill.

Flooring is very important for children's rooms. Adults often forget how close children are to the floor and how much time they spend on it. So many floors are unsuitable. Any form of wood could produce splinters. Pile carpeting is expensive and too easily spoilt; moreover, the pile interferes with car and other games. Consider cord carpeting in tough easy-clean man-made fibres such as nylon and polypropylene or carpet tiles made from synthetic fibres. Avoid rough-textured and abrasive sisal cords and coco matting which hurt tender knees and palms. Sheet or tile vinyls are suitable but choose bright colours and patterns or the effect could be a little bleak. Well-sealed cork flooring is warm and sympathetic. For a low-cost flooring, cover the floor with sheets of hardboard, smooth side up, and stain or paint with a design. Children love chequered or striped patterns which they can use as the basis for their own soldier, farm or car games.

ABOVE *From an early age, children will need a sturdy, stable horizontal surface on which to paint, make models, study and so on.*

dren love to have their own small-size tables and chairs. With a large family, this furniture will probably eventually earn its keep, being passed on from one child to another. Or you could provide the child with a wide shelf as a working surface, mounted on wall-fixed adjustable shelving brackets. The shelf can be raised as the child grows. If you invest in an adjustable office chair, raise

Workrooms

Studies, offices and utility rooms tend to be crowded out of existence in the small modern home. This is a pity for they can make life much more comfortable and smooth running. Moreover they are rooms with activities which do not require a large area so they can be slipped into a space which would otherwise be wasted.

STUDIES OR OFFICES

A study or office need not, for example, be the formal room commonly depicted in Victorian stage sets. It can be a tiny third bedroom almost too small to take a bed or a screened off part of a large landing. If the amount of studying to be done is minimal and the place is to be used simply for paying bills, writing letters and making shopping lists, then a perfectly adequate desk with drawers beneath for files can be fitted up in the kitchen or in a corner of the sitting room or bedroom.

If, however, serious work is to be done and a separate room given over to the purpose, the main aims should be an orderly working area, good lighting and relative quiet. Make sure that the writing and typing surfaces are at the right height, the latter slightly lower than the former. An average height is 650mm for typing, 750mm for writing, but vary these figures to suit the main user of the room. Make sure the telephone is within easy arm's reach of the work desk but preferably not on it: the surface should be as uncluttered as possible and there should be ample filing and book shelving, again within easy arm's reach. It will be clear from all this that in most cases a compact room is a positive advantage as the necessary furnishing and equipment can be easily ranged around the walls within reach of the worker's chair. For someone who needs reference and research material, extra filing and shelving will naturally demand a greater amount of wall space. Good lighting, both natural and artificial, is essential and ideally should come from over the writer's left hand (the reverse for a left-handed person); a desk set against a wall at right angles to the window would suit well. Apart from a good overall light from a central pendant or down-lighter there should be a writing lamp for evening work. As with the telephone, the lamp should not be set on the desk; it could be an angled lamp clamped to shelving above the desk, or a spotlight fixed to the wall, or a tube light concealed beneath the shelving and shining directly down on the working area.

The position of a room in a house will to some extent determine the amount of noise. If it is next to the kitchen or a teenager's bedroom or facing a main road, the noise problem might be acute, and this point should be considered when deciding on the room. Combat noise by double-glazing and by insulating the walls to deaden sounds from within the house. Fitted cupboards or crowded bookshelves do well in this respect and a certain amount of sound insulation can be obtained by lining the walls and doors with materials such as cork, hessian, wool or felt. Do not forget that the incessant tapping of a typewriter can cause distress to others, particularly late at night; stand the machine on a relatively soft surface such as a pad of felt which will help to muffle the noise.

Furniture for a study or office can, if the room is to be used for only occasional writing and reading, consist of no more than a writing desk and chair, a few bookshelves and, perhaps, a comfortable arm-

BELOW *This small extension has made a useful home office. An extended shelf makes an excellent desk and box units provide storage.*

chair. For more serious work, for example when used by a student, a freelance writer or someone conducting a business from home, the requirements will be much more extensive. Both typing and writing surfaces will be needed (and these could well form a right angle to each other), a telephone ledge with storage for directories, plenty of shelving, filing cabinets, stationery storage and so on.

A study or office can be neatly equipped with items from a medium priced shelving and storage range. This could start from modest beginnings – a writing surface, a couple of shelves above and two stacks of drawers below – and be gradually augmented with matching shelving and storage as needs increase. On a less ambitious scale, a length of blockboard or a flush door could be laid across two second-hand filing cabinets, the whole surmounted by home-made shelves, to form, with a second-hand office chair, a cheap and basic but nevertheless satisfactory work station. From a decorative point of view it could be pulled together by brightly coloured gloss paint, with pin-up board over the writing desk covered in a complementary coloured felt and, perhaps, a home-made roller blind at the window.

OTHER TYPES OF WORKROOM

Clothes washing activities should have their own separate area of the kitchen or, ideally, they should be allocated a separate utility room. This, too, need take up only a small space. It should be on an outside wall so that steam can be easily expelled and should, if the operation is not to be too expensive, be easily accessible to existing plumbing and drainage. With those considerations in mind, a utility room can be slipped into an obsolete outside lavatory, an old lean-to scullery, the space under the stairs or a large alcove such as is sometimes to be found on the landings of older houses.

The space should be large enough to take a washing machine, either twin-tub or fully automatic (see the section on 'Kitchens') and, if possible, a tumbler dryer. These machines are undoubtedly expensive to run but are a covetable extra in periods of wet weather or if you live in a flat with no outside drying facilities. A good substitute is a drying cupboard with hanging rails and a low kilowatt heater set at floor level, with an air vent in the door for ventilation. There should also be a large sink, ideally of the deep ceramic kind, for soaking large items and for hand washing, flanked by a laminated plastic counter on which damp washing can be sorted, and with a shelf above for soap powders. The utility room is also a good place to keep the ironing board, and a neat, easily-used arrangement is to have a foldaway board screwed to the wall inside a tall, narrow cupboard. A floor which is at least semi-waterproof against splashing and occasional overflows, wipe-clean walls covered in gloss paint or vinyl, and a good bright overhead light complete the setting for a workmanlike little room. Try to include an extractor fan, as the smell of wet washing can permeate a house as insidiously as that of stale food.

Other work areas in the house could include a handyman's bench set against the wall in a passageway with tools and materials ranged neatly in clips and with brightly coloured plastic storage boxes along the wall above; or a sewing corner concealed within a range of built-in bedroom cupboards — the machine screwed to a pull-up flap, cottons arranged in shallow trays, patterns filed in deep drawers, scissors and tapes hung on a piece of pinboard and a pull-down table for cutting.

BELOW *If you have a small, unused area in your home, consider turning it into a utility room for clothes washing and drying.*

Dual-purpose rooms

Dual-purpose or two-way rooms can be a real blessing to families who find their homes getting too small for them. Putting a room to an extra use usually involves a flash of inspiration to see the possibilities of the basic idea plus some additional and careful planning to put the idea into practice. Exactly how to give rooms an extra function will depend on the needs of the family, and the size and shape of the house. Here are a few ideas as a beginning.

Bedrooms can double up as studies, hobby rooms, reading rooms and so on: for a fuller discussion of these possibilities read the section on 'Bedrooms' earlier in this chapter.

Why not take the idea a little further and turn a bedroom into a proper bed-sitter? This can be very useful for accommodating a student son or daughter or an elderly relative – anybody who likes to have some life of their own apart from the family. In this kind of room, the bed will have to be used for seating during the day, so that it is best to choose a firm edge divan. A fully made up bed always looks bulky and still bed-like even with a neat cover. One solution is to use a fitted bottom sheet and duvet by night. During the day, provide storage for the duvet, perhaps in the base of the bed or in a box on castors to roll away under the bed. The bed can then be covered neatly with a spread and with covers the pillows can look like giant cushions. Remember that a bed which runs along the wall is too deep for comfortable seating so that extra bolsters or wedge-shaped cushions will be needed at the back. Put bolsters at each end and the bed starts to look like a settee. Or buy a convertible settee which opens out by night to produce a bed. For regular use, however, you should only consider designs which allow for folding complete with bedclothes – making up a bed from scratch every evening is very tedious.

You may want to provide some kind of cooking facilities in your bed-sitter. Even an electric kettle and a single electric ring offer considerable scope for small snacks, hot drinks and the like. If a small sink unit can be installed for washing-up, so much the better. But try and screen this area in some manner from the rest of the room – a set of shelves is ideal, providing extra storage at the same time. Or consider putting cooking/washing facilities behind a large sliding-wall storage system, consisting of full length sliding doors running in tracks fixed to ceiling and floor – these doors could also conceal storage for clothes and other possessions. Or make cheaper and simpler screens out of pull-down roller blinds or bead curtains.

In tall rooms in old houses, it might be possible to build some kind of a platform for use with a bed 'on high', reached by a safe ladder. The space underneath could be used as a seating and eating area, or for extra storage. You will need headroom of around 1980mm.

Halls and landings sometimes offer scope for two-way rooms, particularly in older houses built on generous lines. Sometimes there is room for a comfortable chair, where someone can read while others watch a noisy television programme in the living room. Or sometimes there is room for a small desk in a home office area. Where a house does not boast a modern utility room, it has been known for washing machines and freezers to be quite happily sited in odd corners of a hospitable hall!

Living rooms are invariably more than two-way rooms as they are called upon to cope with a constant variety of demands. If, however, you are short of a spare bedroom, remember that there are now many attractive settees on the market which provide a comfortable bed at the flick of a lever.

BELOW LEFT AND BELOW *Two views of the same bedsitter demonstrate how careful planning can produce a room which is restful and relaxed, despite its dual function.*

Halls and landings

The hall-passage-landing part of your home is the circulation area – which people usually pass through without lingering for any length of time. These areas are however just as important to your comfort and safety as any other part of your home. You should not skimp on planning.

Let us look first at the problem of safety. Lighting is vital for safety. In hallways, it is better to have some lighting at a lower level which can be left on for long periods than a bright burst of light turned on occasionally. Eyes need to adjust both when coming in from the dark and when coming out of a brightly lit living room. If possible, have a light with a switch by the front door so that you are in no danger of tripping while moving across the hall in the dark. Good lighting for the stairs is

very important. Light is needed from above to show up the treads clearly, but unless there is also illumination from below in the hall, the risers will be in dangerous shadow. Make sure these fittings are free from glare, and have two-way switches which can be operated from above and below.

Stairs and steps need careful attention at all times. If you have toddlers, protect them with baby gates at top and bottom of the stairs. Does your banister rail provide adequate support, or could you benefit from an additional rail on the staircase wall? This is often a good idea where young children or elderly people are frequently moving up and down stairs. Make sure stair coverings are securely fastened down – do not lay your own stair carpet unless you can make a good job of it. Avoid heavily patterned floor coverings for stairs and steps, as these tend to disguise the edge of the step. A low pile carpeting is best for stairs (e.g. cords or Wilton) in a hard-wearing fibre blend,

ABOVE *You might wish to create a vestibule where there was none before. This simple framework, adorned with plants, effectively and prettily divides entrance from living room without diminishing the spacious feel of the latter.*

sure, however, that there is a sturdy doormat inside the front door. It's a good idea, too, to have a metal boot scraper outside the front door to remove the worst of the mud. If you can provide storage for bedroom slippers or houseshoes near the front door, you can train your family to change their shoes and this can cut down on the cleaning.

Hard floorings make durable long-lasting covering for halls – you can sweep or vacuum from day to day. They will, however, need damp mopping and possibly polishing every week to ten days, depending on use. Consider cork tiles, well sealed; choose as thick a quality as you can afford for added resilience and sound absorption. A good quality vinyl in sheet or tile form is admirable for halls, and some of the brighter more arresting patterns make a splendid welcome. In small houses, the vinyl or cork can be continued from the hall through into the kitchen for a more spacious effect.

Wood floors tend to be noisy as people move around, although sanding and sealing boards provides one of the cheapest floor finishes available. If rugs are added to any of these suggested hard floorings, all of which have some degree of polish, make sure that the rugs are non-slip. Rubberized netting can be affixed to the underside of rugs to top them skidding on polished floors. If a rug curls at one corner, presenting a dangerous trip trap, try coating the underside with latex adhesive; if the curling persists, line the rug completely with hessian stuck down with the adhesive. There must be no loose edges of floorings in doorways from the hall and passageways into living and other rooms. All flooring joins must be secured with metal or plastic binder bars.

Decoration schemes for halls can be more vivid and arresting than the colours and patterns of other areas. Choose durable decorative finishes which can easily be cleaned especially if there are young children – the walls of halls and passages collect dirt and scuffs from shoulder rubbing and trailing hands, particularly so when space is cramped. Vinyl wall coverings are ideal; you might choose one of the exciting large scale patterns for the staircase wall where there will be space to show off the design to good effect. Vinyls also come in a variety of less obtrusive forms, for instance those which cleverly imitate fabrics such as hessian and linen.

Vinyl emulsion paints also make suitable wall finishes for the hall; for example, if it is dark, choose a paler shade in a silk finish for maximum light reflection. Mirrors are useful in narrow corridor halls; run them from floor to ceiling if possible so that they double the apparent width. They will also be useful for last minute adjustments to clothes and hair before going out.

Many older halls have decorative architectural features such as ceiling mouldings and arches which can be emphasized with paint of a contrasting shade to the main scheme. In small terraced

ABOVE *A bold combination of geometric patterns makes the most of a small box-like hall. An empty corner handily takes a hat- and coat-stand while stairs are lit by a spotlight.*

RIGHT *A traditional, terraced hall presented in an attractive manner. The corner is a useful place to put a phone and a pretty picket-type stair-guard protects young children.*

such as a hair or wool/nylon mixture. Stairs can be very noisy unless carpeted. Avoid sisal cords which can be slippery. Adjust your carpet a little every year so that areas of wear are moved around; these areas should never be allowed to develop into dangerous threadbare patches.

Floor coverings for halls and passageways need to be hard wearing and non-slip. If you choose carpeting make sure, as with the stairs, that they are of good quality; if they are not, the flooring will soon show signs of wear and this can be both ugly and dangerous. Choose a cord carpeting made from a good quality fibre rather than a cheap poor quality pile carpeting, even if they cost about the same. Loose-lay carpet tiles can be moved around to equalize wear.

Provided that they are darkish in colour, possibly with a texture or a small pattern, carpetings are easy to keep clean for halls, needing only a vacuum clean and an occasional shampoo. By absorbing sound they keep down the noise level when people are moving around the house. Make

houses, the hall ceiling is usually high in proportion to the width, making the hall seem long and narrow. Consider installing a false ceiling using, say, pine boarding, or even pine slats, which could give an opportunity to fit recess lights at the same time. If, however, you prefer to preserve the original form of the house, a deep colour on the ceiling will make it seem lower.

Storage is important for halls. Unless a space is provided for the everyday clutter, sooner or later somebody will fall over discarded coats or shoes. You will need plenty of hooks for coats, of course, and for children a second line of low-level hooks to take their own and their friends' coats, ponchos, extra cardigans and so on. Simple screw-in large brass cup hooks are quick to fix and take a reasonable amount of weight. A shelf or shallow cupboards, about 300mm deep are useful for shoes; a height of around 500mm is needed to accommodate tall boots. You can sometimes find cheap old fashioned coat racks in junk shops. Strip them or paint them up brightly, and they provide good storage for the average hall. Sometimes they have a built-in tray for dripping umbrellas; if not, a deep metal wastebin will cope with wet brollies.

Some kind of small scale wall storage with small pockets or little pigeon holes is useful for general family clutter. If this can incorporate a pin-up board, it can be used for the important notices, messages, lists etc. which families accumulate.

In large halls, there may be room to provide extra storage over and above immediate needs of the hall. It is often possible to line the walls of a landing with shelves, making a useful extra storage area for book-loving families. Sometimes there is space above doors which can be used for extra cupboards for little used bulky items. Spare cans of paint, and other odds and ends can be kept here until they come in useful.

Don't neglect the space under the stairs. Arrange hooks and shelves to turn this area into useful storage; or it can provide a cosy area for a small work desk, or even a place for the telephone.

Make sure that there is a solid, well-fitting front door with adequate locks and bolts. Provide a large opening for letters at a convenient height for the postman, and fix a basket inside the door to catch the post before the children trample your letters in their mad rush to school! It is useful to have a small rack or basket where the family can put letters to be posted. A small table or a wall fixed shelf makes a useful place to keep a shopping basket where it is not likely to be forgotten; and, of course, it is a place to put it down again when you return.

If you have a very large hall, you may just possibly be able to use it as an extra room — a spare bedroom or dining room. People have been known to have a spare bed in their hall or to use a folding or extending table for entertaining.

7. Walls and Ceilings

When people talk about decorating they generally mean altering the finish of their walls, ceilings and/or woodwork. It must be remembered, however, that no one element in a furnishing scheme should be treated in isolation from the rest. Although the quickest, cheapest and easiest way to give a room a new look is by decorating the walls, either with paper or paint, the aim at all times should be to ensure that the end result harmonizes with the rest of your room. Thus despite the tempting and almost bewildering choice of products, patterns and colours in the shops, decorating choices should be limited. Nevertheless, even within the limitations of one particular shade of one particular colour, there exists a varied range of options. Products available for decorating include emulsion and oil-based paints, wallpapers, vinyls, paper-backed fabrics, grass cloths, tiles of various kinds and wood.

Paint

Paint is the most inexpensive and simplest finish to apply to walls and ceilings. Modern paints are made in an extremely wide range of colours but the standard ready mixed ranges for the home decorator tend only to offer the popular, top selling shades. Several manufacturers now offer machine-tinted paints.

In theory tinting systems can produce an infinite range of colours; in practice the choice is limited to those shown in the manufacturers' selector charts. Even so the ranges usually comprise several hundred colours with the consequent advantage that the chances of finding colours to match or tone with carpets, furnishing fabrics and other items are much greater than with ready mixed ranges. Tinted paints are mixed on the spot in about ten minutes. Inevitably, these custom paints are more expensive than the ready mixed ones. For technical reasons, extra coats or special first coats may be needed with some machine-tinted colours. The selector charts or the stockist will indicate the colours to which this applies.

With most machine-tinting systems, measured amounts of colourant are added to white, coloured or neutral bases. The bases can be oil-based or emulsion and can come in gloss, silk or matt finishes. The same recipes for making up the colours are used for each type of base so exactly the same colour is available in a variety of paint types or sheen levels. This is very useful if, for example, it is intended to use a single colour on ceiling, walls and woodwork, but in different types of paint. Moreover, because most tinting systems offer several tones of many colours, it is possible to build decorative schemes around lighter or darker variations of a single colour. The same effects can be achieved by using the new 'all surface' paints. These can be used on walls as well as on woodwork.

It is of the utmost importance when choosing paint colours to bring the colour charts home and consider the colours in the room for which they are intended. It is also comforting to know, in the face of the great array of colours, that successful colour schemes do not depend on exact matches. Within a range of shades on the selector cards most of the colours close to each other will probably be suitable for a particular room. A lighter or darker finish is simply a matter of personal preference.

For general guidance on colour refer to pages 21 to 26 and for practical help on how to paint see pages 72 to 73. However, the following specific points should be borne in mind while planning the decorating approach.

If you prefer a change of colour and possibly finish for your woodwork remember to consider such items as skirtings, door frames and radiators, as part of the overall look of your walls. Painting these features white often looks smart, but you can achieve more subtle effects with a deeper or lighter tone of your main colour – or even an exact match. Ugly features, such as ill-proportioned windows or door frames, radiators, pipes and telephone cables, will virtually disappear if painted the same colour as their background.

If you have low ceilings paint your skirtings the same or nearly the same colour as the walls. This will increase the apparent height of the room as will painting the ceiling with one of the pale, cool colours which has receding qualities. For high, forbidding ceilings decorate in a warm, advancing colour and continue part of the way down the wall.

Very deep colours for walls tend to absorb a lot of light and will probably need to be compensated for by extra lighting at night. To achieve a restful, one colour effect, with just a few brighter accents, choose different finishes (these range from matt to full gloss) to give different degrees of shine to various surfaces. Avoid sheen finishes on uneven surfaces as they tend to show up the bumps, especially where wall lighting is used. Architectural features, such as cornices, ceiling roses, covings, and door panels, can be highlighted by painting them a contrasting or toning colour to the main scheme.

PAINT TYPES

Most of the paints used for home decorating are either oil-based or emulsion. The choice of paint type will be determined by the effect desired and the surface to be decorated.

● *Oil-based paints* are based on a vegetable drying oil, e.g. linseed oil, generally reinforced with a man-made resin. One widely used resin is alkyd which is often combined with polyurethane.

These paints may be non-drip or liquid. If thinning is required it is done with white spirit which is also needed for cleaning brushes and rollers. With some brands, however, hot water and household detergent will do for cleaning. On new or bare surfaces a primer is necessary. Oil-based paints dry and harden fairly slowly and an overnight interval is required between coats. A typical paint smell persists during application and for a time afterwards.

● *Emulsion paints* contain no oil and are made by dispersing particles of man-made resin in water. The resins used include acrylic and vinyl.

Emulsion paints are usually non-drip. If thinning is necessary it is done with water. Brushes and rollers clean out in water. Priming is needed only on metal or powdery surfaces. The paint dries quickly and surfaces can be recoated within one to two hours. The paint leaves little or no smell.

Although emulsion paints offer some advantages in convenience over oil-based paints, the latter are superior in ease of cleaning, general toughness and protective value. Hence they are the first choice for woodwork and metal, inside and outside, and for ceilings and walls in hard wear situations in such places as steamy kitchens and bathrooms.

Both types of paint are available in various degrees of sheen from matt through semi-gloss (silk or eggshell) to gloss. Emulsion glosses, however, do not have the same brilliance and depth of gloss as oil-based glosses. The required level of sheen is often a matter of personal preference. Many people feel that full gloss looks cold and clinical; they prefer the softer appearance of a matt or silk finish. Moreover, matt or silk finishes are less likely to show up defects such as bumpy walls or rough-grained woodwork. On the other hand where paint has to stand up to tough conditions, hard wear and frequent cleaning, then the glossier it is the better.

The paint guide on page 72 applies to aspects such as durability and ease of cleaning. The choice of paint may be influenced as well by what paint is on the surface already. There is usually no problem in applying oil-based paint over existing emulsion if it is in good condition and adhering properly. Emulsion paint over oil-based is less satisfactory especially if the old paint is glossy and there is likely to be steam and condensation, for example in a kitchen or bathroom. In this case, use a matt or silk oil-based paint if you do not want to repeat a gloss finish.

SURFACES/SITUATIONS	TYPE OF PAINT
Ceilings and walls: in light wear situations, e.g. bedrooms, living rooms, dining rooms.	Matt or silk emulsion
in medium wear situations, e.g. lightly used or well ventilated kitchens and bathrooms.	Silk emulsion. Silk oil-based
in hard wear situations, e.g. well used or poorly ventilated kitchens and bathrooms.	Gloss or silk oil-based
Woodwork and metal: in light or medium wear situations.	Silk or matt oil-based Gloss emulsion
heavy wear situations	Gloss or silk oil-based

HOW TO

Nowadays, most people expect to do at least some of their own painting. The instructions below will guide you to achieve a professional finish.

TOOLS AND MATERIALS

Paint brushes come in a range of sizes from 12.5mm to 200mm wide. For home decorators, a range from 12.5mm to 100mm will do most jobs. Use the size of brush appropriate to the surface, e.g. 12.5mm or 25mm for narrow surfaces such as window frames and picture rails; 50mm or 75mm for broader items like doors and cupboards; 75mm or 100mm for large areas such as ceilings and walls.

When using the smaller sizes of brush, it is often possible to work straight from the container in which the paint is supplied. It is better, however, to pour the paint into a clean paint kettle or bucket and work from that. Then, if dust or grit is picked up from the surface, it does not ruin all the paint. Moreover, there is less paint to carry around.

Paint rollers are usually 150mm–225mm wide with various types of covering materials. The most satisfactory coverings are of synthetic fibre or sheepskin. The short pile types are recommended for use with oil-based paints on smooth surfaces; the long pile rollers are good with emulsion paints, especially on very rough surfaces such as brickwork. For general use, a medium pile type will do for most jobs. Rollers will not paint closely into angles and corners; a brush has to be used for this purpose.

When using a roller, it is necessary to work from a special tray. This has a well at one end into which the paint is poured. The roller is charged by dipping it into the paint and then rolling it on the platform of the tray. It is then rolled over the surface until the paint is spread evenly over a few square feet at a time.

Paint pads consist of a layer of fabric or synthetic fibre similar to that used for rollers, but mounted on a flat, rigid backing.

There are various shapes and sizes, ranging from small pads for painting window glazing bars to larger models for broader surfaces, including walls – although a roller would usually be quicker for these larger surfaces.

In the same way as rollers, paint pads are charged from a tray. The charged pad is placed flat against the surface and drawn along in steady strokes.

PREPARATION

For successful painting, surfaces must be clean, dry and sound. New or unpainted surfaces may need priming. Old paintwork in good condition, i.e. firmly adhering and not cracked or blistered, may need no more than a sponge over with detergent or household cleaner, suitably diluted. On badly grimed areas, over radiators, wall-lights, etc., a little powder cleaner can be used. Greasy areas around door handles or light switches should be cleaned first with white spirit and then with detergent. After cleaning, rinse or sponge with clean water. Allow time for the surfaces to dry properly before applying paint. Rub down glossy paintwork with medium or fine grade (No. 1 or 0) glasspaper. This can be done more effectively if waterproof abrasive paper is used while the surfaces are wet after washing.

If the old paint is in poor condition, it must be removed. Small

areas of defective paint can often be scraped off with a scraper or shavehook. Oil-based paints may be stripped with paint remover or burned-off with a blow-torch. Emulsion paints cannot be burned off and paint removers are not always very effective; usually there is no alternative to rather tedious 'dry scraping'.

Old wallpaper can be over-painted although it is usually wiser to remove it. However, do not paint over vinyl wall-coverings; the vinyl face can usually be pulled away leaving behind the backing paper which can be painted over if it is sticking firmly to the wall. With ordinary wallpaper, make sure that any loose edges are stuck down before painting. If there is gold in the pattern, this may stain the paint; test a patch first. If staining does occur, cover with a coat of primer-sealer. In older houses, ceilings may have been coated with size-distemper. This must always be washed off before painting or papering; if not, the new paint will not stick. If it is not possible to remove the old distemper completely, apply a coat of primer-sealer.

Generally, cracks and holes can be filled with a powder filler mixed with water. Around windows, however, where the glass meets the frame, linseed oil putty (for timber frames) or metal casement putty (for metal ones) should be used.

New or unpainted surfaces may require priming. This will also apply to surfaces from which old paint has been removed. Most manufacturers offer primers, each designed for a particular type of surface and intended for use with their own finishes. Individual brands do not always have the same descriptions so it is necessary to refer to the manufacturers' literature or to the stockist if in doubt. Some makers offer a universal primer, equally suitable for wood, metal and plaster. This avoids having to buy several primers for a small task. Below is a guide to those occasions where priming is necessary, with notes of any special preparation required. Always refer to any instructions given by the manufacturers.

Surface	Preparation	Priming
Plaster rendering, brickwork, asbestos	Allow new surfaces to dry out completely. Wipe off any salts that have formed on the surface	Required for oil-based finishes. Not usually required for emulsions but see maker's instructions
Hardboard, most building boards. Wallpaper, including wood chip, texture and relief papers		As above
Wood	Smooth down with fine glass-paper. Apply a coat of patent knotting to all knots and resinous patches	Required for oil-based and emulsion finishes. Use aluminium primer for wood which is very resinous or has been treated with wood preservative
Iron and steel	Remove all rust and scale with a wire brush or emery cloth	Priming required for oil-based and emulsion finishes
Aluminium and galvanized iron	Rub down with fine glass-paper and white spirit	As above
Previously distempered ceilings and walls	Wash and scrape to remove as much old distemper as possible	Prime with primer-sealer

STEP-BY-STEP GUIDE

Ceilings

Except for a very small ceiling, it is better to work from a proper scaffolding rather than from a step-ladder or stool. Use a stout plank, at least 175mm wide and 38mm thick, supported at each end by a stepladder or strong box. Erect the scaffolding along the shortest dimension of the room. Arrange the plank at a convenient height so that you neither bump your head against the ceiling nor have to over-stretch.

Paint the ceiling in strips about 450mm wide and work methodically from end to end. Join up to the preceding strip as quickly as possible before the wet edge of the paint sets. On a very large ceiling it is desirable to have two people working side by side in order to join up edges before they dry.

Walls

Rollers are excellent for this job, but a small brush will be needed for angles and corners. Paint these first and then roll closely into the angle. If painting walls on your own, start at the top and paint a strip about 450mm wide halfway down the wall. Step down and continue the strip on the lower half of the wall. Then move along and paint the next strip at the top and so on until the whole wall is complete. As in painting ceilings, try to join up the wet edges before the paint sets. The job is made easier if two people tackle it together, one painting the top strips of the wall and the other the lower portions.

Doors

For painting panelled doors, use a 25mm brush for the mouldings and a 50mm or 75mm one for the broader parts. Paint the panels and mouldings first followed by the cross-rails, uprights, edges and last of all, the door-frame.

Flush doors may be painted with a 50mm or 75mm brush or with a roller. When using a brush, paint the full width of the door about one-third of the way down, finishing with vertical strokes. Paint the middle and lower thirds in the same way, joining up to the preceding section before the edge dries. With a roller, paint in strips the full height of the door and complete the edges and frame of the door by brush.

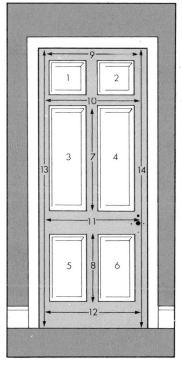

Windows and trim

In painting windows and trim (e.g. skirting boards and picture rails) there is the problem of cutting in—painting up to the glass or adjoining wall—neatly without getting paint in the wrong places. Use a 12.5mm or 25mm brush, preferably one that is worn to a chisel edge. Have the brush fairly well charged with paint, press the bristles firmly into the angle and draw the brush steadily along for a short distance. Repeat the stroke, without re-charging the brush, until the area is evenly coated. If cutting-in is difficult, use a metal shield to prevent the paint from straying. Wipe the edge of the shield after each stroke as paint tends to creep under it. You may find it easier to use a small paint pad, especially for narrow glazing bars.

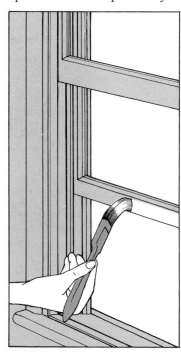

When painting casement windows which open outwards, first open the casement fully and paint the closing edges of the casement and frame. Close the sash and cut in the portions next to the glass. Open the sash again and paint the cross rails and uprights. Complete all the casements and fixed panes before painting the frames. Leave the casement slightly open until the paint is dry. Paint the sill.

To paint double-hung sash windows which slide up and down, start by pushing the bottom sash up and pulling the top one down so that the meeting rail is accessible. Paint this and as much as possible of the lower part of the top sash. Then pull the bottom sash right down again and push up the top sash to within an inch of closing. Paint the remainder of the top sash and the top runners. Raise the bottom sash until it is just clear of the frame at the lower edge. Paint the whole of the bottom sash including the top end. Then paint the frame and sill. Leave the sashes open a little until the paint is dry.

Wall coverings

While the term wall coverings is convenient to use, most of the materials can equally well be used on ceilings. Whatever wall covering is utilized it will be generally more expensive than paint and the hanging will be trickier and will take longer to do than painting.

For helpful hints on pattern selection read carefully the notes on pattern on pages 26 to 28. For guidance on hanging techniques see pages 79 to 80.

There are many different types of wall coverings manufactured and it is worth while becoming acquainted with their different properties.

PAPERS

● *Pulps* are the cheapest type of wallpaper and are similar to ordinary lining paper with a coloured basecoat on which the design or pattern is printed.

The range of designs and effects is limited and, when pasted, pulps are easily torn.

● *Duplex* papers make use of several layers of paper as a base and are therefore stronger and easier to handle when wet. They can also be embossed to produce attractive texture effects.

● *Wood-chip* papers are duplex papers in which wood chips are incorporated to give an oatmeal effect. They are usually supplied 'in the white' to be painted after hanging to enable texture to be combined with individual colour choice. This type of paper is relatively inexpensive and makes an effective cover for old walls with a poor finish.

● *Flocks* are expensive wallpapers intended originally to simulate Italian velvet hangings. The design is formed with chopped silk, rayon or other fibres to give a raised pile effect. They require great care in hanging to avoid spoiling the pile.

● *Relief wallpapers* have a deeply embossed relief effect which may be a formal pattern or a simula-

ABOVE LEFT *Consider carrying your wall covering over your ceiling. You achieve a cosy, enclosed effect which is particularly suitable for bedrooms and bathrooms.*

ABOVE *Wallpapers co-ordinated with soft furnishings such as table linen and with crockery are now available.*

RIGHT *Fabric wall coverings in plain colours (such as hessian) produce a warm, textured look which suits living rooms and studies.*

tion of rough plaster, pebble-dash or other such textures. Some of the most pleasing patterns are the traditional tile effect designs. They are usually supplied 'in the white' for painting after hanging, so remember to add in the cost of the paint when budgeting.

Traditional reliefs are made from stout paper and hung with special adhesive. Once hung, and especially when painted, they can be regarded as a fixture as they are very difficult to strip.

Many wallpapers are supplied in ready pasted form. The adhesive is applied to the back of the paper during manufacture. To activate it, the lengths of paper are placed in water immediately before hanging.

A number of papers are 'dry strippable'. This means that they can be pulled away dry when the time comes to remove them. This avoids the tedious and messy task of soaking and scraping.

Good quality wallpapers have a clear, protective

plastic coating over the pattern and can be sponged. They are not, however, as washable as true vinyls which can be scrubbed if necessary.

VINYLS AND POLYETHYLENE

● *Vinyl coverings* have a layer of vinyl fused on to a stout paper backing; the design is also printed in vinyl. They are tough, moisture-resistant and can be scrubbed so that they are an excellent choice for hard wear situations. Vinyls are patterned to resemble wallpapers although colours tend to be brighter.

● *Textured vinyls* are plain coloured, but textured to imitate fabrics, for example rough weave hessians, smoother linens or silks with an attractive slub weave. By using this type of textured vinyl the look of a fabric wall covering can be achieved at a considerably lower cost than the real thing. The hanging of textured vinyl is far easier than that of fabrics. Fabric-look vinyls wear well and can be cleaned easily.

● *Flock vinyls* have a beautiful pile surface. They are available in a wide range of rich and pastel colours and in various designs. Despite the pile, flock vinyls can be scrubbed clean just like other vinyls.

As with paper, strippable vinyls are available in which the face can be pulled away from the backing paper when the times comes for redecorating. The new metallic vinyls are also worth mentioning as the designs look spectacular but they are expensive.

● *Polyethylene*, a recent development, is an attractive product which looks like paper but is in fact a thick film of foamed plastic printed in a good range of colours and designs. It is very light in weight, warm to the touch and easy to hang because it is the wall or ceiling which is pasted and not the polyethylene itself.

FABRICS

Chintzes, silks, linens, felt and grass cloth have been used in the past as wall coverings. Some of them still are, but hanging the more expensive or delicate materials is a task for a professional.

Many fabrics and other speciality materials, including hessians, grass cloths, linens and corks, are now available mounted on a paper backing, making them much easier for hanging by the home decorator.

Fabric wall coverings are very appealing; they add a touch of softness to any room scheme, and thicker types will also make walls seem warmer. However, they are difficult to clean, tend to be expensive and, in most cases, the joins show prominently.

● *Hessian* is perhaps the most popular fabric covering, providing a pleasant background for modern furniture. It can be used with great effect on one wall, or just for alcoves. It is available in a wide

ABOVE RIGHT *Matching curtains to wall coverings is very effective for smaller rooms. Several manufacturers now produce fabrics and blinds with co-ordinating papers or vinyls. Before you make a final choice always view samples of both the paper and the fabric as in some cases the match is not satisfactory due to differences in printing processes and the materials involved.*

range of colours, but the natural brown shades are least prone to fading. Blues, greens, purples and reds should not be used in very sunny rooms where the colours may dull from fading. Hessian will fade around pictures, leaving bright patches where they hang. Most decorating shops now stock ranges of paper-backed hessian. Rolls may be standard wallpaper width of 53cm–55cm, or they may be wider. Check before ordering. Some shops sell paper-backed hessian by the metre – useful for small areas.

● *Felt* adds a cosy, rich atmosphere to any room. It deadens sound and insulates against heat loss. Felt can be used with great effect to line a small room completely – e.g. a study, or a bedroom. A wide colour range is available and it can be obtained with paper backing.

● *Paper-backed silk, grass cloth and cork* are expensive luxury wall coverings, costing a great deal for just one roll. Even professionals find them tricky to hang and it is not advisable for an amateur to tackle large areas. However you may want to create a special effect by lining an alcove, or a small wall area. Silk has a subtle lustrous sheen, plus a pleasant natural effect created by variations in the weave. Japanese grass cloths come in soft shades of greens and browns in various weave patterns and give a room an oriental atmosphere. Cork wall coverings come in various shades of brown ranging from very pale to dark; some have coloured or metallic ground.

ABOVE *In rooms with plain fitted cupboards you can take the wall covering over the doors for an attractive decorative effect, which can be enhanced by framing the design with wooden moulding or beading to make panels.*

LEFT *Large, boldly-patterned designs, like this one, look good in halls where they make an immediate impact on entering.*

Most wallpapers and paper-backed wall coverings are sold in rolls 10.5m long and 530mm wide, covering about 5.5 sq m per roll. Some imported and specialist materials may be of other sizes or may be supplied in panels instead of rolls.

Wall coverings are printed in batches and there may be slight colour variations from one batch to another. It is important to buy enough material initially to complete the job; if you have to buy more at a later date, the colour may not match exactly. Check that all the rolls have the same batch number and make a note of this in case of a re-order. Even if the batch numbers are all the same it is still advisable to check for uniformity of colour before starting to hang the material. Check also for any printing defects or damage before hanging and, if serious and likely to cause waste, return the material to the stockist.

Today, most wall coverings are supplied ready trimmed. If the material has a selvage, the stockist will usually trim it off for a small charge.

Unless the wall covering is ready pasted, you will need to buy an adhesive or paste. The stockist or the maker's instructions will advise you for the wall covering you have chosen. It is essential to use a fungicidal adhesive for vinyls and heavy relief materials which are to be painted later.

The enormous variety of patterns, colours, textures and styles now available in wall coverings offers exciting opportunities for the expression of individual tastes and ideas. The possibilities can be widened further by mixing and matching and by hanging wall coverings in unusual ways. Here are some ideas.

They require only the basic techniques of hanging described on pages 79 to 80. They must, however, be used with discretion and where they are appropriate; over-elaborate or clever effects can dominate a room and become tiring to live with.

Use the same wall covering for ceiling and walls, a semi-plain or small scale pattern used in this way makes a small room look more spacious.

Exploit the many coordinated collections now available by mixing patterns in the same room or reverse the usual order and contrast a patterned ceiling with plain walls. This can produce a dramatic effect in halls and corridors. For ceilings, try formal abstract patterns which read in any direction. Add interest to feature walls or alcoves with bold patterns or strong colours contrasting with plain textures. Hang stripes or other suitable patterns horizontally – even diagonally – instead of vertically. Coordinated patterns or different colour ways can be used in this way.

You can use the same pattern on the ceiling and in a band around the top part of the wall. Using a bold pattern or strong colour in this way reduces the apparent height of high ceilings. Use motifs (e.g. flowers) cut out from left over rolls to enliven plain wall coverings and painted walls.

ABOVE *This is an idea which may take up a lot more time than it does money. Obtain wallpaper sample books from your local showroom (they may be prepared to let you have discontinued ranges for nothing). Using pattern techniques derived from fabric patchwork build up your wall covering from paper cut-outs. It is probably best to confine yourself to a small area.*

CHOOSING A WALL COVERING

A beginner should choose a ready pasted medium priced vinyl or spongeable wallpaper for the first attempt. Cheap pulp papers are likely to tear easily when wet. Do not risk spoiling an expensive material. It is also sound advice to choose a free match design, that is one that does not require the pattern to be matched at the joints.

Avoid designs with stripes or bold motifs if the wall or ceiling angles are out of true. Do not hang wall coverings on damp walls – certainly not vinyls.

Avoid ordinary wallpapers in steamy kitchens and bathrooms. Vinyls, painted relief papers or the new foamed plastic material mentioned above will give better service. Ordinary papers will not stand up to moisture and vigorous cleaning.

HOW TO

Hanging wallcoverings

Hanging wall coverings is more complicated than painting. Read these notes through completely before embarking on the task. If possible start with a small room with a low ceiling to build-up confidence.

TOOLS AND MATERIALS
With the following tools, most wall covering jobs can be tackled effectively.

Scissors. A large pair of household scissors will suffice but for making long, straight cuts, proper paper-hanging shears with 200mm–250mm blades are preferred. Small household scissors are, however, useful for trimming around fittings and similar awkward jobs.

Folding rule

Plumb-line. Improvise with 4m of thin string and a small weight.

Paperhanger's smoothing brush

Paperhanger's apron with a pocket at the front to hold tools

Synthetic sponge

Wash-leather

Joint roller

Soft lead pencil

Coloured chalk

Paste-table. Unless you are using ready-pasted wall covering, you will need a flat surface on which to cut up and paste. Ordinary tables are usually too wide and not long enough.

Bucket

Large paintbrush

Short steps

PREPARATION
Wall coverings can be applied to most surfaces which are reasonably flat provided that they are clean, dry and sound. Ideally, the surface should be slightly absorbent, e.g. plaster, but, with suitable preparation, wall coverings can be hung on less absorbent surfaces such as painted walls and ceilings. Here are some hints on the preparation of those surfaces usually encountered.

Old wall coverings should be removed, if possible. Soak ordinary wallpaper with water until it softens and can be scraped off. Strippable wallpapers pull off dry. With vinyls, pull away the face; the backing paper can be left as a base for the new wall covering or, if not firmly stuck everywhere, soaked and scraped off.

Painted or varnished papers are difficult to remove because water cannot penetrate them. If the paper is sticking firmly, do not attempt to strip it but rub down prominent joints and stick back any loose paper. If the paper *must* be removed, score the surface with a serrated scraper or a wire brush so that water can penetrate. Consider hiring a steam stripper if large-areas need tackling.

Emulsion painted surfaces, if sound, need only sponging over with detergent and water; do not soak them. If the adhesion of the emulsion is doubtful, scrape off as much as possible, apply a coat of primer-sealer and, when this is dry, cross-line* the surface.

Oil-base painted surfaces should be washed with detergent. If the surface is glossy, rub it down while it is still wet, using waterproof abrasive paper. Then rinse with clean water and dry off.

Ceiling distemper may have been used in older houses. It can be easily recognized because it softens readily when wetted and must be removed or the wall covering will not stick. Wash it off with lots of water and a large sponge or paint brush. If it cannot be washed off, allow the surface to dry and then prime with primer-sealer.

New plaster and repairs to old plaster must be allowed time to dry out, especially if vinyls are to be hung. Plaster from which wallpaper has been stripped needs washing to remove paste residues. Fill cracks and holes with plaster filler. Give plaster and similar absorbent surfaces a coat of size and allow it to dry before the wall covering is hung. Generally, thinned wall covering adhesive is used as a size but always refer to the instructions supplied with the wall covering. Badly cracked or stained plaster should be cross-lined.*

---

*Cross-lining means hanging a stout lining paper as a base for the wall covering. It is usually hung so that the joints come at right-angles (i.e. across) those in the wall covering. On walls this means hanging the lining paper horizontally.

STEP-BY-STEP GUIDE
In hanging walls, it is advisable to start at a corner near a window and work away from the light. In this way, if there are slight overlaps at the joints in the wall covering, they will not cast shadows.

If the room has a large chimney-breast or similar prominent feature, and especially if the pattern has big or dominant motifs, it may be better to start from the middle of the feature in order to achieve a balanced effect.

Wherever the start is made, the length of wall covering must be hung to a plumb or truly vertical line; if not the pattern will run off at top and bottom.

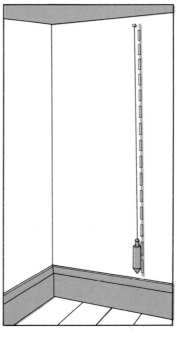

HOW TO SET UP A PLUMB-LINE
Tap in a small masonry nail near the top of the wall and hang the plumb-line from it so that the weight is just above the skirting or foot of the wall. Steady the line and make a vertical pencil mark directly behind it at the bottom. Rub coloured chalk along the line, still leaving it looped around the nail.

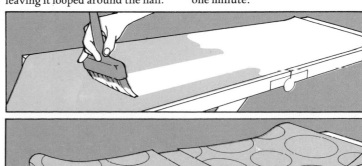

With one hand hold it taut between the nail and the mark at the bottom. With the other hand, draw the line away from the wall and let it snap back smartly to leave a chalked line on the wall.

If a start is made at a corner, set the line up at a distance from the corner about 5mm less than the width of the wall covering. On a chimney-breast or similar feature, set the line up in the middle.

MEASURING AND CUTTING
Measure the space between the top and bottom of the wall, allow about 50mm at each end for trimming and cut the first length. With patterned materials, especially if the motifs are large, try to have complete motifs at the top.

When there is no pattern to match, the whole roll can be cut into lengths. With patterned materials, there is less chance of error if one length is hung before the next is matched and cut.

Plain or free-match wall coverings may be accompanied by an instruction to reverse alternate lengths.

PASTING AND FOLDING
Unless the wall covering is ready-pasted, lay the length on the paste table, pattern side down, with the top in line with one end of the table and the bottom hanging over the other end. Paste the top portion, fold it over, draw the length along and paste the bottom portion. Make another small fold at the bottom to meet the top fold. After pasting, ordinary wallpapers usually require a little time to soak and to become supple; vinyls may be hung immediately.

With ready-pasted wall coverings and vinyls, put water in the trough supplied with the wall covering; immerse the cut length, rolled up from the bottom with the pattern-side outwards in the trough. It is ready to hang in about one minute.

HANGING

Scissors and smoothing brush should be in your apron pocket or ready to hand. With a brush-pasted length, turn the top fold halfway back. Hold the length by the top corners. When in position on the steps or stool, allow the top fold to open and hold the length just clear of the wall. Align the edge against the plumb-line and

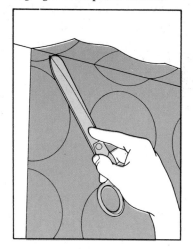

press it down lightly. Smooth down the upper portion of the length with the smoothing brush, working outwards from the middle. Mark and cut the top and press it into position. Deal with the bottom portion similarly, trimming to the angle between the skirting and the wall. Sponge off any paste which has strayed on to adjacent paint-work. With vinyls, a sponge may be used for smoothing down.

With ready-pasted wall coverings, place the trough against the skirting immediately beneath where the length is to be hung. Holding the top corners, draw it out of the trough to the top of the wall and hang it as described.

HOW TO DEAL WITH CORNERS

Wall coverings should not be turned round a corner or angle for more than 12.5mm or there is

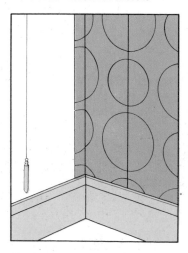

likely to be an unsightly crease. When a corner is reached, cut a strip fractionally wider than the greatest distance between the corner and the edge of the last length. Hang this strip in the usual way; then plumb a line at the correct distance from the corner and hang in the normal way.

TRIMMING AROUND FITTINGS

Remove fittings, if possible. When removing electrical fittings first switch off at the mains. Insert matchsticks into screw-holes, so that they can be located later.

If fittings cannot be removed, they must be cut round. The wall covering is hung loosely over the switch and its centre located. Radiating cuts are made from the centre allowing the wall covering to be pressed flat. The outline of the switch is then marked, the wall covering eased away and the waste trimmed off.

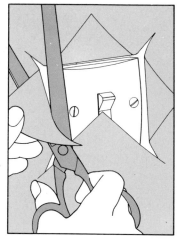

CEILINGS

For ceilings, it is essential to have a proper scaffold as described on page 73. It is usual to hang the first length next to the main window and parallel to the wall. Work at right angles to the window, however, if it means hanging shorter lengths.

A line is required to which to hang the first length. Make pencil marks on the ceiling at each end at a distance from the angle between ceiling and wall or cornice about 5mm less than the width of the wall covering. At one of these marks, tap in a small masonry nail and strike a chalk-line as described on page 79.

Hanging ready-pasted wall coverings on ceilings from a trough is not really practicable. Paste ordinary and ready-pasted types on the paste table, using fairly thin paste for ready-pasted. After pasting, fold the length in short concertina folds.

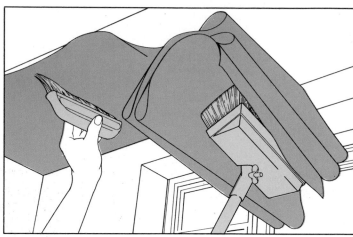

Supporting the folded length with a roll of wall covering or a length of broom-handle, open up the top fold and align the edge against the chalk line. Smooth down the first portion, allow the next fold to open, adjust to the chalk-line, smooth down and so on until the whole length is hung. Then trim away the surplus at the ends and, if necessary, along the edge against the wall or cornice.

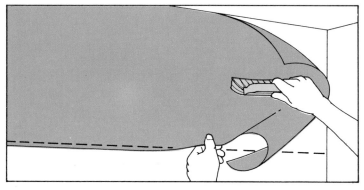

HORIZONTAL HANGING

You will need a scaffold. Strike a chalk-line across the wall, at a distance below the ceiling or cornice angle 5mm less than the width of the wall covering. This provides a guide-line for the bottom edge of the first length. Paste, fold and hang the lengths as for a ceiling.

DIAGONAL HANGING

The techniques are the same as when hanging horizontally but you will need a diagonal line as a guide. To do this, mark a point at the top of the wall mid-way between the two corners. Strike a vertical chalk-line down the wall from this point. Measure from the bottom of the chalk-line, along the base of the wall, a distance equal to the height of the wall.

Strike another chalk-line between this point and the top centre mark. This gives a true diagonal. Diagonal hanging tends to be wasteful of materials so allowance for this must be made when estimating quantities; one extra roll in every five is about right. However, this figure may vary.

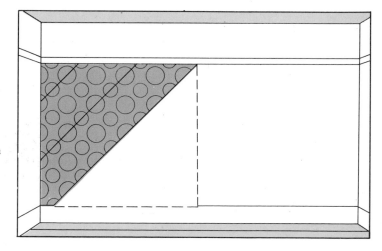

Tiles and other Wall Linings

Ceramic wall tiles offer an easy to clean, durable, stain-resistant and virtually permanent finish for areas of wall which come in for extra heavy wear. Tiles can be used behind sinks and basins to act as a splash back. They are particularly neat on the walls behind working surfaces and cooker hobs in kitchens or where they fill the gap between a working surface and the bottom of cupboards. In the dining room or dining area, tiles behind a carving/serving surface protect the wall from grease and other marks. They can also be used to line bath surrounds and shower enclosures. Although tiles will resist water, and food and cooking stains far better than any wall covering, individual tiles are likely to shatter on impact. Avoid using tiles, therefore, on any wall which is particularly vulnerable to knocks, such as that on a staircase.

There are many ranges of tiles for D.I.Y. fixing at local decorating shops. For a wider selection visit a a builders' merchant, home improvement centre or one of the growing number of specialist shops. Hand decorated tiles are also available from small potteries and craft shops. It is worth while making an effort to explore the market before buying, for tiles are expensive.

CERAMIC TILES

Ceramic tiles are fixed with small gaps between them to allow for movement of the tiles due to expansion and contraction of the surface to which they are fixed. After fixing, the gaps are filled with a compressible material called grouting.

You can tackle small areas of wall tiling yourself (see page 85). Take care in this case to purchase tiles intended for amateur fixing. These will have small protrusions on each side called spacer lugs which help you to achieve even spacing when fixing your tiles. The lugs are concealed at the fixing by the grouting which is applied to fill in the joints. Tiles without lugs are more difficult to fix; over large areas they are probably best left to professionals. When you fix tiles without lugs you must leave a 2mm space between adjoining ones; use a matchstick or a piece of card as a measure. Tiles marked RE have one rounded glazed edge for use around windows and also the last line of tiles when tiling only part way up a wall. Tiles marked REX have two adjoining glazed and rounded edges for use in corners. Standard tiles with unglazed edges are called field tiles.

RIGHT *Tiles are expensive compared with paint and paper. Investigate the market thoroughly before buying. This picture gives an idea of the wide selection available.*

Tiles come in standard sizes; many ranges are sold in packs, but more expensive ranges may be available singly. Small square tiles are 108mm by 108mm – these look particularly neat in small rooms. The larger size of tile available measures 152mm by 152mm. Looking perhaps slightly more old fashioned, this size often suits better some of the attractive designs based on period patterns. Rectangular tiles (sometimes called border tiles) are available, 216mm by 108mm. These offer more exciting design possibilities than squares, for tiles can be arranged in a variety of ways – for example, all vertically, or in alternating horizontal and vertical pairs. A finishing strip of horizontal tiles often looks very pleasant. Border tiles usually do not have spacer lugs, and may have three glazed edges. Many ranges of tiles are imported from France, Italy and Spain, so it is important to check exact sizes and types before determining plans and estimating costs.

In addition to standard squares and rectangles special tile effects are also available – for example, there are the fascinating interlocking ogee shapes sometimes called Moorish or Provençal. Hexagonal wall tiles are also available; they fit together like patchwork. There is also wall mosaic, tiny ceramic tiles in various shapes, including rounds and hexagons, which come in sheets about 300mm square.

A wide range of tile designs is now available. These include exciting modern geometrics which can be combined in various ways to make spectacular patterns. Other ranges are more traditional, being based on delightful revivals of intricate Victorian and Edwardian designs. Victorian tiles are still available second-hand from junk shops and demolition sites but they are growing more expensive as they are becoming highly prized. It is unlikely that you will find enough second-hand tiles of this type to cover a whole wall with one design; try collecting single tiles for an attractive mixed effect.

Many ranges of tiles include patterns and plains in coordinating colours – exploit these imaginatively to plan wall designs. Patterned tiles are usually more expensive (especially hand painted or hand printed tiles). Costs can be saved by planning a feature area, surrounded by toning plain colours. It sometimes looks better to group together all patterned tiles for one large effect, rather than to scatter them individually on the wall.

When choosing tile designs remember that many of the patterns are designed to depend on the repeat of the pattern for the total effect – the whole pattern created may well be far larger than the actual tile. Make sure you see tiles over a large enough area before deciding on a particular design.

Some tiles have an attractive embossed or textured effect. It is possible to find tiles that coordinate with other furnishing products, such as

ceramic or vinyl floor tiles, or wallpapers, or fabrics, or carpets. Tile manufacturers have also planned their colour ranges to complement the colours of baths and basins.

It is very important to plan tile areas carefully so that they blend well with the rest of the room – this is especially true when you intend only to tile a small area, for example around a bath or behind a basin. Make a wall plan. Use squared paper and, taking one square to represent the size of one tile, draw in the wall to scale. This will help to work out how many tiles are needed, and enables you to plan any special design arrangements, e.g. panels of pattern broken up by strips or borders of plains. Consider carefully the treatment for adjoining wall surfaces. Plain tiles for the background to a design can usually be matched exactly with a paint colour; take a tile sample to a shop offering a tint and mix paint service.

In bathrooms it is particularly important to seal any gaps between tiles and the edge of the bath – a proprietary sealing compound for this can be used or a glazed ceramic round edge bath trim.

If you cannot afford new tiles, paint your old tiles – see notes on painting different surfaces on page 72. Or there are several ranges of peel-off self-adhesive transfer designs which can be used to decorate areas of plain tiles. You can also buy hardboard panels with a plastic surface which simulates tiling; unfortunately the colour range is somewhat limited.

When planning to buy tiles for surfaces sub-

ABOVE *Ceramic tiles remain one of the best possible coverings for a bathroom because they will protect your walls from water splashes. They look attractive and are easy to clean. Thinner D.I.Y. ranges are easy to fix yourself and modern adhesives make it possible to tile over old tiles without removing them. In this picture, tiles are effectively combined with wood boarding for basin and bath. Make sure that any wood in a bathroom is well sealed with several coats of varnish. And be sure to seal the gap between bath and wall to prevent water seepage which could lead to rot.*

jected to extremes of heat such as fireplaces, check that the tiles are suitable. Special fireplace tiles which are thicker and stronger may be required.

Tiles, of course, can only offer a good, durable surface, if they are fixed to a sound wall. Walls must be dry and free from grease. Wallpaper should be stripped off, flaking paint removed, and crumbling areas of plaster must be hacked out and made good. Give the wall a good wash down with a solution of hot water and detergent, rinse with clean water and allow to dry before tiling. Modern adhesives and lightweight tiles now make it possible to tile over old tiles provided they are firmly fixed. These hints on wall preparation apply not only to ceramic tiles but also to the other kinds of decorative wall and ceiling tiles discussed below.

CORK TILES

Cork wall tiles, which can also be used on the ceiling, are deservedly becoming more popular. Cork has a warmth and a natural beauty which cannot easily be imitated by other materials. Cork wall coverings improve insulation against heat loss. Cork also deadens noise. The surface is soft enough to take drawing pins, so that an area of cork can make a useful pin-up board. And yet cork wall coverings resist knocks and scratches reasonably well. Cork comes in tiles and panels of various sizes, including 300mm square, 300mm by 900mm and 300mm by 600mm. Thicknesses available include 3mm, 5mm, 8mm and 13mm. Naturally, the thicker panels provide more insulation against noise transmission and heat loss; they also make better pin boards. Try and buy panels sold specifically for wall surfacing. These will be of a greater density than standard cork insulation, which is vulnerable to chipping in use. It is possible to buy even thicker wall panels (up to 20mm thick); some of these are very rough textured as they are made from the bark of the cork tree.

Decorating supermarkets usually sell cork tiles in a choice of pale or medium brown (thinner type) or dark brown (thicker, insulating type). Specialist decorating and tile shops, however, have a wide variety of designs in cork coverings, including chequer board, strip, and granular effects in various shades of brown, ranging from palest honey through to the nearly black. Panels with cork on coloured backgrounds are also available, but they are expensive. In fact cork usually looks most attractive in its cheapest and most natural form. Read the manufacturers' instructions carefully regarding fixing, adhesives, etc.

Wall tiles and panels usually have some form of wax protective finish so that no further finishing is necessary. Varnishes are not usually recommended. Because the material is porous, a great many coats are needed to build up a good finish.

METALLIC TILES

For shimmering reflective wall effects, explore the possibilities of decorative lightweight metallic wall tiles. The aluminium ranges are washable, waterproof and resistant to heat and fire. These tiles can be cut with scissors and even bent round corners. Fixing is simple, as there are no spaces to be left and consequently no grouting. Simply use the self-adhesive pads on the backs of the tiles (for detailed guidance, see page 86). These tiles come in a choice of metallic finishes which include gold, silver, copper, and bronze. Finishes can be bright and shiny, or dull (sometimes called antiqued). Some of these tiles are textured and some have patterns, applied either with colour or contrasting metallic textures. There are interesting geometric designs which can be combined in different ways to make a variety of large scale patterns. Size is usually 108mm square but ogee interlocking shapes are also available. Larger 'feature' tiles or panels, 300mm square are made from metallized plastic in exotic relief designs in gold, silver, copper, bronze and pewter finishes. This type of tile has a polystyrene backing for additional heat and sound insulation. Also available are plastic wall panels in imitation stone or brick. These plastic panels must not be used on surfaces which will become hot.

BELOW *Cork tiles are an attractive and deservedly popular wall hanging. They come in a variety of designs and shades of brown. They impart a warm feeling to a room and are good insulators. They also serve a very useful purpose as pin-up boards in home offices, utility rooms, children's rooms or kitchens.*

ABOVE *For bathrooms, buy a good quality looking glass. It is usually better to have one large mirror area, as above, rather than a cluster of small ones. A light fitting above the glass is a good idea in bathrooms.*

MIRRORS

Make the most of mirrors around the home – their effects can be surprising. They increase light reflection and create an impression of space – height, width or depth, according to the effect required. They can enliven dull corners and enhance paintings and decorations. Fitted at right angles to a window or glazed door, mirrors bounce daylight into a room. Mirrors can lift low ceilings to give a sense of height and even a small mirror fitted to a wall can give an illusion of depth. A square room can appear lengthened by placing a mirror on either side of a chimney breast. Never place a mirror in the traditional place over the mantelpiece, if you have any kind of fire in the grate; it is so easy for a person's clothes to catch fire. In a ground floor room, do not position a mirror where you may be observed by passers-by, or in any room where it will reflect uncomfortable and unnecessary glare.

One large well positioned mirror is normally to be preferred to a clutter of small mirrors. Standard sizes for plain mirrors for wall fixing are 760mm by 440mm, 1200mm by 600mm, 1520mm by 440mm and 1200mm by 360mm.

In bathrooms, because of humidity, buy a good quality mirror designed for bathroom use. When fitting, aim for at least a 3mm gap between the back and the wall so that air can circulate freely.

Glass mirrors must be screwed into plugs in the wall, using the fixings supplied. It may be easier to build up wall mirrors using the wide range of mirror tiles available from D.I.Y. shops as these usually have self-adhesive pads. The wall must be sound, as for all tiling (see above). Sizes available include 102mm by 102mm, 150mm by 150mm, 150mm by 300mm, 300mm by 300mm and 300mm by 450mm. Porous surfaces such as plaster must be sealed before fixing. Mirror tiles can be plain, or with designs, or in smokey grey and antique gold finishes. Some stores may also stock quarter and half rounds. By varying the tile size attractive effects can be achieved.

POLYSTYRENE TILES

Old fashioned ceilings with small cracks or blemishes can be concealed successfully with insulating polystyrene tiles or panels. These come in thicknesses from 4.5mm to 14mm. Popular sizes are 300mm square, 408mm square and 610mm square. The thicker the tiles the more they will insulate against heat loss. Tiles and panels are available plain or in various abstract and geometric designs. When applying polystyrene tiles, always spread adhesive over the whole of the back of the tile. Do not use the blob method formerly recommended – this can constitute a fire hazard. Always use adhesives recommended by the manufacturer.

Tiles and panels can be left undecorated as a snowy white or they can be painted with any kind of water-based (emulsion) paint. Do not use oil-based (gloss) paints; they are a fire hazard. Polystyrene purchased in rolls 2mm thick can be used for insulating walls; 4mm and 7mm thick is needed for ceilings. Polystyrene on walls is best covered with some form of decorative wall covering as it is rather vulnerable to damage from knocks.

To finish off a ceiling, use polystyrene coving in 3ft, 4ft, 6ft, 1 metre and 2 metre lengths, with mitred corner sections. Coving fits neatly into the angle between wall and ceiling. Slim-line modern or moulded period versions are available, 38mm, 63mm and 98mm deep. It is useful as a finishing touch for any form of wall or ceiling decoration (paper, paint, etc.) as it conceals uneven trimming etc. and covers cracks which often appear at the ceiling/wall junction.

HOW TO
Applying tiles

There are basic tools and methods of application which are common to all types of tiles. Read through the introductory notes before the specific details for the tile-type you have chosen.

TOOLS AND MATERIALS

Two sets of tools are required : one for setting out and another for fixing.

For setting out you need the following :

Folding rule or steel measure tape
Spirit level
Plumb-line
Chalk
Straight-edge, preferably about 2m long
Hammer
Masonry nails
Lengths of wood battens or laths about 25mm by 8mm

For fixing you will need the following :

Notched adhesive spreader, usually supplied with the tiles
Tile cutter. The simplest is a bar of metal with a carbide steel tip, but more sophisticated types incorporate a measuring gauge.
A broad paint scraper or filling knife
Folding rule
Pencil
Synthetic sponge
Fine-cut flat file or oil-stone.

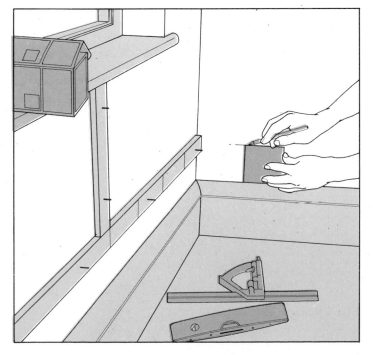

PREPARATION

Tiles can be fixed to most flat and smooth surfaces provided the surfaces are clean, dry and sound.

Plaster and concrete must be dry and level. Fill holes and cracks and level any low spots with plaster filler. If the surface is very porous or dusty, apply a sealer or priming solution. A stockist or the makers' instructions will advise on what to use.

Painted surfaces can be tiled if the paint is sound and adhering properly. To check this, apply a length of adhesive tape to the surface and pull it away sharply. If this detaches the paint, the paint should be removed. This is best done by dry scraping or sanding. If paint remover has to be used, ensure that all residues are removed after stripping. Sound gloss paint must be well rubbed down.

Wall coverings must be stripped before tiling.

Old ceramic tiles, if they are adhering firmly, provide a good surface. Re-fix loose tiles and repair any which are cracked or broken with plaster filler. Manufacturers may recommend a special adhesive for use over ceramic tiles.

STEP-BY-STEP GUIDE

Accurate setting out and careful planning is essential for a neat, professional-looking finish so that it is worth spending time on this.

Do not be tempted to use the skirting or floor-line as a guide to fixing the tiles. They are rarely true. Instead, find the lowest point of the skirting top or floor-line and mark the wall one tile-width above this. Draw a line through this point around the base of the wall using the straight-edge and spirit level to ensure that it is exactly horizontal. Fix the battens against the line with masonry nails to provide a base for the first row of tiles.

Starting from the middle, measure the number of full tiles required at either side (allowing for the spacing lugs in the case of ceramic tiles) and mark the position of the end tile. Fix a batten vertically at this point, using the plumb-line or spirit-level for accuracy. This is where the first tile will be placed unless, for example, there is a window opening and the tiles are to extend above the sill. In that case, the starting point will be immediately below the centre of the window opening and the vertical batten should be fixed there.

If the tiles are unpatterned, each wall can be centred in the same way so that any narrow pieces of tile are to be fitted in corners. With patterned tiles, however, the pattern has to be kept going around the corners, if possible. If the corners are reasonably true, this should not be too difficult and you can probably make use of the two portions of a cut tile at either side of the angle. If not, you may have to cut two tiles to fill the spaces. It is essential that the tiles run vertically and do not follow the corner if it is not true.

HOW TO FIX CERAMIC TILES

Ceramic tiles are usually fixed with a water-thinned adhesive either ready for use or in powder form to be mixed with water. Follow the manufacturer's instructions, especially if the tiles are to be fixed in damp or hot situations, where special adhesives may be required.

Having set out as described above, apply the adhesive evenly with the broad scraper to the wall where the first row of tiles is to be laid. Do not attempt to cover an area of more than about 18 tiles. Then comb the surface with the notched spreader to form ridges. Press the tiles firmly into position, sliding them against the previous tile or the batten. Most ceramic tiles have spacing lugs to ensure that the joints between are uniform in width. If not, insert short pieces of split matchstick or thin card into the joints. Fix all the full tiles before filling in where necessary with cut tiles, including those at the

bottom of the wall.

To cut ceramic tiles, measure the space to be filled after the last full tile. Transfer the measurement to the tile to be cut, making sure with patterned tiles that you leave the correct edge for matching to the preceding tile ; mark the line with a soft pencil. Score the glazed side of the tile along the line with the tile cutter. Place the tile on a flat surface, slip a matchstick under the scored line, and press with your thumbs on each corner to snap the tile.

If you have to cut a portion out of a tile, mark its shape with the tile cutter and then carefully nibble away the surplus portion with pincers or pliers.

Cut edges of tiles can be smoothed with a fine-cut flat file or coarse oil-stone used dry.

To complete tiling, allow 24 hours for the adhesive to dry and then fill or grout the joints using one of the proprietary materials made for this purpose. These are available ready-mixed or in powder form for mixing with water. Rub into the joints with a damp cloth or sponge. When the grout has set, the excess is removed with a damp sponge. A neat finish can be given to the joints by smoothing before the grout has set with a piece of thin, flat wood rounded at one end.

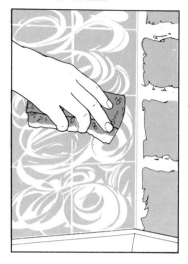

HOW TO FIX MIRROR TILES
It is possible to cover walls entirely with mirror tiles, as with ceramics, but the cutting of the tiles is more difficult and there is a much greater risk of breakage. You are, however, more likely to use mirror tiles as feature panels or over wash-basins or around baths.
Setting out should follow the lines described above, i.e. fix a horizontal batten at the base of the area to be tiled. If you are tiling a small area, say over a wash-basin, start tiling in the middle and work outwards.

Fixing is done either with self-adhesive pads or tape or with a special adhesive, as recommended by the tile manufacturer. Adhesive is usually best for tiles which are to be used in damp or steamy conditions, such as in kitchens and bathrooms. Handle the tiles very carefully as the protective backing can easily be damaged.

Cutting is done with a glass cutter in the same way as with ordinary glass. With a felt pen mark the position of the cut on the face side of the tile, place a ruler or straight-edge over the line and then, holding the glass cutter upright against the ruler, draw it firmly and steadily across the tile in one stroke. Do not go back over the cut or it will not break cleanly. Holding the tile between thumbs and fingers at each side of the cut, bend the tile away from you sharply to break it along the cut. The cut edge can be cleaned up with an oil-stone.

HOW TO FIX METALLIC TILES
Metallic tiles are usually made of thin aluminium which can be bent around corners or cut with scissors. They are supplied with adhesive tape or pads for fixing. The tiles usually have a protective film on the face which is peeled away after they are fixed.

HOW TO FIX CORK TILES
Some cork tiles have a self-adhesive backing, protected with film which can be peeled off; others require fixing with contact adhesive. They are easy to cut with a sharp trimming knife and a straight-edge. Cork tiles may be pre-finished with a clear matt or semi-gloss coating or they may be coated after fixing; polyurethane varnish or floor seal is suitable for this.

HOW TO FIX POLYSTYRENE TILES
These are fairly soft and easily damaged. They are generally suitable only for ceilings or the upper parts of walls. However, they have very good insulating properties and so help to cut down condensation in steamy kitchens and bathrooms. They are also excellent for covering cracked or uneven ceilings.

Polystyrene tiles can provide a fire risk. To avoid this, the maker's instructions on fixing must be followed precisely. For the same reason, they must never be painted with oil-based gloss paints; emulsion paint is safer.

Setting out is similar to that described for floor tiles (page 98), i.e. strike two lines at right angles to each other through the centre of the ceiling and work from the centre outwards.

Fixing should be undertaken with the adhesive recommended by the tile manufacturer. Apply it fairly thickly with a broad scraper over an area equal to that of about a dozen tiles before starting to fix them. Ensure that the whole area is covered so that no air pockets are left. Use a flat piece of board covered with felt or soft cloth to press the tiles into position. Cutting is easily done with a sharp trimming knife. Polystyrene ceiling cove is fixed in a similar fashion. It is useful for hiding cracks which often develop in the angle between ceiling and walls.

Fixing wood and fibre boarding

Wood adds a warm, natural look to any room and with care wood linings are not difficult to fix.

TOOLS AND MATERIALS
Timber battens, 50mm by 25mm
Masonry nails
Drill
Wall plugs
Screws
Rust-proofed nails or pins
Hammer
Contact adhesive

PREPARATION
Wood and fibre-board linings are usually fixed to timber grounds nailed or screwed to the wall or ceiling although fibre board can also be fixed with contact adhesive to smooth, level surfaces. In order to allow for the thickness of the grounds and the board, it is usually necessary to remove skirting boards, door architraves, light switches and power points, so the job is definitely one requiring a fair amount of D.I.Y. skill and experience. For the grounds, use 50mm by 25mm timber. If fixing to sound plaster walls, use masonry nails; if the plaster is weak or crumbly, drill and plug the walls

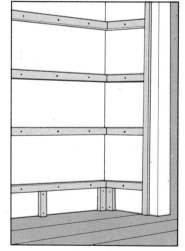

and fix the grounds with screws. For ceilings, locate the joists and nail the grounds to these.

With tongued-and-grooved boards, the grounds should run at right angles to the boards, i.e. if the boards are to be fixed vertically on a wall, the grounds should be placed horizontally and vice versa. They should be located at intervals of about 400mm. For fibre-board linings, assuming that 2.4m by 1.2m sheets are being used, the grounds running along the length of the sheets are placed at 600mm intervals and those across the sheets at 1.2m.

On wavy or uneven surfaces, the grounds may require packing out to ensure that their front faces are level with each other.

STEP-BY-STEP GUIDE
Start from a corner or angle and ensure that the first board runs truly vertical or horizontal. Fix it with small rust-proofed nails or pins driven through the face of the board. Fix succeeding boards with nails or pins through the tongues at an angle of 45 degrees. If it is necessary to join boards end-to-end, stagger the joints so that they do not coincide on adjacent boards.

At light switches and power points, it may be necessary to fit

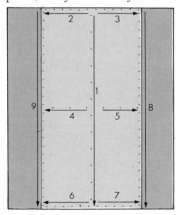

new junction boxes flush with the surface of the boards, cutting the latter to fit. Some trimming around door frames to make a neat finish will also be required. Skirtings can be refixed or may be dispensed with if the boards have been neatly trimmed along the bottom edges.

Fibre-board sheets may be fixed either by nailing or with contact adhesive. The former is usually more convenient especially for large sheets or on ceilings. Use small rust-proofed nails or pins at 100mm intervals along the edges and 200mm elsewhere. Nail in the sequence shown to avoid bulges in the sheets. With wood-grain or tile effect sheets, nail at the grooves and punch the nails below the surface.

If fixing with contact adhesive, use one of the thixotropic types which allow adjustments of the sheets after placing. Apply the adhesive to the grounds and to the corresponding places on the sheet. Position the sheet as accurately as possible before pressing it into place.

FINISHING
Wood boarding may be finished with a clear wood seal (see page 98) Nail holes in fibre board sheet should be filled with plastic wood and then, if necessary, touched up with matching paint.

WOOD CLADDING

Wood, in solid or in veneer form, provides a warm, attractive finish for walls and ceilings. Part of its charm is that no two pieces are ever exactly the same. Walls lined with solid wood are especially useful in kitchens; small pins or hooks can easily be fixed to take a wide variety of lightweight cooking implements.

Solid wood for walls and ceilings usually comes in strip form, called tongued-and-grooved boarding (known as 't-and-g'), because each board has a groove along its length on one side and a projecting tongue along the other. The tongue from one board fits into the groove of the next. T-and-g is a convenient way of disguising walls with an uneven or cracked finish – provided that the walls are sound enough to take the fixing battens.

Pine (complete with all its natural knots and marks) is the most easily obtainable wood and its yellow/brown colour fits in well with an informal style of furnishing. However, it is possible to obtain other wood from specialist timber merchants, including cedar which, because it is darker brown in colour, is perhaps better suited to a more

formal furnishing style. T-and-g for walls and ceilings is usually vee-jointed on the facing side to emphasize the lines of the panelling. Common strip width is 100mm but strips 150mm wide are also available. When estimating allow for the space taken up by the tongue as it fits into the groove of the next board. Thus a board 100mm wide will only take up about 90mm when fixed to the wall. Wood boarding can be run vertically; this is the most popular way and is very attractive. Some people prefer the boards to run horizontally or even diagonally. This is an expensive method of wall-covering, but wood looks good when confined to small feature areas; whole rooms enclosed with wood can be rather oppressive.

A wide variety of wood (or wood-effect) panels is also available in standard sizes up to 2400mm by 1200mm. Many of these panels have a planked effect which simulates boarding and so disguises the panel joins. Real wood is available in veneer form, affixed to a plywood or chipboard backing. Various kinds of simulated woods are also available, including printed plywoods and plastic-faced chipboards and hardboards.

Tongued-and-grooved boarding, most commonly available in pine, looks most effective for a country-style kitchen. It will conceal bumpy walls and take small hooks on which you could hang all kinds of kitchen utensils. Make sure that you treat your boarding to several coats of sealer before it becomes soiled with greasy kitchen fumes.

BRICKWORK

An attractive feature of many old houses, especially those of the 16th and 17th centuries, is the original brickwork exposed by the removal of defective plaster or layers of limewash. The old bricks, perhaps hand-made from local clays, lack the precision of present day common bricks and with their variegated colourings, have an appeal to those who favour the natural look in decoration and furnishing.

Not all old brickwork is worth the very considerable amount of work that is needed to remove plaster or thick coatings of limewash. It was probably not originally intended to be seen and so may have been rather crudely laid. Also, over the years, there may have been structural alterations, using different colours and sizes of bricks. It is certainly unlikely that the backing bricks used

in houses built in the last 100 years or so would be found particularly attractive.

Increasing use is being made of the decorative qualities of brickwork in modern houses, often as a single feature wall. A wide range of colours is available, including white or cream, blues and browns as well as the more usual reds and russets. There are many interesting textures and further possibilities in the use of coloured mortars for the brick joints.

Brickwork requires very little maintenance but, in some situations may require protection against soiling, or treatment to allow easy cleaning. And, if you acquire an older house with feature brickwork, it may be necessary to clean it before treating.

If it is not too badly soiled, scrubbing with a solution of household detergent may be all that is required. If it is badly stained or discoloured,

ABOVE *In many older houses you can make an attractive feature by stripping your wall back to the original brick. It is not necessary to do the whole room—an alcove or chimney breast or just one wall can look most effective.*

chemical treatment or 'dressing' the face of the brickwork to expose a clean surface may be possible but these are jobs for the professional builder or bricklayer. Often raking out and re-pointing the joints can improve the appearance of soiled or stained brickwork considerably but, again, this is a professional job.

If you are starting with new or clean brickwork, a simple and effective way of preventing soiling or staining of the actual brick is to apply a coating of a clear emulsion. A material of this type, sold for application to wallpaper to prevent soiling, is quite satisfactory for brickwork although you may have to apply several coats because the bricks will absorb it rapidly. It may have a whitish, semi-opaque appearance when first applied to dark coloured bricks but will become transparent as it dries. Coated in this way, the brickwork will resist staining and can be cleaned easily when necessary.

COLLAGES AND MURALS

It is relatively simple to create special effects for your walls and ceilings which, as they are designed and implemented exclusively by you yourself, will be both unique and original.

You can, for example, create a wall collage from pictures cut from magazines. If possible, use high quality glossy pages. Use new copies straight from the book stand, or old copies that have hardly been touched – creases can be pressed out with a warm iron with a fair measure of success. Best results are achieved by basing a wall collage on a particular theme – for example, pictures of animals, fashion pictures, or pictures all in one colour, say, brilliant reds or sunny yellows. Cut your pictures carefully, all to one shape, or overlap them for a patchwork effect. Treat the wall first with sizing powder. Follow the directions on the packet. Use ordinary wallpaper glue for pasting up your pictures.

Good results can be achieved with newspapers or children's comics – the latter can give an amusing pop-art effect. To prevent the yellowing of this type of paper, coat your finished wall collage with a very weak solution of glue size and finish with varnish (see below).

Attractive collage designs can be cut from old wallpaper sample books which can often be obtained free from decorating shops. Patterns can be made from hexagon or diamond shapes, basing ideas on designs for patchwork bedspreads. Choose colours carefully so that they blend with each other and with the room.

Paper wall collage will benefit from the extra shine and protection of a coat of varnish. First give a weak coat of glue size. For small areas brush on polyurethane varnish. For large areas not subject to heavy wear it is quicker and cheaper to use clear spirit varnish, which is simply brushed on and allowed to dry.

Murals for walls and ceilings can be painted on to any sound surface. Hardboard, plasterboard, plywood, insulating board and the like should first be sealed as directed in the painting section. If the mural is painted on to panels attached to the wall, you can take them with you when you move. However, the most attractive murals owe their effect to being painted directly on to the wall and thus becoming part of the room.

Plan your designs carefully so that they fit into the room. Let patterns flow off the wall on to the ceiling; alternatively continue a pattern from the wall on to a piece of furniture. Stripes are very effective if they are allowed to exploit the features

BELOW *A collage made from pictures cut out of magazines is a simple, inexpensive and an amusing way of decorating a portion of a wall or even plain furniture.*

of a room – for example, running across a wall, round a door or even across the door. An attractive effect can also be gained by the use of a stripe to outline the shape of furniture against a wall.

People often think that murals are beyond their ability because they are not capable of executing complicated designs. In fact, it is possible to make murals out of very simple shapes, like stylized trees, clouds or flowers, which can often be copied from magazines. Try, for example, a grass pattern in dark green along the skirting board, with one tree in the same colour and some white clouds, all against a pale blue 'sky' background. Geometric shapes are easy. For circles, use a pencil on the end of a piece of string as a large compass. To make smaller circles, simply wind the string around the end of the pencil. For a staggered bull's eye effect, simply move the centre of the circles a little each time. A pattern with curves is easier than one with stripes. As a guide for curves, draw round any suitable large round or oval objects which may be in the house – round trays, tennis racquets, large cans and so on. For geometric designs, a spirit level is necessary to find true horizontals. Find true verticals with a plumb bob, or a level with a vertical mark. A large set square is required for right angles. Masking tape is useful for getting a clean edge to straight lines – where there is any possibility that your tape is going to pull off the base paint (if the walls were previously papered, for example) use a special low-tack drafting tape obtainable from office stationers. Masking tape is best on high sheen base coat, such as an oil-based gloss, or vinyl gloss or silk.

Most kinds of paint can be used for murals. Emulsions from the tint and mix systems are ideal because they offer such a wide colour range. Their shade cards are useful for providing ideas for colour arrangements – a design based on graded tones of the same colour can look very good.

Ordering paints from these ranges can, however, be expensive as the minimum quantities on sale are normally half a litre for gloss paint and one litre for emulsion.

For murals many people use up odds and ends of paints in their possession. Strain the bits out of old paints by passing the paint through material cut from a pair of tights or a stocking. As you grow in confidence, you will find that you can mix your own colours. There is no reason why you should not use oil-based paints for some areas and water-based paints for others; but for oil-based paints, you will need white spirit to clean your brushes. For small areas of colour detail, tubes of artist's p.v.a. colours can be used.

No special equipment is required for murals. Use large wall brushes or rollers for filling in background areas; small paintbrushes and artist's brushes are needed for any fine detailing.

Where possible, paint paler colours first before proceeding to darker. Always allow adjoining areas to dry before moving on to a fresh section. This will only take around one hour for emulsions, but could take up to eight hours for oil-based paints. Use a very soft pencil, or charcoal, or perhaps a brush, for outlining your designs.

To enlarge a sketch of your own design, or an idea from a book or magazine, on to the wall, use the grid technique. Using soft pencil or charcoal cover your wall with faintly-drawn 300mm squares. Count the number of squares along the bottom of the wall. Measure the base of the picture area you wish to copy. Divide the latter figure by the former to give you the square size for a small scale grid which you draw over your picture for reference. Copy your picture one square at a time, from the small scale picture reference to the large scale wall grid. Mark all the points where the lines of the design cross the lines of the grid – then join up the lines, according to the original reference.

RIGHT *Murals are at their most stunning when designed to fit in with the architectural features of a room.*

BELOW *Draw the largescale grid onto the wall and transfer the picture one square at a time from the small-scale one.*

8. Floors and Floor Coverings

Of all surfaces in the home, floors take the hardest beating. It is a common mistake to put down floors which are not of sufficiently good quality to cope with the kind of traffic and wear they get. The result is a surface which soon looks scruffy and worn. With floors, the surface must be able to cope with the wear it will receive. There is one cardinal rule – buying the very best you can afford.

There is a bewildering variety of floorings on the market, some smooth (such as vinyls, woods and cork), others soft (such as different carpetings). Their decorative and practical advantages are explained on the following pages. Many of the smooth floorings are cheaper than carpets. If you cannot afford carpeting of sufficient quality for a high traffic area, consider having a smooth flooring instead and adding one or two rugs at strategic points. Smooth floors are sometimes referred to as hard floors. But, as you will see, these types of alternative flooring to carpets differ in their hardness – cork and cushion vinyl, for example, are much more resilient than ceramic tiles or wood strip.

Buying floorings is complicated at present by the fact that some shops give sizes and prices in metric dimensions, others in imperial. Where metric sizes are quoted, make sure you have the *exact* metric conversion, rather than the nearest approximation in convenient round figures. When comparing prices, remember that a square metre is about one-fifth larger than a square yard – i.e. 5 sq m are about 6 sq yds, and £1 a sq m is about 84p a sq yd. When estimating costs, include the price of any preparation or treatment of the under-floor (see below) and any necessary underlays. Also include laying charges unless attempting the job yourself, in which case take into consideration the cost of any necessary fixing materials (nails, pins, gripper strips, adhesives) or finishing products (stains, sealers, sanders) so that a true cost comparison can be made between different flooring finishes.

Patterned floors, available soft as in carpets, and smooth as in vinyls, are invaluable for families as they disguise dirt and stains. Plain colours, however, can make rooms seem larger and will harmonize better with other patterns in the room. You could compromise with one of the large number of floorings which have a texture or a natural pattern rather than an actual design – such as wood with its graining, or a twisted pile carpet with its knubbly surface. Using a single colour throughout one level for flooring is a useful device for making a place look larger; it is not necessary to use the same material throughout, but the colour could be the same. In this way you will create a unified interior that will feel spacious.

As with all decorative finishes, floorings are only as good as the surface on which they are laid. No floor covering can survive for long if the floor underneath is damp. Damp will rot carpets and lift tiles and sheet material. To test for damp, place a small piece of glass or polythene sheet on the floor and seal around the edges with sticky tape. Leave in position for about a week. If droplets of water condense on the under surface, then the floor is damp. Consult a professional for the remedy.

With all flooring products, particularly those designed for D.I.Y. laying, read carefully the manufacturer's instructions regarding the treatment of

the under-floor on which your flooring will be laid. In general, under-floors should be free from damp, clean, and level. It is possible to level a solid uneven floor of quarry tiles or concrete with a 'self-levelling' powder compound, which will smooth itself after you have mixed it with water and spread it over the floor. Do not use these compounds for wood or wood block floors. To level wood floors, lay sheet hardboard (smooth or mesh side up, as recommended by the flooring manufacturer). For fixing instructions, see page 98. Hardboard underlay is particularly recommended for vinyl sheet and tiles, cork tiles and some carpet tiles.

Before laying any kind of floor covering, deal with squeaky floorboards. Screw through the faulty board in two places and pull it tight to the flooring joint. Try lubricating its edges with talcum powder. Be careful that you do not pierce pipes or wires running under the floor.

WOOD

For budget-priced floors you could consider sanding and sealing, staining, or painting the existing board floor (see page 98). When painting use the board lines as the basis for different designs. However, this kind of treatment is usually rather draughty and noisy. Old sheet floorings, such as lino and vinyl can be painted with lino paint with some success.

Standard hardboard sheets, suitably varnished, act as an inexpensive floor covering. In damp conditions or in heavy traffic areas choose oil-tempered hardboard.

Natural hard wood floors, laid on top of an existing floor have a warm and pleasing effect. These floors while not cheap are no more expensive than good quality grades of carpeting. Unlike carpeting, wood floors can add to the value of your house. Choose from strips or parquet panels.

BELOW LEFT *One of the cheapest ways to achieve an attractive floor is to sand and seal the boards. Floor-sanding machines can be hired in most areas.*

BELOW *Although more expensive parquet floors add value to a house and have a very warm and pleasing effect.*

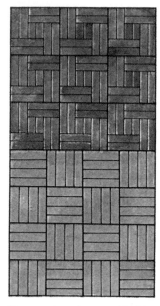

Parquet panels: top, Haddon Hall; above, basket weave.

Strips are of different lengths of between 760mm and 3040mm (which cuts down on waste) and in a choice of wood. Some are tongued and grooved, others have interlocking 'ears'. Woods available include maple, oak, afrormosia, and iroko. The width of strips varies from about 45mm to 70mm according to the wood. Nail or stick these floors to your under-floor as recommended by their manufacturers. (For general laying instructions, see page 100).

Parquet panels give the attractive look of the traditional parquet floor at a fraction of the cost. These panels are about 8mm thick and are usually in squares of 305mm and 457mm. Some are felt-backed and can be stuck directly to the under-floor, carefully following the instructions provided by the manufacturer (for general guidance, see page 99). Others are tongued-and-grooved so that they can form an interlocking floor which can be lifted and relaid elsewhere if you wish to change your flooring or place it elsewhere.

Within the panels, the wood blocks can be arranged in different patterns. The most common pattern is a simple basket weave design. The traditional Haddon Hall pattern has a more complicated chequerboard effect. Some manufacturers also do herringbone designs.

With all these wood floorings leave expansion gaps around the walls to be filled with cork expansion strip or quadrant moulding as recommended by the manufacturer.

Wood colours vary greatly, from the palest of yellow shades to deep reddy browns. In all cases, obtain a small sample before making up your mind – even if you have to pay for this it will be worth it.

VINYL SHEET

Types of vinyl flooring are improving all the time as manufacturers develop new techniques and expand their ranges of patterns and designs. Sheet vinyl flooring has to a great extent replaced sheet linoleum; it is easier to handle and comes in a wide range of colours and patterns. Lino, however, can still be ordered through some stores, in thicknesses from 2mm to 6mm and in plain or marble patterns, 1830mm wide.

Vinyl floorings are in sheet or tile form. Both types have their advantages. Tiles are small and easy to handle and can cover the most awkwardly shaped room with the minimum of wastage. You can plan your own orig.nal designs. Sheet vinyl, however, is usually quicker to lay, but may need two people. Sheet floorings give an unbroken stretch of jointless flooring which helps make rooms look larger and, in rooms such as bathrooms, withstands water more effectively. With sheet vinyl choose a cushioned type (not available in tiles) with its added warmth and resilience.

The cheapest kind of sheet covering is merely felt printed with garish designs and with a plastic coating. Designs are not very attractive, and in any event this kind of covering should be restricted to rooms which receive little wear.

The cheapest type of vinyl is made with asbestos fillers usually in tile form in plain colours with a marbled effect. The colour goes right through the tile. These tiles are hard-wearing but care must be taken in laying, as they can be brittle; it is easy, for example, to snap off corners. These tiles need regular polishing to maintain surface sheen.

Brighter colours and patterns are made by photographically reverse printing a pattern on to a layer of clear vinyl – i.e. the pattern goes underneath the vinyl wear layer which then protects the pattern. The vinyl film is then laminated to a vinyl backing. This type of vinyl flooring is available in sheet or tile form. In sheet form its disadvantage is that it tends to shrink back after laying. Allow for this when trimming or delay trimming until the flooring has been down for a few weeks. This thinner type of vinyl sheet will also show up clearly any

(as with the slate tiles) to add to the effect.

Cushioned vinyl sheet is an attractive flooring available in various thicknesses. It gives a springier, more resilient feeling underfoot, making it pleasant in rooms where you are on your feet a lot – for example, in kitchens. It is less prone to shrinkage after laying, and shows up irregularities in the under-floor less than does the thinner type of sheet vinyl. The foam interlayer is formed during the manufacturing process. The thickness of the foam usually determines the quality and price of the product. The pattern is printed directly on the sheet and this type of flooring is often embossed or textured. The cushion-effect is vulnerable to scratching and indentation from grit etc., so provide adequate door mats and boot scrapers. Tiles are not available in cushion vinyls at present. The range of designs is increasing every year. Small-scale tile patterns are useful for smaller rooms, and the pattern can be carried on to splash-backs or the sides of the bath. Do not use it behind a cooker hob as it will not withstand heat. Large-scale patterns are attractive over wide areas, especially if you can take the flooring through from one room to another – for example, from the hall to the kitchen or dining room. Colours are more subtle than formerly, with plenty of russets, terracottas and natural stone colours. In addition to bright and subdued ceramic tile patterns, there are designs which imitate natural stone and, newest of all, cork. Surfaces have an attractive shiny look imparted by the clear vinyl wear layer.

Vinyl sheet flooring comes in imperial widths of 4ft (1220mm), 6ft (1830mm) and 12ft (3660mm). Some manufacturers, however, have now changed to metric, the 2m width being the most common. With tiles, some are made to imperial sizes of 9in or 12in (229mm or 305mm) or in new metric sizes of 250mm or 300mm sq. Hexagonal, octagonal and ogee shapes are available in some ranges.

TILES

Tiles give greater scope for individual designs than sheet vinyl. Plan designs carefully. Using squared paper, take one square to represent the size of your tile and then draw the room outline to the same scale. Some manufacturers incorporate these planning grids in their brochures or leaflets. There is plenty of scope for making your own patterns; they can include large or small chequered effects, stripes, borders, or diagonal laying. One expensive range of tiles offers 'feature' strips to lay between the tiles to increase the choice of patterns. Tiles laid as horizontal stripes can increase the apparent width of a floor area and this can be useful in small rooms such as halls and kitchens. A tile design can be used to separate one part of a room from another – for example, an area for a dining table or an area in front of a settee.

Cork tiles are an increasingly popular form of

LEFT *An excellent substitute for ceramic tiles is cushioned vinyl sheet.*

ABOVE *Cork tiles are warm and easy on the feet. For areas of heavy usage buy tiles finished with a layer of PVC.*

imperfections in the under-floor and these can result in patches of uneven wear. On old wooden floors a hardboard underlay is advisable. A sophisticated range of patterns in both tile and sheet is available in various price ranges including some attractive designs based on tile and brick floorings. There are also designs which imitate natural materials such as wood, brick, or marble; perhaps the most effective are those which imitate slate. This type of vinyl flooring may be embossed or textured

Common tile size is 300mm or 305mm square but it is also possible to buy long strips for a planked effect, usually 150mm wide and about 900mm long. Tile thickness is usually 3.2mm but thicker versions are also available. Thicker tiles are not necessarily harder but they offer greater insulation and resilience.

For heaviest areas of wear, tiles which are factory finished with a layer of clear PVC are recommended. These tiles are also available finished with a wax polish, they are suitable for most areas in the home, including bathrooms, but not for very heavy duty areas such as a family kitchen. Unsealed tiles available in cheaper ranges must be sealed with several coats of varnish, applied as recommended by the manufacturer, before any wear takes place. Before laying cork tiles, always read carefully the manufacturer's instructions relating to the under-floor; for laying hints see page 98.

Ceramic tiles have a good claim to being the most durable and hard wearing of all floor coverings. They can, however, be hard on the feet. Therefore, in an area such as a kitchen a more resilient flooring such as cork or cushion vinyl is to be preferred.

Most types of ceramic tiles require specialist laying as they are set into a bed of mortar, although recently techniques have been simplified by the development of 'thin bed' adhesives. There are, however, some ranges for D.I.Y. laying with spacer lugs on the edge of each tile – little projections which help to keep the tiles even. Solid concrete floors are the best base for ceramic tiles but they can also be laid on timber floors provided that the floor is strong enough to take the weight of the chosen tile; consult a flooring specialist on this point. The floor must be lined with plywood or blockboard to prevent timber movement from disturbing the level of the tiles.

Quarry tiles are unglazed tiles in shades of buff and reddy-brown. Domestically, they are popular in sizes 101mm by 101mm and 152mm by 152mm. They have a natural, rustic look suitable for country style kitchens. They are the cheapest of all ceramics, comparing in price with a medium quality carpet and available through builders' merchants or specialist tiling shops. Other types of unglazed patterned tiles are also available.

Patterned glazed ceramic tiles, though richly and exotically decorated, are very expensive – as dear as luxury carpet. Some are made in this country, but many are imported from France, Italy and Spain, where this type of flooring perhaps better suits the climate! Sizes available are 101mm by 101mm, 152mm by 152mm and 202mm by 101mm. Interlocking ogee shapes are very attractive – these are sometimes called Provençal or Moorish. If the real thing is too expensive try the cushioned vinyl sheeting ranges which can imitate floor tile ranges most effectively and are reasonably priced.

ABOVE *Unglazed quarry tiles in shades of buff and reddy-brown look good for rustic-style kitchens. Continue the tiles up the wall or over a working surface for added sophistication.*

flooring. Warm and resilient, the pleasant brown natural colour blends well with many decoration schemes. Shades range from pale and fleck to dark brown and there are also some attractive strip effects in the more expensive ranges. More elaborate cork designs must be ordered from specialist flooring shops but the most simple versions are often available from decorating supermarkets.

HOW TO
Laying floorings

This section describes how to prepare surfaces and apply or lay: stains, seals and paints; hardboard; vinyl and cork tiles; vinyl sheet; parquet squares; hardwood strip; and ceramic floor tiles.

The basic preparation and many of the tools and methods used are common to most of these. Read, therefore, these general notes before referring to the detail on individual treatments and materials.

TOOLS AND MATERIALS
For applying paints, stains and seals you need paint brushes and cans. The tools required for laying and fixing other flooring materials are:
Folding rule or steel tape-measure
Lengths of thin string
Small nails
Steel straight-edge
Trimming knife
Stout kitchen scissors
Large pair of dividers or scribing block*
Broad paint scraper
Notched spreader (usually supplied with adhesive)
Tenon or pad saw (for hardboard and wood flooring)
Hammer and nail-punch (for hardboard and wood)
Small Surform or block-plane (for wood floors)

PREPARATION
Floor surfaces must be dry, clean, reasonably smooth and level. Solid floors, such as concrete or quarry tiles, must be tested for dampness. Borrow or hire a moisture meter; this is the most reliable method. Otherwise, tape a 300mm square of glass or thick polythene sheet to the floor with adhesive tape and leave it in position for at least a week. If beads of moisture form under the glass or film, it would be unwise to apply paint or lay impervious floor coverings. Rising damp can be prevented by brushing on a damp-proof coating (usually a thick bitumen-based product) over the floor surface. Old paint, varnish and polish residues must be removed, before

*Make a scribing block by cutting a piece of wood 150mm long, 35mm wide and 20mm thick.

new floor coverings can be stuck down.

Most floor coverings can be laid over existing vinyl tiles if these are clean and sticking properly. If they have to be removed, warm them gently with a blowlamp and lift them gently with a paint scraper.

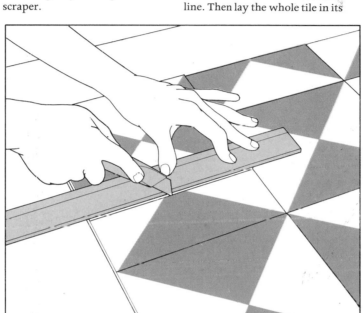

Mechanical sanding is best for rough or uneven wood floors and for removing old paint, varnish and polish. Machines can be hired by the day – time enough to sand quite a large floor. Although they are usually fitted with a dust-bag, a lot of dust is likely to escape so keep the door shut and the windows open. Wear a piece of thin cloth around your mouth and nose so that you do not inhale the dust.

Re-fix or replace loose and broken floorboards, or, if they are in very poor condition, cover the floor with hardboard. Punch upstanding nail heads below the surface. For rough or uneven concrete or quarry tile floors there are 'underlayments' or levelling compounds. These are supplied ready for use or as powders for mixing with water. They are poured on to the floor, spread roughly with a float trowel and left to flow out level. Very rough concrete or quarry-tiles need cement-topping but this is a job for a professional.

TRIMMING
With all types of flooring materials it is usually necessary to trim to skirtings and around hearth slabs, door architraves and similar obstructions. You may also have to cut round such things as wash basins or lavatory pedestals. Most trimming can be tackled by one or other of the following methods.

To cut tiles for spaces less than a tile's width, lay in place, but do not stick the last full tile in the row. Lay another tile on top with its edge tightly against the skirting or wall. Using the opposite edge as a guide, mark across the first tile and cut to the line. Then lay the whole tile in its

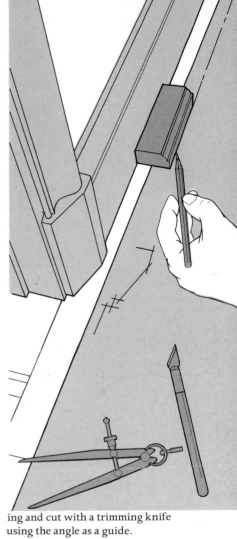

ing and cut with a trimming knife using the angle as a guide.

Scribing is a more accurate method and should be used for thick vinyl sheet and hardboard. Use either a scribing block or, for even greater accuracy, a pair of dividers. To scribe the long edges of a sheet with a scribing block draw the material away from the wall a distance less than the width of the block. Place the long edge of the block against the wall and, using the other edge as a guide, mark the surface of the sheet.

place in the row; the cut part will fit the gap left perfectly.

Knifing-in may be used to trim sheet vinyl to fit against a skirting or a wall although it is only suitable for trimming thin, flexible sheet and it requires a very steady hand. Press the sheet tightly into the angle between floor and skirt-

Using the dividers for the same purpose, draw the sheet away from the wall to about 50mm and set and lock the dividers 6mm wider than the greatest distance between the sheet and the wall. Hold the dividers upright and at right-angles to the wall with one point against the wall and the other on the sheet. Draw the dividers along so that the sheet is marked to follow the line of the wall. Door openings and architraves can also be marked very accurately in this way.

To scribe the ends of sheets for trimming, lay the sheet in position (having trimmed the edge if necessary) with the ends overlapping the end walls. Draw a line on the floor surface about 450mm long along the edge of the sheet. Draw the sheet away from the wall (allowing it to ride up the wall at the other end) a distance less than the width of the scribing block or about 50mm if using dividers. Ensure that the edge of the sheet is in contact with the guide-line on the floor surface. Then proceed as described below for edges.

MAKING A TEMPLATE
To fit floor coverings around complex shapes such as wash basins or toilet pedestals, it is best to make a template from stout paper or thin card. Cut a rectangle of paper or card larger than the base of the fitting and align it against the base so that you can locate its approximate centre and dimensions. Make a cut from one edge to the centre and radiating cuts from the centre outwards, enabling the template to be fitted round the base of the object. Tape or pin it in position and mark round the base with a soft pencil. Remove the template and cut away the waste. Tape it in position on the floor covering and re-trace the outline.

PROTECTING THE EDGES
With sheet and tile floor coverings, it is desirable to protect the edges in door openings if the covering does not continue through. For this, you require an aluminium cover strip which nails or screws across the opening. These strips may also be suitable for thicker parquet squares and hardwood but some manufacturers supply angled wood finishing strips for this purpose.

HOW TO PAINT FLOORS
Painting is perhaps the cheapest way of brightening up a shabby floor although frequent repainting may be necessary if the floor receives more than very moderate wear.

Softwood boards, concrete and quarry tiles can be painted successfully provided that they are dry, clean and sound. Old linoleum can be painted but, if it is shabby, it may be better to take it up and cover the floor with hardboard before painting or sealing. It is not advisable to paint vinyl tiles as their constituents may prevent paint from drying properly. For preparation guidance see the general notes on page 72.

Ordinary household paints are not usually suitable for floors. Tell the stockist what you want to paint and he will advise. Floor paints are usually applied directly to the surface without primer or undercoat but a primer may be required for concrete.

HOW TO SEAL AND STAIN WOOD FLOORS
Softwood floors can be made very attractive by using stain or a clear finish if the boards are in reasonable condition. If there are wide gaps or the boards are cracked or broken, cover the floor with hardboard. Fill nail holes with plastic wood or cabinet stopping; plaster filler can be used but it absorbs the stain or seal and will turn dark.

For a natural look after the floor has been cleaned or sanded, finish with clear floor varnish or seal, preferably polyurethane-based. Varnishes and seals are available in gloss, satin and matt finishes; gloss stands up best to hard wear. Two coats applied by brush are usually sufficient but follow the maker's instructions.

If you want a darker finish, apply a stain or wood-dye before the clear finish. Stains and wood-dyes are available in wood colours such as oak, walnut, mahogany, etc., but the finished colour will be influenced by the colour of the

wood itself. Also available are semi-transparent varnishes in clear, bright colours. Unlike paint, they do not obscure the grain of the wood. One coat of coloured varnish over the first coat of clear varnish is the usual method of proceeding.

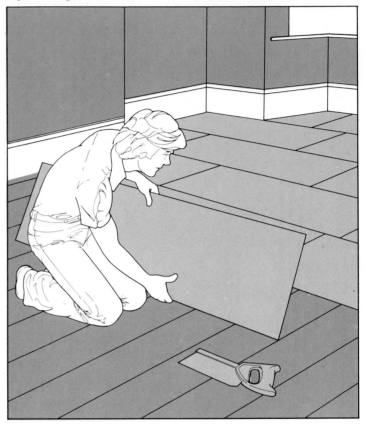

HOW TO COVER FLOORS WITH HARDBOARD
Hardboard can be used as a base for other floor coverings on floors which are in poor condition. It also makes an excellent floor covering in its own right.

Hardboard comes in sheets in a variety of sizes but the most convenient size for floors is 1.2m by 610mm. This size can be cut to make two 610mm square tiles.

Hardboard should be conditioned before use to ensure that it lies flat after fixing. To do this, bring the sheets into the room 24 hours before they are to be laid and brush or spray about a pint of water over the mesh or rough side. Lay them flat, in pairs, with their mesh sides together.

If laying hardboard as a base for another floor covering, start by laying a line of 1.2m by 610mm sheets end-to-end along the longest wall. Start the next line with a 610mm by 610mm sheet, so that the joints are staggered. If laying the board as square tiles, set out and lay from the middle of the floor in the same way as described for floor tiles.

Except for use as a surface finish or as an underlay for thin vinyl tiles, hardboard should be laid with its smooth side downwards. Fix the sheets with 20mm rust-proof nails at 100mm intervals along the edges and at 150mm intervals elsewhere. Nail along one edge first, setting the nails 12mm in from the edge. Work across the sheet in rows 180mm to 280mm apart. If you make the mistake of first nailing all the edges, the sheets will tend to bulge in the middle. Drive the nails well home and, if the board is to be left as a finish, use a hammer and nail-punch to sink the nail-heads below the surface. Fill the holes with plastic wood or cabinet stopping. Where trimming is necessary, mark or scribe by one of the methods described above and cut with a tenon or pad saw; if only a small amount of board has to be trimmed, use a Surform or block plane. Hardboard can be painted, stained or sealed by the methods described above.

HOW TO LAY VINYL AND CORK TILES
Some tiles have a self-adhesive backing with a peel-off protective film; with others, adhesive is applied to the floor.

Vinyl and cork tiles are usually laid outwards from the middle of the floor. To establish the starting point, stretch two lines of thin string between small nails tapped into the floor at the middle of opposite walls; if the floor is solid, tap the nails into the base of

the skirting. Using a tile, check that the two lines intersect at right angles. From the intersection, loose-lay a row of tiles along one line to the wall. If the space between the last full tile in the row and the wall or skirting is less than about one-third of the width of a tile, move the second guide-line exactly one half-tile width away from the edge of the first tile, and then move the whole row of tiles up to the repositioned line. Now loose-lay towards the wall another row of tiles starting from the middle and at right-angles to the first row. Again, if the space at the end is less than about one-third of the width of a tile, move the first guide-line and the row of tiles exactly one half-tile width away from the wall. If the spaces at the ends of the rows are more than one-third the tile width, leave the lines in their original positions.

The first two tiles are laid at the intersection of the guide-lines. If adhesive is required, remove the lines, leaving the nails in position; apply the adhesive, spread it evenly with a broad paint scraper and then comb it with the notched spreader. Cover an area sufficient for about eight tiles or as recommended in the instructions. Then refix the guide-lines before starting to lay the tiles. With self-adhesive tiles, there is no need to move the lines. Lay one half of the floor at a time, working outwards from the middle in the manner of a pyramid.

When the skirting or wall is reached, trim the last tile by the 'tile-on-tile' method described on page 97, using a steel straight-edge and a trimming knife.

Cork tiles may be pre-finished or you may have to apply a seal. The maker's instructions will guide you on this.

HOW TO LAY VINYL SHEET FLOORING

Vinyl sheet flooring is made in 1.2m, 1.8m, 2m and 3.6m widths although not all makes and patterns are available in all these sizes. The two smaller widths are the most popular and easiest to handle. Most materials are suitable for laying by D.I.Y. users but laying by a professional is recommended for some of the heavier grades of sheeting.

Most materials require sticking only at their edges and seams; others have to be stuck down overall. This must be remembered when choosing material and when estimating the quantity of adhesive required.

Some manufacturers recommend that the sheets are cut to length, allowing 50mm–75mm for trimming at each end, and that the lengths are then laid on the floor for some hours before trimming and fixing.

Lay the first sheet with its edge against the wall or skirting and turned up the wall an equal amount at each end. If the wall is straight, no trimming is necessary; otherwise, scribe and trim.

Lay succeeding lengths edge-to-edge or with overlapping edges as advised in the instructions. Scribe and trim or 'knife-in' the last sheet. Then trim the ends. If there are fitments or complex shapes to cut round, make templates.

When the sheets have been overlapped at the seams, cut through the centres of the over-laps, using a steel straight-edge and a trimming knife. Turn back the edges, apply a 150mm band of adhesive centrally under the join and press the edges into position. Similarly, stick down the outer edges with a 75mm band of adhesive. Double-sided adhesive tape can be used instead of adhesive, but it may show a ridge through thin materials.

HOW TO LAY PARQUET SQUARES

A readily available and easily laid type of parquet flooring comes in squares about 460mm by 460mm by 8mm. Each square is composed

of four smaller squares with three, four or five 'fingers' of hardwood and backed with bitumen felt. They can be laid on most dry, clean surfaces and are stuck down with adhesive.

Because parquet squares are so much thicker than vinyl sheets and tiles, it may be necessary to trim door bottoms to give clearance. This should be done first of all. If possible, the squares should be laid out to condition for several days before fixing.

Lay the first row of squares to a line stretched parallel to the longest wall; the line should be the width of a square plus 12mm away from the wall or skirting. This ensures that a gap for expansion is left between the squares and the wall; a similar gap must be left at the ends of the rows. Work from the middle of the rows outwards to the ends so that an equal width of square is left at each end. Apply a layer of adhesive about 1.5mm thick to 3 to 4 sq metres of floor surface. Lay the squares into the adhesive, aligning them to the guide-line.

When the end of the row or the other side of the floor is reached, cut the squares to fit using the tile-on-tile method described on page 97. Cut the squares with a tenon or pad saw. Cover the expansion gap with 15mm quadrant moulding fixed to the skirting with panel pins; alternatively, use cork expansion strip.

If the squares have been laid to a smooth level surface, little or no sanding will be needed although a mechanical sander can be used if necessary. Sand down any 'high spots' with fine abrasive paper wrapped around a cork block. Sweep and vacuum-clean the floor thoroughly and apply floor seal as recommended by the manufacturer.

Some types of parquet squares and tiles have interlocking edges and can be laid 'dry'; others have 'ears' enabling them to be pinned to wood sub-floors with panel pins. Another variety has a self-adhesive backing with a peel-off protective film. The same general principles of preparation, laying and finishing apply to all these different types.

HOW TO LAY WOOD-STRIP FLOORING

This is supplied in the form of solid hardwood strips about 45mm to 70mm wide and 10mm to 12mm thick and in random lengths from 650mm to 2.5m. The edges are tongued and grooved. Wood strip is usually laid on a wood sub-floor and fixed by nailing; adhesives are available for sticking the strips to solid floors but this is a method more for the professional floor-layer.

Strips should be brought into the room a few days before they are to be laid. They should be fixed at right angles to the floorboards of the existing floor. If this is not possible, lay hardboard panels first.

Stretch a line parallel to the skirting and about 10mm less than the width of a strip away from it. Fix the first line of strips against this guide-line by means of panel pins driven through the face along each edge of the strips every 200mm. The grooved side of the wood strips must face the skirting.

Subsequent rows of strips are fixed with panel pins just above the tongues at an angle of about 45 degrees and punched below the surface. Tap the strips closely together, using a piece of waste strip to prevent damage to the tongues.

Start each line with a strip of a different length so that the joints are staggered. To fit strips into the gaps left at the start and finish, saw or plane off the tongue and the required amount from the opposite edge. Fix with panel pins through the face side.

It is normally necessary to use a mechanical sander on a wood strip floor. Sweep and vacuum-clean the floor after sanding it and finish with a floor seal as recommended by the supplier.

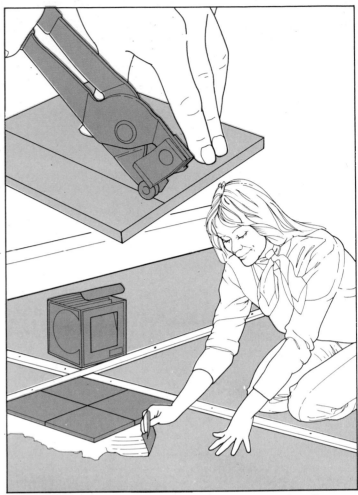

HOW TO LAY CERAMIC FLOOR TILES

Solid concrete floors are an ideal base for ceramic floor tiles but these can be laid on timber floors. However, there is a risk of flexing which will cause cracks. The floor tiles are thicker than the wall tiles, usually about 9mm to 12mm, so that the lower edges of doors will almost certainly need adjusting. In addition to the tools required for ceramic wall tiles you will need a float trowel and a rubber squeegee (piece of thick rubber tacked on to a strip of wood is a practical substitute).

With ceramic floor tiles, the lines of the joints are prominent, so that accurate setting out is essential. It is usually best to arrange to run the joints at right-angles and parallel to the door-opening.

Strike a line from the middle of the door-opening and at right-angles to it. Starting with a full tile at the door, loose-lay a row of tiles along the line to the opposite wall. Unless the tiles have spacers (usually not) allow 3mm between each. Mark the position of the last tile and, through this point, fix a batten at right-angles to the guide-line. If the floor is solid and will not take a nail, fix the batten with

patches of double-sided adhesive tape. Now loose lay another row of tiles along the batten and adjust until there is an even space at each end. Mark the position of the last tile in the row and fix a second batten at right-angles to the first. The angle between the two battens is the starting point.

Spread adhesive with the trowel to about a square metre of surface or as advised in the instructions. Lay the tiles into the adhesive with pieces of matchstick or thick card between the joints as spacers. Continue until all the full tiles have been laid. Remove the battens and fill in the spaces around the edges with cut tiles.

Measure and mark each tile. Score each on the face side with the tile cutter. Hold the tile with both hands, face side down, and strike it smartly across the edge of another tile held upright between the knees. If necessary, smooth the cut edge with an oil-stone used dry. Apply adhesive to the back of the cut tile and press it into position.

Allow 24 hours for the adhesive to harden, then remove the spacers and work grout into the joints with the rubber squeegee. When the grout is dry, polish the surface with a soft cloth.

CARPETS

Of all floorings, carpeting is the most popular. For carpets offer a comfortable, soft, appealing surface, insulating against heat loss, sealing out draughts and deadening noise. By the very nature of their soft surface, however, carpets are more vulnerable to wear and staining than other smooth or hard flooring surfaces. As with all floorings generally, it is essential to buy carpeting of a suitable quality for the wear it is likely to receive; thus, for example, living rooms need better (and usually more expensive) qualities than bedrooms. Many British carpets are labelled with the British Carpet Mark, a quality grading which indicates whether a carpet is suitable for a particular room.

Carpets are graded as follows:

1. **Light Domestic.** Suitable for little used bedrooms.

2. **Medium Domestic/Light Contract.** For main bedrooms and dining rooms.

3. **General Domestic/Medium Contract.** For living areas, except where really heavy traffic is to be expected (e.g. stairs).

4. **Heavy Domestic/General Contract.** For heavy wear areas of the home.

5. **Heavy Contract.** Unlikely to be needed in most homes and very expensive.

6. **Luxury Use.** This describes carpets usually with a long pile and of at least grade 3 quality, suitable for creating a luxury effect.

Carpets can be made in various ways. Contrary to popular belief, the method of construction (e.g. Axminster or Wilton) is in no way a guarantee of quality, as you will see from the notes below on fibres. The traditional way of making carpets is by weaving the pile at the same time as the backing. The two main British types of woven carpets are world famous.

Axminsters are usually of intricate patterns, and up to 35 colours may be used in any one design.

ABOVE *One of the most luxurious types of carpet now available is the long or 'shag' pile. Choose a good quality for a living room where you may sometimes need to use a carpet 'rake' to revive the pile. Bedrooms can take cheaper qualities in synthetic fibres. Note the attractive feature in this room of carpeting carried over a seating platform. This is an idea you could copy with any kind of carpet, even inexpensive carpet tiles.*

They are available in wide choice of qualities and designs and the pile is usually cut.

Wiltons are widely available in plain colours either in cut or looped piles. The Wilton weaving process is usually limited to five colours but those not appearing in the surface pile are carried behind in the backing to create a pad of fibres which cushions wear and so gives a Wilton its traditional reputation for 'hidden value'!

The tufted way of making carpets has the pile needled into a hessian backing and then secured on the back with adhesive. A secondary hessian backing is added for strength. Some qualities also have an additional foam backing eliminating the need for an underlay. The tufted method of manufacture is quicker and requires less labour than weaving. Cheap tufteds made from synthetic fibres are for light or short term use. More expensive tufteds, however, made from fibres such as wool or acrylics, have hard wearing qualities and offer excellent value for money.

Cord carpets can be made in a number of different ways. They can be woven rather like Wiltons but with an uncut pile. They can also be made from a bonded mat of fibres attached to a hessian backing and then given a ridged surface. Alternatively, cords can be made by tufted methods with tightly packed uncut loops.

The most important factor for determining wear is not the construction of the carpet but the type and amount of materials used in making the pile. One should always consider the composition of the pile together with its density (i.e. how much pile there is to every square centimetre or square inch of your carpet).

Wool, the traditional and natural (but expensive) carpet fibre, still remains unbeaten for warmth, resilience, hard wear and low flammability. Wool carpets come in a wide range of colours and patterns, and are strongly resistant to soiling. However, the addition of 20 per cent of nylon increases wearing qualities up to five times. Many carpets are made from 80/20 wool/nylon blends.

Acrylic fibres (e.g. Acrilan or Courtelle) are man-made and most resemble wool in appearance and in feel. They are resilient and hard wearing, whether used on their own or with one or more other fibres in budget priced blends.

Nylon fibres (e.g. Bri-Nylon or Enkalon) are also man-made; they are hard wearing and are available at medium prices. They tend to attract dirt but they can easily be cleaned by home shampooing. New soft spun fine denier nylons offer a greater degree of luxury and resistance to soiling. Rayon (Evlan and Evlan M) man-made fibres are suitable only for areas of light wear unless blended with other more hard wearing fibres; they tend to flatten and soil easily. There are also attractive long pile polyester (e.g. terylene) carpets and stain-resisting poly-

propylenes. Sisal, a natural fibre, is used in cord constructions for hard wearing carpets but they are rather rough to the touch.

For good, hard wear, select a carpet with a dense and firmly packed pile; it will wear better than a sparse pile which 'grins' (the trade term for showing the backing) when the carpet is bent back on itself. Given the same densities, the longer the pile the better.

Naturally you will want to choose a colour which blends with your overall room scheme. A carpet of good quality is likely to be down for at least seven years; with care, some families make their carpets last for ten or more years. The colour and pattern selected may have to survive several changes of paper and paint so avoid high fashion by choosing neutral or subdued colours. We all know that pale colours show marks and stains, but often we do not realise that very dark colours show bits of fluff, cotton thread, talcum powder, crumbs, etc. Perhaps a good choice is somewhere in between – a medium shade of brown, for example, is very practical as it is dirt-coloured at the start and also provides a possible basis for a number of different future schemes. Other practical colours are shades of mid-grey, green, or gold.

Many of the carpets featured in the room set-

ABOVE *This patterned carpet makes a luxurious bathroom. Make sure you choose a carpet with a synthetic pile for bathrooms. The backing too should be rot-proof. Always protect your carpet with an additional bathmat.*

RIGHT *The British Carpet Mark indicates the quality grading of a carpet.*

British Carpet MARK

LEFT *Some of the variety of carpets available. First row (far left), top to bottom: a standard wool/hair cord carpet, a sand-coloured, wool pile Berber carpet and a peat-coloured wool Berber. Second row (centre), top to bottom: a cream-coloured, woven sisal carpet and a wool pile figured Berber carpet.*
Third row (left), top to bottom: a March-green, wool pile velvet Wilton, two examples of wool pile Brussels weaves, a midsummer-green wool pile velvet Wilton and a heavy-duty wool/hair pile cord carpet.

ABOVE *A simply-patterned carpet adds elegance to this bedroom.*

RIGHT *Cord carpets come in a variety of attractive colours and are hard-wearing.*

tings of glossy magazines are entirely plain, and very chic they look. A sense of space and continuity can be added to small homes by continuing the same plain carpet from room to room. Some manufacturers make carpets of different grades with this continuity in mind.

Patterned carpets on the other hand have the advantage of concealing dirt and wear. There are plenty of designs available which are neat, small and unobtrusive. With a large patterned design for the carpet, it is usually wise to have plain or textured effects for walls, curtains and upholstery.

Some carpets, though plain, gain extra surface interest from their texture. Loop pile carpets have an interesting knubbly surface formed by their continuous series of loops. Long or 'shag' pile carpets have long pile strands, usually all the same length, to create a luxurious shaggy effect. They are practical and tend to need less vacuum cleaning than shorter pile carpets of the same shade. A flattened pile can be revived with a special plastic carpet rake. Hard twist carpets have a kink or twist set into the pile to impart a rough textured look – often found in Wilton qualities where they contrast markedly with the smooth velvet piles also available. Sculptured piles have a pattern created through variations of cut or through looped high or low tufts; the colour may be

identical but a pattern is created through the texture.

The carpet industry is gradually changing to metric widths of 1m, 2m, 3m and 4m. But machinery is expensive to replace so that manufacturers of woven carpets in particular will be making carpets in the imperial sizes for some time. Broadloom widths are 15ft (4.6m); 12ft (3.7m); 10ft 6in (3.2m); 9ft (2.7m); 7ft 6in (2.3m); and 6ft (1.8m). Not all qualities, however, will be made in all those widths. Narrower 'body' widths of 36in (90cm) and 27in (70cm – called 'three-quarter body' in the trade) are good for corridors and stairs. Some woven carpets (especially Wiltons) are only made in three-quarter body and have to be seamed together to cover larger areas – this is a job for professionals.

FITTING CARPETS

Accurate estimating and planning are essential to find the most suitable and economical way to lay a carpet. Draw a plan of the room, preferably to scale, and mark in carefully the sizes of any

recesses and bays. Your retailer will then help you to work out how much carpet is needed. The length of the carpet should run down the length of the room. Plain carpets can look patchy when laid; this effect, which is called shading, will be lessened if the pile leans away from the light.

Carpets are expensive and it is courting trouble in attempting to lay them yourself unless you feel completely confident. Foam-backed tufted carpets and carpet tiles (see below) are within the scope of most amateurs (see the 'How To' sections at the end of the chapter) as are stair carpets for straight flights. But unbacked woven carpets (Axminsters and Wiltons) are difficult to lay as they need to be stretched by professional techniques. The trade uses a tool called a 'knee kicker' which in the hands of the inexperienced can damage both knees and carpet. Certain types of cord carpeting such as sisals and non-woven cords will also look better if they are professionally stretched. They may sometimes need a second stretching when they have been down for a short period.

Any carpet without a foam backing should have an underlay to cushion wear and to add resilience and extra insulation. Use a good quality felt, or rubberized felt or good quality foam rubber.

CARPET SQUARES

Seductive, luxurious, fitted carpets are warm, easy to clean, and make a room look larger. But they are relatively expensive as they cover also the little-used areas of the room in alcoves and under furniture. You cannot easily and economically take them with you when you move. 'Squares' are available in a wide range of colours and standard sizes and shapes, including circles and ovals, and with attractive designs and special features such as central motifs, borders and fringes. Squares can be adjusted from time to time to spread the wear; and they can go with you if you move. Smooth floorings (such as cork, wood and vinyl) can look attractive as a surround for carpet squares or rugs; or you can use low cost cords as a background, making a feature of your squares.

CARPET TILES

Carpet tiles, a relatively new idea, have many advantages. Most have special backings which make an underlay unnecessary, and most ranges can easily be laid by amateurs. You can create your own patterns, as with vinyl tiles. There is far less waste in cutting and fitting tiles than with broadloom carpeting. Common sizes are 300mm, 305mm, and 500mm square. Tiles are usually sold in packs although some brands may offer loose tiles. Cheapest brands resemble non-woven cords or needle felt but tiles are also available in pile carpetings, including shags. Many brands are loose laid and can therefore be moved around to spread wear or be taken up for removing stubborn stains.

MATTINGS

Alternatives to expensive carpeting include various mattings, such as rush matting and coconut matting. Their rough texture and natural brown shades blend well with informal or country styles of decorating. They can be loose-laid without fixing but with an underlay if possible. Secure cut edges with latex adhesive or with carpet binding tape, stuck down with the adhesive. Trim edges neatly first, and conclude by tapping lightly with a hammer to improve adhesion.

RUGS

Furnishing stores offer an enormous variety of rugs and mats. Rugs, like cushions, often provide that vital touch needed to finish a room scheme. Rugs can break the monotony of large areas of plain dark flooring and can highlight and define particular floor areas, such as the space in front of a settee; they can also provide extra comfort to smooth flooring. Use them where people like to sit on the floor – in front of the fire – or where bare feet are likely as in bedrooms. Use them in bathrooms for added protection and comfort. Make sure, however, that they are able to withstand the effects of water and are non-slip. Combined with cheaper floorings, rugs add a touch of luxury to a home without depleting the budget.

Traditional oriental rugs are available new or secondhand. They are hand-made with subtle and intricate patterns which have been passed down for hundreds of years. They come from a variety of countries including India, Persia (Iran), China, Turkey, Afghanistan, and Morocco. Oriental rugs should always be purchased from a reputable dealer, preferably a specialist, who can explain the intricacies of the different types, and can select rugs which will blend with a particular furnishing scheme. Unlike most floor coverings, a well chosen oriental rug is likely to increase in value. There are, however, many imitations of oriental patterns which are machine-made in this country on Axminster looms.

Many attractive rugs of good value come from India. These include plain off-white rugs and carpet squares in all-wool and these blend well with modern furnishings. There are also inexpensive Indian flat-weave cotton rugs in brightly coloured stripes called dhurries. Numdah rugs are also inexpensive, made from off-white felt with embroidered designs. They soil quickly, but can be dry-cleaned.

Chinese rugs and carpets are famous for their soft subtle colourings (blues, greens, golds) and feature traditional motifs with symbolic significance – such as the dragon (representing the forces of nature) and the lotus flower (the sacred Buddhist emblem). The designs are often offset by beautiful borders, and the pile is frequently 'sculptured' to give a high/low effect. Carpets and small rugs in a plain colour often have a design sculptured into the pile.

Long pile Rya rugs with wool or wool-like pile originally came from Scandinavia but many imitations are now woven in this country. Designs usually feature geometric motifs in bright colours and blend well with modern furniture.

English manufacturers make a wide choice of plain, textured and patterned rugs in various fibres. They offer a huge range of sizes from small hearthrugs to long runners and carpet squares; they are also available in ovals, circles and half moons to emphasise different floor areas.

Various kinds of fur and skin rugs are produced in all price ranges. At the lower end of the price range there are fleecy sheepskins in white and in shades of cream and these can usually be washed; or try a long-haired goatskin but beware of this on a dark carpet as it tends to moult!

Long pile fluffy rugs made from synthetic fibres such as nylons and acrylics offer a luxury touch at modest cost. The pile often has an attractive sheen which adds to the effect and there is a good range of deep and pastel colours. There are also long pile cotton rugs which come in attractive colours.

Inexpensive rush matting looks attractive on wood or tile floors. It comes in various weaves and in square, oblong or round shapes.

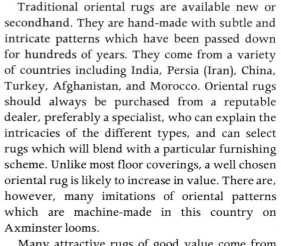

HOW TO
Laying carpets

HOW TO LAY A STAIR CARPET
It is essential for safety that stair carpet should be well-fitted. If in doubt, consult a professional.

TOOLS AND MATERIALS
Suitable carpeting
Pads for unbacked carpets
Tackless carpet grippers with fixings
Carpet tacks
Hammer

PREPARATION
To estimate the amount of carpet required, measure the depth of the tread and height of the riser, add together and multiply by the number of stairs in the flight. Add 450mm to the figure reached to allow carpet to be moved periodically to shift wear. For un-backed carpet use stair pads as an underlay to guard against wear and to deaden noise. Pads should be deep enough to fit against the riser on one side and to extend at least 50mm over the nosing of the tread.

STEP-BY-STEP GUIDE
Secure the underlay pads with tacks. Into the angle made by each tread and riser, tack pre-cut lengths of angled metal tackless carpet gripper, fixing these lengths over the stair pads. They will hold the carpet safely and invisibly across its whole length on angled pins. Special plastic versions are available for foam-backed carpets. Stroke the carpet to

determine the direction of the pile. Pile runs the way which feels the smoothest. Lay the carpet with the pile running downwards. Starting from the top of the stairs, turn and tack the carpet into place along the riser of the top step. Then, using the special tool sold with gripper

fixings, press the carpet onto the first set of gripper pins. Take it taut over the step, down the riser, and onto the second set of gripper pins. Continue to the bottom, turn in the surplus on the bottom riser and tack in place.

HOW TO LAY A FOAM-BACKED CARPET
Unbacked carpets are best laid by a professional. However, laying a foam-backed carpet is within the scope of the competent home handyperson.

TOOLS AND MATERIALS
Paper felt
Carpet adhesive
Carpet seaming tape
Hammer
Carpet tacks
Trimming knife
Chalk
Double-sided adhesive tape or staple gun

PREPARATION
Remove any protuberances such as nails which may damage the carpet. Remove doors where necessary. Sweep the floor.

STEP-BY-STEP GUIDE
Line the floor with paper felt to prevent the foam backing sticking to the floor. This is particularly important if carpet is ever to be moved. Stroke the carpet – pile runs the way that feels the smoothest. Lay the carpet with the surface pile running away from the light. Unroll the carpet. Try to keep the surface smooth and in line. If you do not, bad bulges will result; roll up the carpet and start again. Use adhesive carpet seaming tape for joins. Turn back the carpet on one side of the seam. Chalk a line on the floor along the

other edge. Turn back the other edge. Tack down the tape at one end, sticky side up. Unwind the

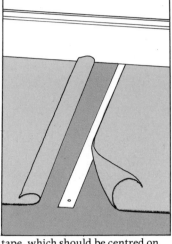

tape, which should be centred on the chalk guide line. Tack down at the other end. Then press down the carpet edges onto the tape. Remove the tacks and press down the ends.

To fit the carpet at the skirtings, trim as necessary with a sharp knife. If large amounts need to be cut away, for example at chimney-breasts, mark with chalk the estimated cutting line on the

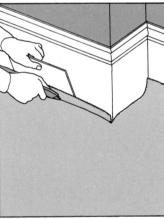

carpet. Cut, leaving a margin which allows a final trim for an exact fit. Instead of tacking, you can secure the carpet at the edges with double-sided adhesive tape or with a staple gun.

HOW TO DYE A CARPET
Carpet dye colours are suitable for wool, nylon and rayons such as Evlan and mixtures of these fibres with acrylics, such as Courtelle. They should not be used on cotton or 100 per cent acrylics, nor on carpets which are foam or rubber backed. When a carpet colour is changed the dye used will blend with the existing colour so that, for example, a gold carpet dyed blue will become green. For good results, keep to a colour in

the same family – dye red or burgundy over pink and brown over beige. Dyeing a patterned carpet will not obliterate the design but a colour-change will give it a completely new look.

TOOLS AND MATERIALS
Vacuum cleaner
Carpet shampoo
Newspaper
Small bowl
Stiff scrubbing brush
Carpet dye
Rubber gloves

PREPARATION
Vacuum. Protect the skirting boards and any surrounding floor area with newspaper. Shampoo, removing as many stains as possible as these might otherwise show through the dye.

STEP-BY-STEP GUIDE
Dissolve the dye in boiling water following the manufacturer's instructions. Start at the corner furthest from the door and work the hot dye well into the pile with

a stiff brush. Dye faded areas first and give them a second applica-tion when the whole carpet has been dyed. If it is necessary to stop before finishing the carpet, break off in a zig-zag rather than a straight line. Leave to dry for approximately 24 hours and then vacuum.

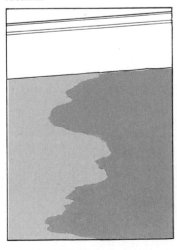

9. Windows and Doors

Enter a bare room during daytime and your eyes are automatically drawn towards the source of light. The windows invariably give the initial impression. How many are there? Are they large or small? Which way do they face? Do they offer a pleasing view?

Windows help set the mood of a room. With skilled treatment they can do more to create mood than almost any other furnishing feature. Treat them with the care they deserve and they will reward you by turning the most uninspiring box into a handsome room.

Often the largest focal point above floor level, a window holds the greatest scope for improvements. With a little know-how it is possible to perform prodigies even with the most unattractive of windows. A small window can be made to appear large, a narrow one look wider and a badly placed one seem well situated. Whatever your budget, clever use of shape and colour works wonders.

Before planning a treatment, remember that a window exists to let in both light and air and nothing must be allowed to interfere with these functions. Whatever is done should improve them both by providing warmth and insulation in cold weather or shading and ventilation in summer – in addition to enhancing the appearance of the window itself.

Ask yourself these questions: What is there to see from the window? If there is an attractive view not overlooked by neighbours or passers-by, you will want to make the most of this by leaving as much of the window as possible bare and uncluttered by day. By night, however, it will need hiding for it will merely be a blank, dark screen. If, on the other hand, the view is of little consequence, you may wish to keep it out while still letting in light. For this you can use open-weave sheers or nets or café curtains which hang prettily from a rod half-way down the window and remain permanently drawn.

What about the window's shape; is it elegant or ugly? Uninspiring windows can be given the full treatment by trimming with a pelmet, or swags and tie-backs or by adding a blind to match the curtains. Stick to simple methods with a beautiful window, leaving as many of its ornamental features on show as possible.

What are the other furnishings in the room like? Any treatment should be in keeping with them. Colour and pattern of window fabrics need to be coordinated with floor and wall coverings, other soft furnishings, and with the design and even the colour of furniture.

How will it all look from outside? What may seem a brilliant idea from indoors (a low pelmet or a painted window pane) may spoil the symmetry of an exterior wall.

There are other points to consider. Should you have short or floor length curtains? Short curtains

BELOW *An attractive way of treating a window without obscuring light is to place plants on the sill.*

(not more than 5cm below the sill) require less fabric and therefore cost less. They are also more informal and most convenient where there is a radiator or a large piece of furniture under the window; they tend to suit windows which are set well back into a wall. Floor length curtains, on the other hand, are more luxurious (and expensive), make a room look larger and add cosiness at night time. They should clear the floor by at least 3cm.

Finally, is the treatment practical for your needs? Select washable fabric for curtains likely to come into contact with small, grubby fingers, a wipe-clean blind for a hot, steamy kitchen and insulating lining for a draughty sash. Make sure that before deciding you have investigated all the possibilities from the wide choice of fabrics, blinds, shutters and screens which are available.

Should you choose plain or patterned fabric and which colour? This depends on the remainder of the room. Read carefully the section on choosing colours, pages 21 to 26.

WINDOW TYPES

● *Sash (or double-hung) windows* are typical of Victorian homes. Two frames balanced by counter weights slide up or down. Traditionally made of wood, some are now being made in metal. Large and well-proportioned, with attractive wooden architraves (surrounds), they respond best to simple treatments in keeping with the house, such as a plain but substantial wooden pole painted to match the frame colour, hung with full length pencil-pleated curtains. As sashes do not open inwards, they can have blinds or fixed daytime curtains (sheers, nets or cafés) if desired.

● *Casement windows*, fixed in part so they cannot open, with inner frames which swing from the top, or sideways like a door, are a feature of many smaller houses. Make sure the treatment selected does not interfere with the opening of the window. Fixed daytime curtains are not suitable. If there is more than one window on a wall, long curtains on a single track which pull back in sets between windows give unity during the day and soft colour at night.

● *Leaded windows* have small panes joined together with lead strips. They date from the days when glass could only be obtained in small sections. Found in cottages and Tudor-style houses, they lend themselves particularly well to pretty treatment and can effectively take such items as frills, valances and draping.

● *Picture windows* and floor-to-ceiling sliding windows are found in many new houses. Big windows

BELOW *Café curtains (this one has a scalloped heading) are pretty, easy to make and can add depth to a shallow window*

so that curtains can be pulled clear of the window frame to reveal its shape. Professional curtain makers can make arched curtain headings, but these are difficult to tackle at home.

● *Recessed windows* in a row could create a problem. A neat solution is to use patterned wallpaper and matching roller blinds inside the recess with plain curtains and wall outside them.

● *Windows above doors* may let in light but they may also mean that someone at a higher level can see inside. Consider net curtains or obscured glass. Net curtains can be cut to the shape of an attractive semi-circular fanlight, cutting the lower edge twice as wide as that of the window. Fix them round the curve of the fan with slim openweave heading tape and flexible track; along the straight lower edge of the fan, gather the curtain on to a wire slotted through a pocketed hem.

● *Dormer windows* are fixed into an extension projecting from the roof so that they give light to an attic room. You can blend a dormer window in with the rest of the room by using curtains or a blind that match or tone with your paper or paint. Alternatively, this type of window lends itself to special treatment. You could frame the dormer with a broad painted border and echo the border by painting the window frame to match. Finish off with a neat, plain blind, perhaps branded with braid to match the border and the window frame. To make a focal point of the dormer, paint and curtain it in a colour contrasting strongly with the rest of the room.

● *Skylights* provide extra light in an attic by letting in light through the roof. Since most of them are at an incline they cannot be curtained. Skylights on a shallow incline can be fitted with standard roller blinds to run under retaining wires on either side. Pull-cords which can be run along the walls, over pulleys if necessary, must be fastened around a cleat. On steep slopes and horizontal surfaces specially ordered blinds, stiffened with metal strip, must run along metal channels.

● *Strip windows,* set high up in a wall, short and very wide, provide light but no view. They leave a wall free to take furniture but can look bare and untidy if furniture is placed at random beneath. Try sill length curtains, with a wall unit below. Or make the window look longer by a run of café curtains starting just above the bottom of the window, with a second set of curtains from the top of the window to the lowest edge of the café curtains.

Windows which do not match and face each other (such as a casement and French windows) need grouping together. Give them bold matching curtains in the same style; long curtains with pelmets are very suitable.

Here are a few tricks with awkward shapes. Extend tracks so that curtains cover the wall at the sides of windows which are too narrow, and pull back as far as possible during the daytime. If a

like these need important treatment. They let in plenty of light, but their vast expanse of glass can look cold at times. Warm, open weave sheers kept drawn all the time are an answer. Deep headings and simple tracks make the most of these windows. If the window is not centrally placed, curtain the entire wall and pull the fabric back on one side only.

● *Bay windows* are an attractive feature. If the ceiling of the bay extension is lower than that of the main room, you can hang short curtains against the windows. Tall bay windows can be given royal treatment with individual pairs of full length curtains, tied back between windows and linked by a single pelmet. Half-length daytime café curtains usually look good in bay windows, perhaps with a blind to pull down over the top half at night. Alternatively, blinds on their own are a simple low-budget solution to the bay window problem.

Make the most of attractive arches by leaving visible as much of them as possible. Run enough simple track straight across the top of the window

window is too short, add a deep pelmet which starts well above the window and ends just below the top of the window frame – longer curtains will add to the illusion of height, or instead of the pelmet use a blind and keep it partly pulled down. When there are several narrow windows on one wall, run one length of track across all the windows, so that the curtains create one sheet of colour at night time. Draw them back over the wall areas between windows, so that this gives the illusion of one large window. When a window is situated at one end of a wall, you could curtain the whole wall and leave all except the window area drawn the whole time. This is also a good way of hiding an unwanted door and furniture can be placed in front of the curtained wall.

POLES AND TRACKS

The means of supporting curtains are an integral part of the overall style and help to give finish and balance to the whole. Select track or pole, therefore, at the same time as headings and fabrics: all three should successfully combine to suit the window shape.

Read manufacturers' leaflets very carefully. There are a great many different types of track on the market. Make sure you choose the right one for your purpose. Tracks which are purely functional should be as unobtrusive as possible when curtains are drawn back. Consider also how silently the system operates; whether it will take the weight of heavy fabric; and whether it has a cording set (to open and shut curtains without handling) or whether this can be fitted – an important consideration for fabrics such as velvet which mark with constant handling.

The cheapest tracks are plastic and I-shaped in section, and are usually sold in chain stores. Along the track run plastic gliders with attached rings (from which curtains hang on hooks) and they are held to the wall or ceiling with brackets. Attachments (which include end stops so that gliders cannot slide off and curtain ends can be secured) are bought separately. Extras which may be needed include an overlap arm so that curtains overlap at the centre of the window, another track and carriers for the valance, a bridge to join two tracks into a double length, and a cording set. As I-shaped tracks are functional rather than beautiful, these should be screened behind a valance.

More sophisticated 'no-pelmet' tracks have hidden wall fixings, with a neat and almost invisible groove on the under-side or rear to take gliders. In addition to plain white they include a variety of self-adhesive wood-grain or metallized laminate finishes which are designed for curtains with stiff, deeper headings and no pelmet, as they resemble decorative bars when installed. When drawn, the curtain heading should cover the track. Tracks can be bought in standard lengths and cut down to the

required window size. Most plastic tracks can bend gently to fit round bays but special tracks are needed for angles or excessive curves; some bend one way only, so that care is needed if curtains are to go round an S-bend. Some metal tracks can be bent to order before delivery, or they can be curved at home by using a special tool. For right angles, it is possible to adapt some straight systems by adding a length of L-shaped track which allows curtains to run continuously. Alternatively, angle end stops can join two tracks at an angle but in this case separate curtains are needed.

Brackets are designed for face fixing to wall or vertical surfaces, or for top fixing to ceiling or horizontal surfaces. Top fixings are necessary where there is no wall space above a window (e.g. if a window reaches ceiling height). Some tracks

can be fixed directly to a wall and flush against it. Extendable brackets can make tracks stand away from the wall; this is necessary for old windows which have been double-glazed later.

Curtains with straight formal pelmets (to hide plain gathered headings) hang from a curtain track fixed under a wooden pelmet board. The pelmet fabric is backed with stiffening and then tacked to the board or attached with Velcro so that it can be removed easily for cleaning.

Decorative pelmets need no fabric cover-up – and come in a variety of finishes such as reeded aluminium, white-painted coving and natural pine. These are available in standard sizes. Some have adjustable track and can be cut to size.

Simple gathers or more formal deep headings can hang from rings beneath a pole. Old-fashioned brass and wood poles with matching rings are still available in a wide range of diameters. Alternatively, there are several newer decorative corded, adjustable poles/tracks available in different finishes and thicknesses. Round the pole are regularly spaced semi-circular curtain rings which are attached to gliders at the back. Finished to look like metal or natural, or painted and gilded wood, there is a pole to suit almost every type of fabric.

Brass and wooden curtain poles with matching rings have an appeal of their own. Metal poles can be elegantly plain or reeded with finials (decorative ends) round, pineapple or fleur de lys in shape. To finish off the effect, there are beautiful architrave brackets which support the poles.

With a little ingenuity, very attractive homemade hang-up systems can be invented. Try, for example, a length of bamboo for a looped café-curtain heading, or plain wooden dowelling (or even a broomstick), polished and varnished or painted and combined with wooden or brass rings. Rest the rods on brass cup hooks and anchor them by sewing decorative ties at the outside corner of each curtain, knotting pole and cup hook together with them.

ABOVE *Make sure that curtains do not obscure the pretty shape of the arches during the day. Here, a simple rod runs along the top of the windows with plenty of space to pull the curtains well back on either side.*

RIGHT *Tracks, poles and headings: (a) a decorative heading with the tape placed so that the heading hides the plastic track; (b) a track designed to accommodate a decorative heading and separate lining. The glider and hook are combined to make installation easy; (c) a track specifically designed for use with pelmets or valances. These hook directly onto the top track, while the curtain hangs from the bottom one; (d) a curtain with fanned pinch pleat heading hangs from a corded, adjustable pole; (e) a wooden, curtain pole with pencil-pleated curtain. Note that the heading tape must be placed at the top edge of the curtain; (f) a skylight blind.*

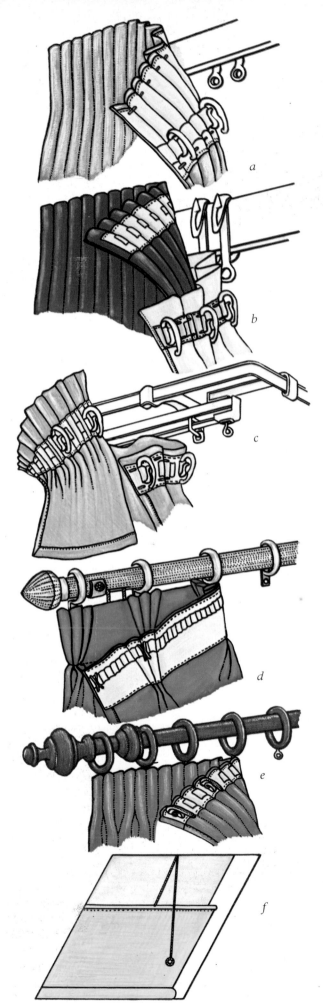

ABOVE *A simple cotton print fabric makes lovely curtaining for a bedroom. Some fabrics are available with matching wallpaper. Consider too making a matching bedspread.*

FABRICS FOR CURTAINS

Picking curtain fabrics worries many people. A large outlay is required, and mistakes have to be lived with for a long time. However, with care, an informed selection of material will solve many problems.

Texture as well as pattern sets style and mood. Rich fabrics suit formal rooms; cosy corners appear attractive in dainty, informal cottons. For a cheerful, bright area, you can choose something unpretentious, such as gingham. Textured fabrics make a room look and feel warmer; smooth materials make it appear cooler.

Wearability and laundering are of importance. For example, kitchens need fabric which can stand up to frequent washing; materials which need dry-cleaning should be for rooms used by adults only. Curtains will need cleaning more often in the city than in the country. Furnishing fabrics come in several qualities, from fixed upholstery weight to lighter curtain materials. It is a waste of money to buy heavy duty quality on tight budgets.

There is a wide choice of silks, cottons, linens, wools and man-made materials. Silk is the most lush and most formal but the least hardwearing. It has several man-made substitutes. One range in beautiful sheeny colours looks like slub silk. Other fabrics with a silken look include rustling taffeta and its watermarked sister, moiré.

Cotton has many textures: velvet, traditionally

silk, is now mostly cotton or man-made, and it cleans better. It can bring warmth to formal rooms and fits in well with other fabrics. Corded velvet is usually reserved for upholstery, but it makes distinctive long curtains, particularly in a really wide stripe.

Shiny chintzes and cretonnes with flowery prints are associated with cottages and polished floors, but look graceful across a picture window in a modern room, colour-linked to plain walls and carpets.

Cotton repp comes in plain colours with a slight rib to the texture; budget priced, it takes on almost any style, according to its treatment. However, sateen repp (cotton satin with a ribbed backing) falls stiffly and formally.

Linen is combined with cotton to make closely woven linen union; an extremely hard-wearing furnishing fabric, it is usually pre-shrunk, colour-fast and washable. In bold clear prints, there is a pattern to suit most tastes, from stylized William Morris to geometrics, or to suit any room or house whether solidly Victorian or cosily contemporary. Linen unions make satisfactory upholstery coverings, as well as curtaining.

Some wallpaper and vinyl patterns are repeated in furnishing cotton. Small, pretty prints which look attractive in bedrooms can curtain windows and cover walls, giving an overall look to a small room cluttered with fussy windows. For bathrooms and kitchens there are laminated cottons with a wipe-clean finish.

Warm and resilient wool or wool-look fabrics include nubbly tweed and graceful open weaves which hang in soft folds allowing light to filter through. Mostly in neutral shades, they add texture rather than pattern and suit walls in strong colours.

Many man-made materials look like natural fabrics. For example, nylon plush looks like cotton velvet, acrylic sheers look like wool, rayons look like slubbed silk. Mostly they wash well and need little or no ironing. Net curtains, which give privacy and can be matched with thick outer curtains, are usually in nylon or polyesters such as Terylene. Shrink-resistant, fibreglass curtains are usually sheer, and have insulating properties; but they require hand washing and drip-drying. Man-made fibres are often mixed in blends with natural fibres to improve wear and washing properties, and to stabilize costs.

More unusual materials can also be made up into curtains; but do not expect them all to wear as well as furnishing fabrics for they are not being put to their intended use. Dress fabrics, for example, though pretty and cheap, may shrink substantially when washed.

An inexpensive buy, hessian is available in almost any colour but is cheapest in its natural shades. It is plain enough to dress up with ornate braiding and it can also be used on walls, but it is best hung at windows without much sun as it will almost certainly fade. The natural shades of brown fade least, the blues and greens most.

Tough denim improves in appearance as it fades and creases – think of well-washed jeans! You can even consider patchwork curtains made from old jeans.

For quick, virtually no-sew curtains at relatively little cost, try felt which needs no hemming. Just. cut, attach the heading and hang it up. Decorate, if you like, with felt cut-outs such as flower shapes, stuck or sewn on at random. Or try a whole collage, but balance the pictures or pattern and carry them over both curtains. However, these curtains will need dry-cleaning.

Natural cotton duck is inexpensive and hard-wearing. A creamy off-white, it can be really attractive trimmed with a double border of contrasting ribbons of different widths.

Towelling is a versatile material. You could add an appliqué design in printed cottons – testing for colour-fastness first.

A cotton lace cloth is more romantic than net curtains. Hang one with a wavy hem straight across a thick pole so that the pattern shows. But since lace shrinks, remember to buy a cloth larger than the window and wash it first!

Sheeting, old or new, can be tie-dyed with beautiful results. Large amounts of fabric are involved – you can cold-dye in the bathtub, or cold or hot dye in a washing machine.

Linings give body, add insulation, and protect the main fabric against sunlight and dirt. Cotton sateen, the traditional fabric for linings, is available in many colours. Twill can also be used – indeed any close woven fabric with the same sewing and cleaning properties as the curtain itself. There is a polyester/cotton curtain cambric for lining easy-care fabrics.

Interlining with bump (cotton padding) gives even more warmth and makes curtains look weightier. For warmth without weight, use a special insulating lining, which eliminates interlining. This is cotton sateen backed by a coating of aluminium particles which reflect heat and light. The fabric side is available in many colours.

DIFFERENT HEADINGS

For an immaculate, well finished appearance, it is the top edge or heading of a curtain which should receive priority treatment. Ready-made heading tapes with hook pockets and drawstrings (sold by the metre in most department and specialist stores) make light work of most styles; even intricate pleating can be handled quite easily at home, and there is a special tape for detachable linings.

The cheapest tape is the narrow standard type, up to 25mm wide, which is sewn on slightly below the curtain top to give a ruffled effect. Since this

BELOW *(a) Tie-backs give a simple bay window height and elegance.*
(b) Do not obscure an attractively shaped window; a simple treatment is best.
(c) Wide-spaced curtains on a narrow frame give an impression of depth.
(d) A small, modern window benefits from café curtain treatment with a mock lower half.
(e) Linking windows into a continuous run adds to a room's width.
(f) Using an L-shaped curved rail allows you to draw curtains completely clear of dormer windows. You might consider matching wallpaper to curtain to blend the window in with the rest of the room.

a   b   c

d   e   f

kind of tape is available in cotton in about 20 colours, or in man-made materials, it can easily be matched to curtain fabric. Pull up the drawstrings and the fabric falls into simple gathers. Standard tape requires minimum fabric—the curtain width need only be $1\frac{1}{2}$ times the length of the track; other headings require 2–3 times as much fabric as the track length. Gathers are not quite as neat as other taped headings. Use this tape behind pelmets, valances or swags, or combine with rod and rings.

Several narrow tapes are specially designed to give a neat finish to net and light fabrics. Take your choice, depending on whether you want miniature or fanned pinch pleats, even folds, or an open weave tape which will not show on the front of filmy curtains.

Wide tapes, sewn across the top edge, give a deep, crisp heading and a neat upright finish concealing the track completely when the curtains are drawn. They are designed to be used without pelmets and can be combined with modern track or traditional rods and rings. They average about 7.5cm in width. The amount of fabric needed varies according to the heading and the fabric used – the lighter the fabric, the more of it is needed. Stitched on and pulled up with drawstrings like standard tape, the fabric is formed into even folds called pencil pleats which look particularly attractive across modern picture windows. More elaborate deep headings can be made with pull-up tapes by working four rows of stitching instead of two. The results are smocked effects.

Fanned pinch pleats are easy to achieve. Use automatic pleating tape (used with special two-pronged hooks) to form the fabric into regularly spaced sets of triple pleats when the drawstrings are pulled. There are variations of both pencil and pinch pleating tapes, according to whether curtains are to hang below the track or stand well above it. The manufacturers offer comprehensive literature for guidance.

For other pleats there is wide tape with pockets woven at regular intervals but without drawstrings. By inserting four-pronged pleat hooks in the correct pocket, a variety of effects can be obtained, such as tailored single, double or triple pinch pleats as well as box pleats, which need stitching flat to finish.

Cartridge pleats are an elegant variation and are ideal for velvet as they do not crease the fabric. They are made with tape like narrow box pleats with a roll of buckram inserted in each pleated section of tape to give a stiff rounded effect.

More intricate pleats, such as diamonds (box pleats pinched together in the centre with top and bottom outwards), or scalloped pinch pleats for poles and rings, have to be hand-sewn. They add detail and interest to plain fabrics. These are a little ambitious to tackle first-time round at home.

Making your own headings without special

tapes can save both fabric and money, and produce decorative results. Scallops are half circles cut out along the top edge of a curtain and are best teamed with poles and rings. A pretty variation on this theme is to cut away Vs instead of half circles.

Rings are not needed for café or long curtains which are never pulled back; try creating one of several looped headings to hang from an ornate pole. A traditional café-curtain heading, for instance, consists of deep scallop shapes with the ends looped over the pole. A castellated café heading with rectangles instead of scallops is an easy variation which lends itself to contrast binding trims, and requires very little fabric for it looks best hung straight across a window.

Even trimmings can make good headings: a little braid can go a long way. For a soft pretty look, hang light, pale curtains from a slim pole with bold coloured loop braids; then run a band of it along the curtain hems.

TRIMMINGS

The most humble of curtains can be made to cut a dash with a little clever trimming. Indeed trimming is an easy way to turn mass produced ready-made items into stunning individual creations!

The simplest of all ways is to add straight bands of braid or ribbon down the edges which meet at the middle of the window, and also along the hemline. Dozens of different braids are available. It is important to choose a texture which blends with the curtain fabric and that both fabric and braid have the same cleaning qualities.

An economical trim is easy to make from a length of contrasting fabric by cutting bands across the full fabric width, joining them end to end, and turning under edges ready for stitching to a curtain. Geometric patterns can be cut on the bias. Take care not to stretch strips, and therefore the pattern, out of shape when sewing.

Trimming ready made curtains with patchwork gives them a style of their own. Make up bands of patchwork in hexagons, diamonds and rectangles, filling in the sides to obtain straight edges, or merely joining patches end to end for a shapely border. Patchwork groups, like hexagon flowers, can also be added in a border or at random.

Tie-backs give curtains instant drape. Lengths of fabric, cord, ribbon or chain are fixed to the window sides and used to keep curtains pulled back. Tasselled dressing-gown cords are a good substitute and there are also large decorative metal hooks which are equally effective although expensive. Some fabric tie-backs are shaped and stiffened – their widths vary from 5cm to 15cm depending on the height and fullness of the curtains. You can make a very simple curtain tie-back using a length of ribbon sewn to a curtain ring at each end, and attached to a cup hook screwed into the window frame on each side.

Valances, pelmets and swags can be used to create style at the top. Gathered or pleated in different ways, valances are really mini-curtains: you can gather or pleat them, choosing a style you like from the ideas already outlined for curtain headings. Make them between 10cm and 30cm deep, according to the proportions of the curtains. They can box in and hide the curtain's heading.

Pelmets box in headings too but are more formal. The fabric is given a stiff backing to keep it flat. Depth depends on curtain proportions, and it's a good idea to experiment with paper patterns.

Draped swags, with tails, are elegant at tall windows in high ceilinged rooms. What appears to be one length of fabric – but is in fact several pieces carefully cut, pleated and joined – is swathed in graceful folds (swags) over the curtain top, and the ends (tails) allowed to fall at each side. This, however, is too ambitious for the novice curtain maker.

LEFT *To retain the shape of an arched window during the evening when the curtains are drawn across, you must make a special arched heading or valance. This project would be too ambitious for the novice curtain-maker.*

RIGHT *Curtain tie backs can be created from loops of cord or ribbon. They add style to any simple curtain treatment.*

BLINDS

Blinds can be a relatively inexpensive way of covering windows. For more intricate window treatments, you can combine curtains and blinds, but this can be much more expensive. There are several types and each is designed for a particular purpose.

Venetian blinds consist of horizontal slats supported by tape uprights. The slats can lie flat or be tilted forwards or backwards until they are almost edge to edge, slightly overlapping, and the blind as a whole can be pulled up or down. This gives complete control over the amount of light which can be let into a room; direct glare can be excluded, light can still be allowed in. Available in a wide variety of colours and styles, there is one to suit any budget or décor.

Price differs according to the materials used and the neatness with which the mechanics of the blind are concealed. Slats can be made of stove-enamelled aluminium or plastic, and there are some attractive wooden slats. Tapes are of cotton or Terylene. There are several points to consider when buying.

Can the headrail which holds the mechanics be fitted behind a curtain rail or pelmet? Are there snap fastenings for easy removal to clean? Are all components resistant to rust? How wide are the slats and will they fade, buckle, chip or snap?

Venetian blinds can be made to fit almost any size of square or rectangular window and it is possible for them to be custom-made for awkward shapes. There are even those which fit between double-glazed windows with pull-up mechanisms operating from indoors. Slat widths vary between 25mm and 50mm.

Venetian blinds can blend with curtains or be made the main feature. Some have multi-coloured slats with a rainbow effect; others have slats in different colours assembled so that they form a special pattern which can be tied in to a design on the wall. To preserve the uniformity of an outside wall, some blinds even have two-tone slats with a colour on top and white on the underside. Even with a different colour of blind in each room, they will all look white from the outside.

Vertical blinds are a more recent innovation.

Slats which run from floor to ceiling are operated on the same principle as the Venetian blind by altering their angle to diffuse or reflect light. Designed to be drawn back to left or right, or to divide in the middle, their advantage is that they can be parted or partly drawn to provide entry and exit through French and floor to ceiling sliding windows. Slats, of open weave vinyl-impregnated fabric, slide along a ceiling track, are weighted to hang straight, and are linked together by a guide chain at the foot. Wider than horizontal blinds, slat widths vary from 12.5cm to 9cm.

There are also fashionable slatted natural or green wood blinds, reminiscent of the tropics. Made of fine wood strips woven together with cotton they roll up from the lower edge. Designed solely as screens, they are non-fade and are ideal for giving a warm feeling to an exposed area such as a sun room, which is also used at night or in dull weather.

Roller blinds act as screens and offer the greatest scope for adding a personal touch. Use them as cheap doors against shelving as well as at windows. There are scores of easy ways of trimming a plain blind and beautiful trims can be teamed with those

of cushions, curtains and upholstery. Ready-made blinds in specially treated and stiffened wipe-clean fabric can be bought off the peg in standard sizes trimmed at the shop to fit your window or to be assembled and trimmed at home. Roller blinds are also made to measure in an enormous variety of colour-ways and patterns. Some ranges match wallpaper and furnishing fabrics so that they can be matched with curtains and other furnishings in a room. There are some very attractive blinds in new, scenic patterns and some are designed with a panel of pattern at the lower edge which creates a pelmet effect when the blind is rolled up.

Roller blinds can be made from scratch at home using a D.I.Y. kit which contains a wooden roller and all necessary components except fabric. Stiffened blind fabric is available by the metre. Close woven untreated fabric can also be used if it is sprayed with stiffener; the finish is less stiff but looks attractive.

A decorative trim – added below the lath which keeps the bottom of a blind taut – softens its severe lines. Its lower edge can be scalloped, castellated or finished in many ways. Add a matching pelmet and a blind has enough elegance and style to dress a

ABOVE *Attractive moulded window surrounds are often found in older houses. They can be obscured by curtains. Consider simple roller blinds as an alternative. You can paint your own designs or choose one from the excellent ranges of mass-produced patterned blinds.*

RIGHT *Roman blinds are a very pretty alternative to roller blinds. They too can be made at home.*

window formally without the aid of curtains. It is the addition of detail which adds to the style. Ornate tasselled or rounded pulls, bobbles, broad bands of braid or ribbon can be used – but take care that the thickness of the trim does not prevent the fabric from rolling up smoothly.

Roman blinds can also be made at home. In unstiffened fabric, they are operated by a system of fine cords which run through vertical lines of rings attached on tape at the back of the blind. Pulling the cord at the side of the window raises the blind in horizontal folds which can be made to look most attractive.

Painted blinds can provide fun. An old metal Venetian blind can be updated by using gloss enamel to paint a bold design, which is visible only when slats are closed. Or, for a window which needs to be screened off during daytime, try a pretty illusion by painting a mock window complete with view on white sheeting using fabric paint. To paint a ready made blind, use the kind of shoe dye which is suitable for plastic.

OTHER IDEAS

It is not essential to have a curtain or a blind for every window. There are some alternative unusual treatments.

There are two possibilities for windows which look out at a blank wall or an uninspiring basement area – either to improve the outlook or to hide it without blocking out the light. Ideas for improving the view could include adding plants outside the window in tubs or window-boxes or growing creepers or climbers up the wall or a trellis. Alternatively, paint a mural on the wall.

There are many pleasing ways of hiding a view without blocking the light. For example, erect glass shelves in recessed windows and stand pot plants on them. The glass will scarcely reduce the amount of light – and the plants will thrive!

For painting on glass to be successful, use a special paint which gives the effect of translucent coloured glass. Self-adhesive imitation lead strip can be added to create realistic leaded windows. A delightful way to pretend spring is round the corner, even in mid-November, is to paint on the pane what appears to be an overhanging branch laden with blossom, or refreshing spring greenery.

For a rustling screen which flutters at the hint of a breeze, try beads. Ready-made screens can now be bought in wood or in plastic which looks like glass. The simplest way to make one is to thread rows of beads of the same colour and shape sequence, and hang them vertically from a rod across the window to produce horizontal stripes of colour or shape. More intricate designs can be worked out on squared paper, each string assembled by working down a line of squares and hung in sequence. As a variation from beads use curtain rings linked into chains or chain bought by the yard or metre.

Airy macramé wall hangings show to great advantage against a window. They can be made to perform a double duty both as a screen and as wall hanging at a recessed window where the sill is occasionally put in use. Use a swivel free arm towel rail – these look good in perspex – as a base for working the macramé. Put the rail outside the recess, so that the macramé hangs in front of the window; or swing it against the wall leaving the window free.

Functional shutters can also be decorative. Louvres allow light to penetrate. Alternatively make shutters in pine board, with shaped top and bottom edges and a peephole. Plain shutters found in old houses can look attractive with painted flower borders on the outside, visible when folded back and with a larger design on the inside to add interest at night when they are across the window. Shutters in a recessed window can be colour-linked to carpet or walls; adding a window seat covered in carpet gives added warmth. Pretty daytime shutters made of fretwork hardboard give a lace-like look and allow light to enter.

BELOW *A bead screen is an attractive and unusual way of treating a window. Screens can be bought ready-made or you could try making your own.*

RIGHT *Shelves across a window screen an ugly view. The natural back lighting enhances any objects displayed. In this picture, the old-fashioned iron brackets add interest.*

Doors

Doors have a great deal of decorative potential. But consider first whether you have the kind of door best suited to your functional needs. Sometimes a very simple adjustment such as hanging a door round the other way can make a big difference to a room, making it possible to position furniture or storage in a better way. If you are very short of space, consider a sliding door. There are also doors made of soft materials which fold up concertina-fashion into very little space and there are bi-fold doors split vertically down the middle and hinged so that when they are opened, they fold into two. Louvre versions of this bi-fold are very popular. If a door is left open most of the time, e.g. the door from the hall into the kitchen, and the house is well heated, you could consider removing it completely and substituting a bead-screen. (See also pages 14 to 20.)

Of course you may not want to change the door itself, but are content to decorate what you already have. In small, busy rooms where wall space is limited, it may be more pleasing to decorate a door to suit the rest of the room by painting the wall, frame and door in the same colour, or at least in tones of the same basic colour. This is often the best solution where the door or frame is crooked or unattractive: one colour treatment often camouflages defects.

When papering a wall, you could cover a flush door with the same pattern, painting the door frame in a toning colour to resemble a picture frame. This is a very effective method for panelled doors, too, where the panels only are lined with the wall covering pattern. Panelled doors lend themselves to many different finishes. The panels themselves can be painted in colours which contrast with the rest of the paintwork and you could even add a third colour to the mouldings. Or the panels could be lined with any one of a number of exotic decorative materials – marbled or metallic papers, felts or corks, paper-backed hessians or even mirror mosaic!

For many years it has been popular to modernize old properties by covering the original panelled doors with sheets of hardboard to provide a flush finish. In some cases, for example in rented properties, this is necessary to meet fire regulations, but in a private home is it really an improvement? The recessed and moulded panels of the old doors often seem to suit older properties much better than their smooth surfaced replacements. Careful filling and painting can restore the surface of even the most battered paintwork. Or consider stripping off the old paint to reveal the beauties of the natural wood. You can do the stripping yourself, following the procedure outlined on page 131. Or you can take the door off its hinges and have it stripped pro-

fessionally by one of the many antique furniture dealers offering this kind of service. Stripped doors must be sealed thoroughly to prevent dirty marks from penetrating the wood.

The knobs on a door can make all the difference to its good looks. Try and choose knobs in keeping with the style of the door. Modern lever handles in aluminium are out of keeping on beautiful old panelled doors; replace them with large round knobs of the same shape as that which the doors had originally. Brass knobs are becoming expensive; sometimes you can find the odd pair in junk shops. Consider also the very attractive knobs made in Perspex which, although plastic, have a look similar to clear or coloured crystal. Visit an architectural ironmonger specializing in handles and door fittings; the stock of the ordinary hardware store tends to be rather limited.

Fingerplates in china, Perspex or metal are also attractive on old doors and are useful for covering up marks left by old handles, etc.

Most modern houses are fitted with simple flush faced doors and with no panels to provide decorative inspiration. You could consider adding your own panels. You can achieve a panelled effect with wooden moulding mitred at the corners. Ready made complete plastic panels are also available and

BELOW *Plain modern flush-panelled doors provide a suitable surface for your own painted designs. One based on diagonal strips, as shown, is easy to do. Obtain crisp edges by using masking tape and make sure each strip is dry before tackling an adjoining area.*

these can be glued or pinned into place and painted. When finished they look exactly like wood. They soften the appearance of the door and blend particularly well with antique or traditional styles of furnishing.

You could also exploit the flush face of a modern door by covering it with ready-painted door-sized pictures available from good decorating shops, or by covering the door with your own collage of cut-outs from magazines, postcards, photos, etc. For a more permanent effect, stick down the cuttings with wallpaper paste and cover with varnish for protection from dirty marks. Or cover the door with thin cork tiles, and turn it into a pin-up area so that you can change your cut-outs and cuttings as the mood suits you. Some people have even covered a door with mirror tiles, making a useful full length mirror and adding extra light and a sense of space to a room.

If you are artistically inclined, use a flush door to provide a good surface for your own murals. Incidentally, these always look more attractive if they are allowed to flow off the door onto the adjacent walls; try a large stripe, for example, running along the wall, over the door, and on to the wall again.

Children love to have their own names on the outside of the door of their room. You can add these quite easily—or have the children do it—with stencilled letters or with rub-down lettering.

ABOVE *You can use translucent glass-paints, available from hobby shops, to decorate doors with glass panels. If you do not want to design your own pattern, you could use stencils.*

HOW TO
Making curtains

HOW TO ESTIMATE QUANTITIES FOR CURTAINS

The first step in making any kind of curtain is to purchase your fabric, estimating the quantity you need as described below.

TOOLS AND MATERIALS
Use a steel rule for accurate measurements – a tape sags or stretches.

PREPARATION
Work out the track length using the window width or adding 15cm more at each side; where necessary to go across several windows.

STEP-BY-STEP GUIDE
To find the total width according to the curtain heading, multiply the track length by $1\frac{1}{2}$ for standard gathers, by 2 for pencil pleats, by $2\frac{1}{2}$ or 3 for pinch or box pleats. Add 10cm per curtain on the track to this measurement.

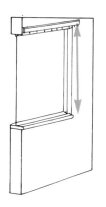

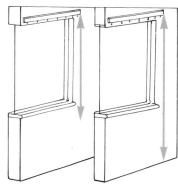

To find the length, work out the curtain drop as in the diagram – from track to sill, or 10cm to 15cm below sill, or 2.5cm from the floor. Add 20cm to the drop for top and

bottom turnings. To find the number of lengths required divide the total width by the width of the curtain fabric.

To find the total quantity multiply the length measurement by the number of lengths required. If the fabric has a pattern repeat (i.e. a definite design recurring at regular intervals) extra fabric is needed so that the pattern can be matched across total width. Proceed as follows: find the number of repeats per length by measuring the distance between two repeats, then divide the length measurement by this figure. If the answer produces several whole repeats plus part of one, add one repeat per number of lengths required to the total quantity. Further, in all cases add one repeat so that a whole pattern can be positioned along the lower edge.

HOW TO MAKE AN UNLINED CURTAIN WITH GATHERED HEADING
This is the simplest type of curtain to make and is well within the scope of any beginner.

TOOLS AND MATERIALS
Fabric
Enough heading tape to go across total width plus 10cm per curtain
Thread

PREPARATION
Pre-shrink the fabric if necessary. To get an absolutely straight line at right angles to curtain sides, pull a thread across the fabric width before cutting. Work out the length (see estimating quantities).

STEP-BY-STEP GUIDE
Cut the first length so that there is a whole pattern along the hemline. To match up the design so it runs across the full width of both curtains, lay each length cut alongside the uncut fabric and match the pattern at selvedges before cutting off the next.

If the number of lengths required for your track add up to an odd number and has to be made up into two curtains, cut the last length down the middle and put the half widths at the sides of the window.

Join together the lengths for each curtain with a long stitch, along the selvedges, snipping into seam allowances to prevent puckering; press the seams open. Turn the side edges under first 1.5cm then 3.5cm, tack and press. Hand or machine hem to within 16.5cm of the lower and 3.5cm of

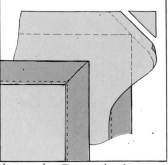

the top edge. Turn under the top edge 3.5cm and press, mitring corners and trimming away excess. Lay the curtains flat, wrong side up.

To head each curtain: with the pockets for the hooks facing you, pin tape across the top 2.5cm from the foldline, distributing the excess equally and leaving the ends unpinned.

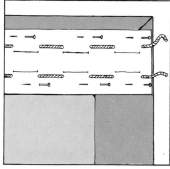

Now pull out the cords for about 5cm at the end which will be at the centre of the window so that the loose ends hang from behind the tape. Knot the cords together firmly, trim away most of the excess tape, turn under a tiny hem (flush with the curtain side) and pin down the folded end to hide the knot.

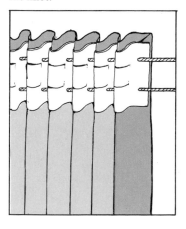

At the opposite end (i.e. at the side of the window) pull out the cords so that the loose ends hang *in front* of the tape, then finish off as before, leaving the cords free for pulling. Stitch the whole tape in place round its four edges taking care not to catch the free ends of the cord.

Lay the curtains flat, right side up, and mark off the finished length, measuring from the top edge, *not* from the level of the tape. Turn under and tack; hem, but do not finish. Hang the curtains for about a week; then before the final hemming adjust any unevenness caused by the fabric dropping.

To put up, gather the curtains by pulling together both loose ends of cord; the required width for each curtain of a pair is half the length of the track plus about 2.5cm so they meet closely. Knot the cord ends firmly together and tuck the excess into the mitred corners. Do not cut them off as the curtains will need flattening out for laundering.

Now fit the hooks into the tape – one at each end, the others spaced evenly about 12.5cm apart. To insert each hook, push the straight end through a tape pocket from bottom to top, then turn it over until it is upright.

To finish, adjust the hem, mitre the bottom corners, tack and press. If needed, sew small weights inside the hem so that it hangs evenly; then slipstitch in place by hand.

HOW TO ADD A CURTAIN LINING
All curtains benefit from lining. It improves the drape, allows less light through and increases the curtain's insulating capacity.

TOOLS AND MATERIALS
Enough lining fabric to cover the same area of curtain
Thread

STEP-BY-STEP GUIDE
Cut the main curtain fabric and join the widths as for unlined curtains. Cut and make up the lining in the same way so that it is 5cm shorter and 5cm narrower than the curtain.

Turn in 5cm allowances at each side of the curtain. Tack and press but do not hem. Repeat with the lining. Turn up the lower edge of the lining, first 6mm then 2.5cm, mitring corners. Tack, press and machine stitch. Turn up the lower edge of the curtain 10cm; tack and press but do not hem.

Lock the lining and curtain together: lay the curtain out flat, wrong side up; place the lining right side up over it so that the top raw edges are flush and the excess width of curtain is equal at both sides; pin the layers together down the middle. Leaving the curtain flat, fold back the lining sides so they meet over the middle pin line. Make a loose buttonhole stitch down each foldline, picking up a thread of the curtain fabric at the same time so that stitching does not show on the curtain front; stop 20cm from the bottom of the curtain.

Open out the lining again and slipstitch the side turnings to the curtain stopping 20cm from the bottom.

To attach the heading turn back

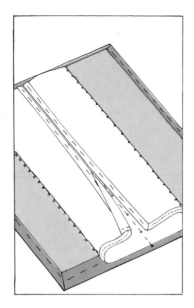

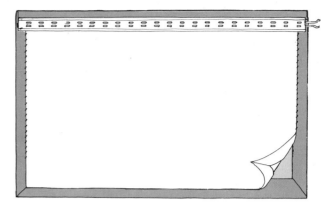

double-thickness at the top edge after measuring off the length from the bottom of the hem; then prepare and stitch on the tape as for unlined curtains, treating both lining and curtain fabrics as one.

Hang curtains for a few days, adjust the hem of main fabric and complete as for unlined curtains; then finish slipstitching down the sides, allowing the bottom hems to hang free from each other.

Making a simple blind

Blinds can be both decorative and useful in a number of different roles. Special kits are available for those who wish to make their own.

TOOLS AND MATERIALS
Fabric to cover window
Internally sprung wooden roller with metal ends
Special fixing brackets with screws
Tacks
Bottom lath required to weight fabric
Cord to pull blind down
Acorn, ring or tassel pull for free end of cord
Covering plate with screws
Thread
Fabric stiffener, if required

PREPARATION
Roller. Measure across the width of the window. Make sure there is enough space for the pins projecting from the roller ends to turn in the brackets without scraping the sides in a window recess. Allow more than the width of recess if the roller is going outside it.

Cut the roller to size at the end opposite the spring. Fix on the metal cap and hammer home round the pin. Fix the brackets to the wall following the manufacturer's instructions, making sure there is at least 1.5cm clearance between the top of the roller and ceiling, or the top of the recess, when the roller is in place.

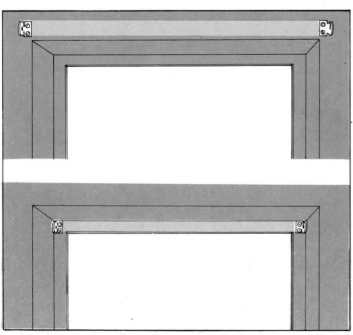

Fabric. The finished width should be 2.5cm less than the length of the roller. Add 2.5cm for each side turning to this measurement. To work out the finished length, measure from the middle of a bracket to the window ledge; add 15cm to 25cm for an extra turn round the roller, depending on its thickness. Add 5cm to this measurement for the bottom hem.

STEP-BY-STEP GUIDE
Measure out the fabric. Make sure it is absolutely straight across the top edge and that the pattern runs down it. To do this, pull a thread from the selvedge or, if the fabric is stiffened, use the corner of a table as a guide, taping a side edge of the fabric flush with the edge of the table. Cut the fabric, centring the pattern.

So that turnings do not pucker, snip into the selvedges at regular intervals where they have not been removed. Turn the side seam allowances under, tack, press and machine with a zig zag stitch to oversew raw edges. If this is not possible, sew with two rows of straight stitching close together. Do not turn in raw edges before stitching: the extra bulk will prevent the fabric from winding smoothly round the roller.

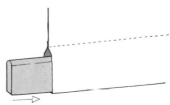

Turn the lower edge first 1.5cm then 3.5cm to the wrong side. Tack, press and machine along the top of the hem to make a pocket.

Trim the length of lath to 1.5cm less than the width of the finished blind; then slide it into the pocket. Fix one end of the cord to the lath on the centre front of the blind with two upholstery tacks. Cover the tacks with the plate, fixing with screws. Attach the pull to other end of the cord.

If using thin fabric, turn the top raw edge 5mm to the right side and press, ready for tacking a double layer of the fabric to the roller.

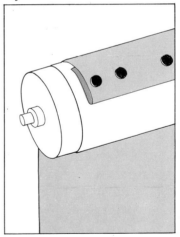

Lay the blind out flat and attach to the roller with tacks (or staples) and put up as directed by the manufacturer. Blind kits are designed so that the fabric hangs behind the roller when the blind is down, so that you will probably need to have the fabric the right side up. Tack the fabric to the roller working from the middle outwards so that the blind hangs properly.

Rollers are usually sold with a special slotted bracket for the spring end. Make sure that this end is the right way round for its particular bracket before tacking on the fabric.

10. Furniture and Soft Furnishings

Good quality new furniture is expensive. And so-called cheap modern furniture is only cheap when compared to expensive furniture – it still costs a lot of money.

However, second-hand furniture can be obtained at a fraction of the price of new modern furniture. Victorian and Edwardian pieces have become rather fashionable, and in consequence their prices have unfortunately risen substantially in the last few years. Nevertheless pieces made in the thirties or just after the last war are still reasonably cheap and can be given a new lease of life with some of the techniques outlined below.

Make a note of the measurements of your main room in a notebook or diary, carefully recording the sizes of any recesses and the heights of ceilings. This will prevent you buying a beautiful but out-size wardrobe which will not fit the room when you get it home. Always take a rule or tape so that you can check measurements in the shop.

You need vision when you are buying second-hand – the vision to see how the piece can be transformed and fitted into your home. On the whole, if you have large rooms of Victorian proportions it is easier to furnish second-hand than for a small modern flat. But there are older pieces around which are small – mirrors, small tables, little cupboards, small upright chairs and so on – and the addition of something old can often soften the effect of a severe modern setting.

An attractive way to treat old furniture is to strip off the varnish and stain and so to reveal the natural appeal of the original wood. This is particularly so with pieces made from pine (chests, dressers, small tables and the like), which assume a delightful golden yellow colour when stripped.

STRIPPING FURNITURE

Stripping furniture can be a long and arduous business. Avoid tackling an item like a large chest of drawers or a dresser unless you are sure you have the time and endurance to see the job through. Start with something small. People often find that the work is harder than they had imagined. Most large towns have shops specializing in selling old furniture which has already been stripped. These firms use large caustic baths in which they dip items to remove the varnish and polish. They are usually prepared to take in items for stripping and so to save you the work involved. Of course you

can still do the finishing for yourself if you want to. In addition to furniture, these firms can also strip doors, but you yourself will have to tackle any woodwork which is part of the structure of your house, such as skirtings, banisters and so on.

Before you embark on stripping, try to find a piece of wood on your furniture which has not been finished—look on the inside. This will show you the likely appearance when you have finished stripping. If your furniture has been stained as well as varnished, you may have to use a sander to remove the stain as it may have sunk deep into the grain. For notes on stripping woodwork, see page 131.

You may also need to make small repairs. Loose joints can be glued with a modern woodworking adhesive; take care to follow instructions on the pack. Tie, weight or cramp the joint together while the glue sets. There may be need to glue down small mouldings or edgings, but if any new wood has to be used, stain it to match the original. Often handles are missing so that a complete new set will be required. It is best to take care to buy handles concealing the fixings of those you have removed (take an old handle with you to the shop, and compare it for size).

PAINTING FURNITURE

Second-hand furniture not suitable for stripping can often be painted effectively. In any event you may prefer a painted finish – for example, a large piece which has been stained and finished with a varnish may seem much less oppressive if painted in white or in a pale colour to blend with the furnishing scheme.

Paint will not, however, adhere to a greasy or dirty surface. You can paint over old varnish, provided that every scrap of old wax is removed with white spirit and wire wool. If furniture has already been painted, it should be washed down thoroughly with a solution of detergent, rinsed well, and then sanded with a medium grade glass paper to provide a key for the new paint. Prime any patches of bare wood and any areas where filler has been used to patch small holes and other damage.

If the wood has been treated with a stain which is bitumen based this could work its way (or 'bleed') through your own final paint film. A coat of button polish, available from a hardware store, will seal the stain before painting begins.

On woods with a very open grain, a better finish is obtained if a fine surface filler is used before painting; this fills the grain and leaves a flat surface for the paint film. Apply with a wide bladed filling knife. Wait until the filler has hardened

LEFT *Furniture bought from junk shops can be transformed by stripping off its layers of varnish. Always read carefully the instructions on the container which holds the stripping agent before starting work.*

ABOVE *The flat fronts of cupboards and wall-cabinets provide a good surface for decoration. You can use stencils to create a design or go to town with your own painting.*

then rub down with a fine grade glass paper and prime before painting.

For hints on painting different articles of furniture, see page 131.

When painting, you have at your disposal the whole vast range of colours produced by paint manufacturers today. Read once again the notes on choosing colours for rooms on pages 21 to 26. Choose your colour for your furniture to harmonize with your room scheme – bulky, rather unattractive old pieces will be minimized in this way. But smaller pieces make delightful colour accents or contrasts and this effect is intensified by a glossy finish. There is no need to limit yourself to one colour. Consider picking out doors or drawers or mouldings or panels in a contrasting colour. Or use a range of shades, grading from light to dark on a set of drawers or down a louvre door. You can integrate your painted furniture with your room, for example by painting a stripe on the wall which frames the piece of furniture, or carrying a stripe across the wall over the piece of furniture and back on to the wall again.

There are all kinds of extra decorative touches which can be given to old furniture old and new to create individual articles of great charm.

The ideas which follow can be used on painted second-hand furniture. They can also be used for new whitewood furniture, which is available in a wide choice of different designs mainly for kitchen, bedroom and nursery. Modern whitewood designs often lend themselves particularly well to decorative ideas – some, for example, have louvred or panelled doors which cry out for special treatment. Paint them in a contrasting colour or in a lighter or darker shade of your chosen colour.

Whitewood furniture is simple to decorate but to obtain a really professional finish, take a little time and trouble preparing the wood before applying the final coat of paint. Firstly, the units should be wiped over with a damp cloth to remove any dust particles. A primer should then be applied to seal the whitewood – a quick-drying acrylic based primer is ideal. Follow this in turn with an undercoat. Allow both to dry thoroughly before applying the next coat of paint, which can be gloss or matt as required.

STAINING FURNITURE

As an alternative to painted finishes, consider colour stains. These are suitable for whitewood furniture or for older stripped pieces in paler woods such as pine. Stripped furniture sometimes benefits from treatment with a wood bleach before staining. Colour stains allow the natural grain of the wood to show through and will not chip in the same way as a painted finish.

Colour stains are available as powders for mixing with water, or with half water/half methylated spirits if a concentrated colour is required. An alternative range is available ready mixed in cans. Both these types of colour stains require a finishing coat of clear gloss or matt polyurethane varnish to protect the wood. Polyurethane varnishes are also available with colour ready mixed in the varnish; although quicker to apply, these do not give such a clear colour effect as with stain and varnish used separately.

Colour stains can be applied with a brush, cloth or sponge, and work should be along the grain. Apply a second coat for a deeper colour. An 'antique' look can be achieved by using a stronger solution of the stain at the edges of the furniture.

MOULDINGS

There are many ways for giving furniture your own personal touch. You can, for example, add mouldings to plain flush doors and panels. Choice ranges from simple wood beadings and moulded strips to intricate plastic fleur de lys, scrolls and lovers' knots. Spend time working out the arrangements which you find most pleasing before you pin and glue mouldings into place. Measure carefully for accurate positioning. Many of the plastic mouldings can be bent round curved surfaces if they are first heated in hot water. Paint mouldings to match the main colour of the furniture or highlight them in a contrasting shade.

STENCILS AND TRANSFERS

Furniture decorated with stencils can be most attractive – but keep the colours bright and simple. At its most effective this method of decoration is reminiscent of folk art. Ready-cut stencils are available from art and craft shops, including letters for adding names to children's furniture. There is a wide range designed specially for furniture and walls. Make your own stencils by folding and cutting paper in the way shown in the diagrams; and protect your home-made stencils with a coat of varnish. Applying stencils is simple once you get the knack (see page 131).

The effects you achieve with transfers may be more perfect than stencils but the result will not be as original or personal. Department and D.I.Y. stores have wide ranges of transfers covering all kinds of subjects, including birds, flowers, animals, cartoon characters and so on. Water-slide transfers must be soaked and then slid carefully off the backing paper on to the furniture. Easier to apply are the decorative motifs with peel-off self-adhesive backings.

Decoupage is an old craft enjoying a modern revival. The name derives from the French word *découper* meaning to cut out; the craft involves decorating furniture with paper cut-outs. Choose suitable motifs and pictures from magazines and prints. Colour supplements are not suitable, as the paper must be of a good quality. Cut motifs from wallpaper scraps or sample pages – build up, for example, a paper patchwork pattern of hexagons. A pair of small sharp scissors are needed for the cutting out. Stick the paperwork to the furniture with white p.v.a. adhesive or use wallpaper paste. Seal the front of the print with a thin coat of glue

BELOW *Wooden, rush chairs can be enlivened by the use of cushions and a spot of paint. The chairs illustrated have received a delicate floral treatment. However, plain colours will do the trick.*

size and finish off with several coats of varnish, lightly sanding between each coat. Build up the layers of varnish until the edges of the paper cutout 'sink' into the varnish coating, making the paper decoration look as though it has been painted on the furniture.

Very useful for quick furniture face-lifts are the thin plastic coverings with peel-off self-adhesive backings available by the yard or metre from most hardware, decorating and department stores. Designs have improved tremendously in the last three years or so. There are now many good plain colours in various ranges, including glossy finishes which look like paintwork. Use these for simple cut-out motifs, or stripes or even large letters. Some of the most attractive designs resemble fabrics, such as cotton mini-prints, attractive ginghams or textured weaves. Thicker heavy duty designs can be used for covering horizontal surfaces such as tabletops. Allow extra material for overlaps, and for turning over edges, rims and curves. The squares on the backing paper are a useful aid to measuring and straight cutting.

Real fabrics can be used most effectively to decorate the fronts of furniture – in particular large expanses of fitted cupboard doors. Stick fabric directly to the wood with a fabric glue. A better effect will be obtained with a fabric already paper backed for use on walls. In specialist decorating shops, there are good ranges of felts, hessians, silks and rough textured weaves already prepared in this way. Fabric-finished furniture looks particularly good if the edges are finished off with some kind of trim such as a contrasting braid.

Simple stripes can be a most effective form of furniture decoration, particularly if the stripe is allowed to run off the furniture on to the wall. The easiest way to add stripes is to use bands of coloured adhesive tape. A more professional effect, however, will be obtained by painting the stripes on the furniture. Use masking tape to ensure neat edges. Make sure that your base coat is thoroughly dry before applying the tape; if not, the paint will come away when the tape is removed.

Mirror tiles can be used most effectively on cupboard fronts; they are particularly useful for bedrooms. Sheets of mirror mosaic can also be purchased. They are tiny squares of mirror with a self-adhesive backing and can give cupboards and small tables a glamorous art-deco touch.

ABOVE *This inexpensive whitewood kitchen unit has been transformed with a bold use of colour and a design applied with stencils bought from an art-supply shop.*

HOW TO
Stripping woodwork

Stripped woodwork adds a mellow, soft look to any interior. Start with a limited project, such as a small piece of furniture or a single door.

TOOLS AND MATERIALS
Paint stripper
Rubber gloves
Old newspapers
Paint scraper and/or shavehook
Steel wool
White spirit
Matt varnish

PREPARATION
Allow plenty of time; stripping is a lengthy process. Cover the floor with old newspaper. Use a proprietary paint stripper, available from hardware and D.I.Y. shops. Thixotropic or jelly types are easier to use as they will not run. Read carefully the instructions on the container. In general, strippers should be used in well-ventilated rooms, away from any kind of naked flame – and do not smoke! Protect your hands with rubber gloves. Take care not to get any stripping solution on your skin or in your eyes. If you do, wash affected areas thoroughly with cold water. Do not use a blow-lamp for stripping furniture – there is a danger of scorching the wood.

STEP-BY-STEP GUIDE
Confine your work to small areas at a time. Apply stripper liberally and wait for the time specified in instructions. When paint or old varnish have softened, remove with the scraper or shavehook. Take care not to dig into the wood with the scraper. Use steel wool on awkward mouldings. Stand legs of furniture in a bowl so that the stripper which trickles down can

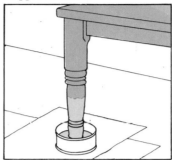

be reused. Immediately an area has been stripped, apply more stripper and scrub with steel wool to remove any lingering flecks.

When stripped down to the bare wood, rinse the surface to remove all traces of stripper. Then sand thoroughly to remove any stain from the grain and to smooth the wood. Use a fine grade

glasspaper, wrapped round a small block of wood. If using the sanding attachment on a power drill, take care not to score the wood. Hand-sanding is always preferable for the final finish. Remove all dust with a vacuum cleaner or dry cloth. Wipe over with white spirit. Carry out any minor repairs necessary and, if desired, either bleach or stain wood to a more acceptable colour. When staining, experiment first on a scrap piece of timber. Finally, finish furniture with polyurethane varnish.

Painting furniture

Read carefully the general notes on painting woodwork given on page 72. These are hints to help you to obtain a good finish on furniture.

TOOLS AND MATERIALS
Suitable paint such as oil-based matt, eggshell or gloss or vinyl gloss (follow manufacturer's recommendations for undercoat and primer)
Old newspapers
Fine grade glasspaper
62.5mm, 25mm and 12.5mm paint brushes
White spirit (if using oil-based paint)
Fine steel wool

Sponge
Warm water
Detergent
Rags

PREPARATION
Find a place where furniture can be left for several days. Cover the flooring with old newspapers. Remove any handles. Rub down old varnished finishes with steel wool and white spirit. Wipe over with clean damp cloth. Wash down old painted finishes with detergent solution. Rinse, then sand with fine grade glasspaper to provide a key for the paint. Carry out any necessary small repairs.

STEP-BY-STEP GUIDE
Apply a coat of primer followed by an undercoat and two or three top coats, as recommended by the paint manufacturer. Leave for at least eight hours between coats of oil-based paints – for a whole day if possible. Each coat should be rubbed lightly with fine grade sandpaper and thoroughly dusted before the next coat is applied. Use a wider brush on large areas and a small brush for awkward places. To avoid paint runs, do not overload your brush and always draw it outwards towards an edge. Fix a nail or screw partway into the underneath of each leg. This raises the furniture clear of the working surface so that the brush does not pick up dust from the floor and the

furniture does not stick to the newspaper. Turn chairs upside down and place on a sheet of newspaper on a table if possible so that the underside can be painted first. Tables should also be turned upside down first.

Chests of drawers and small cupboards can be raised on battens. Remove the drawers, paint the cross-rails and then paint the rest of the carcase. Put back the drawers. Paint the top drawer, pulled open just sufficiently to be able to paint the front and the inner edges. Pull out the next drawer a little further; work in a similar fashion down the chest. Cupboard doors on white-wood ranges can often be simply lifted off their hinges for easy painting.

Applying a stencil

Stencils can give painted furniture that extra personal and decorative touch. They are also fun to do.

TOOLS AND MATERIALS
Medium size stencil brush
Paint (emulsion, eggshell or gloss)
Flat 'dabbing' board
Ordinary paintbrush to take paint from tin to dabbing board
Masking tape or pins
Practice paper (newspaper)

PREPARATION
Practise on the paper first to familiarize yourself with the technique. Plan out the spacing before you start.

STEP-BY-STEP GUIDE
Stencils may be applied to any flat surface. Attach the four corners of the stencil with tape or pins to the furniture, making sure it is flush with the surface. With an ordinary paintbrush, place two dabs of

paint on the board. Hold the stencil brush vertically and dab into the paint on the board. Remove any excess as the paint must be evenly distributed on the brush. To distribute paint evenly, make a few short strokes with the vertical brush on the practice paper. *Never* put a stencil brush directly into a tin of paint; this will cause paint to run and blot behind the stencil. *Always* dab new colour with an ordinary paintbrush. Start from the top left and apply paint to the holes of the stencil with short quick strokes. Hold the brush vertical. Continue until all the holes are filled with colour. Then start at the top left again and dab over the same area. Remove the stencil carefully to avoid

smudging. Make sure that the stencil is dry before repeating the pattern. If, after lifting the stencil, paint has seeped under the edges making them blurred, either the paint was too thin or it was not evenly distributed on the brush.

TABLES

There are some good table bargains to be found in junk shops. Often they may be less than beautiful, and their surfaces may be beyond any restoring but solid enough to be hidden under an attractive cover.

Cloth-covered tables have a festive look. Victorian linen cupboards boasted crisp white linen, beautifully embroidered. More colourful and informal embroidered designs are now usually reserved for tea tables.

A table needs dressing up with fabric right both for its surroundings and for its use. Proportions are important, too, so that sizes must be determined with care. If the drop of the cloth (i.e. the amount which overhangs the edge) is skimpy, the table will appear too high; too much drop and the chair seats will brush against it. Allow 5cm clearance between cloth and seat tops.

Fabrics which need little ironing, or are wipe-clean, can make simple yet beautiful tablecloths. Plastic-coated fabrics, plain and patterned, can be bought by the metre. Alternatively, a length of polyester or terylene/cotton sheeting – available in a wide range of co-ordinating patterns and colours and in widths of up to 228cm – can make a most attractive cloth. Narrow fabrics can be seamed together to produce the right width so long as patterns are matched accurately.

Tableware items should be looked upon as the accessories of a tablecloth. One with a busy overall pattern can look overdressed with ornate china, whereas a plain cloth may seem stark with simple crockery.

Make a special feature of napkins. Highlight a plain cloth with boldly-patterned napkins echoing its colour theme. Or repeat the cloth pattern, but in a different size or by reversing the colourways. To make them stand out, always allow napkins to be bolder and brighter than the tablecloth.

The focal point of a table is its centrepiece which should be in proportion and low enough for people to see over. It can be almost anything – for example, a piece of napkin fabric cut to the table shape, a delicious looking dessert attractively presented, or a conventional flower and candle arrangement.

Spur-of-the-moment arrangements can be made from items at hand. Flowers from the garden or even from a windowbox can be placed in a gravy boat, colourful exotic vegetables piled on a white cake icing stand, or a bowl filled with Christmas fruit and nuts.

There are decorative paper cloths and napkins in the shops and some can be washed and re-used; or you can make your own. Box in a trestle with crêpe paper, adding frills, fringes or festoons. Left-over wallpaper can be used; match the pattern across several lengths and tape edges together. Lining paper makes a cheap cover up for tables at a fête; decorate with a stripe of coloured tape and trim away the corners.

Full-length tablecloths as a permanent part of the décor give tables an upholstered look and can suit many settings. Tweeds look tailored in a masculine study; lace on a contrasting background is sophisticated enough for traditional elegance; an intricate patchwork of silks looks exotic and rich. Cloths should always clear the floor by 2.5cm and be the same shape as their table, with any corners rounded off (see page 138). Make fitted cloths for a more sophisticated effect, with one panel on the top, separate sides, kick pleats and piping round the top edge.

Try topping a long plain cloth with a patterned cloth in another shape (e.g. square on round, or diamond on square). Or throw a rug over an ugly low table and make matching floor cushions. In this and many other ways an old table can be given a bright new look.

BELOW *Small tables can be dressed to provide a decorative focal point. Here the effect has been enhanced by using a square cloth over a round one and by the three pendants with their pretty, bead shades.*

BEDS

Good looking beds have progressed a long way since the heyday of the candlewick bedspread. With the advent of the continental quilt, many people have discarded the bedspread completely, replacing it with bed linen which is both pretty and practical.

Sheets, pillowcases, quilt covers and valances are now available in such a wide selection of colours and patterns that mixing and matching them with a colour scheme of a room is as important as choosing other soft furnishings. Traditional linen, flannelette or cotton is still available, but as sheets are now mostly in a blend of polyester or Terylene and cotton (which machine washes and tumble dries speedily) the agonies of washday have disappeared and smaller stocks of linen are needed for each bed. Moreover, coloured and printed sheeting can be bought by the metre from big stores and by mail order, in widths of up to 274cm so that it is not difficult to make distinctive bedding to choice.

Beds which are left uncovered during daytime need careful colour-linking to their room. Their main colour should match the floor or wall. Dress the bed top (quilt and pillowcases) in a pretty print, then match it with a plain fitted sheet and valance; or choose a variation of this idea, depending on the other furnishings. Co-ordinated prints (one basic design in different sizes and shades) can, for instance, be matched in many ways – so long as one smaller print reappears on more than one item to give the scheme unity. One neat solution is to have one design on the top of a quilt cover with a less obtrusive design on the underside to match the bottom sheet and pillow; when the bed is turned down, all bed linen matches. Several prints can be used on the quilt cover either in stripes or in a patchwork of squares. Contrasting sheeting can be used as a border or to add appliqué motifs to quilt covers both of which have a pleasing effect.

ABOVE *Patchwork bedspreads add a unique personal touch to any bedroom. Intricate patterns can be created from simple shapes such as squares and rectangles.*

133

BELOW *Bedheads need not be staid and unobtrusive. They provide a marvellous opportunity for a touch of flamboyance as in this cherry design. The idea, however, can be adapted easily to a design of your choice.*

Plain, ready made sheets and pillowcases become special once they are decorated with an elegant patterned fabric or painted border. To ensure that proportions are correct make up the bed, showing as much topsheet as you want and work out the depth of the border by experimenting with paper patterns. By-the-metre trims, such as broderie anglaise, are also suitable but they must be washable and dye-fast. Traditionally, topsheets have straight edges but a scalloped or scrolled edge at the head of the bed is a decorative alternative.

A dated eiderdown which is clean and in sound condition can be re-covered quite simply by making a new cover out of sheeting to match bedclothes. Make a giant, piped cushion cover, fit the eiderdown inside, close the gap, and top-stitch all layers together along an outer quilt line of the old cover to create an attractive, new cover.

BEDCOVERS

Bedcovers can also be matched to bedclothes or be teamed with curtains or other soft furnishings. Fitted covers with sides and valances look formal and neat, and are particularly suitable in a room which performs a double duty as a bedsitter. Like curtains, bed valances can either have gathers or box pleats, or be straight with kick pleats at each corner. A plain bedcover calls for really bold trimmings.

A separate valance falling from under the mattress will disguise an ugly bed base. It will stay in position at all times. Match it to a fitted cover which fits like a lid over the bedtop and over the sides of the mattress. Short throwover bedspreads with decorative edges, dropping halfway down separate and permanently fixed contrast valances are a decorative alternative to the fitted variety.

Throwover bedspreads are simpler to make than fitted spreads. Because of their basic shape, texture, detail and pattern are important for style. The more austere the bedroom, the more intricate a bedspread can be. For those not lucky enough to possess heirloom patchwork, there are several designs (such as log cabin) which can be made by machine. Simple patchwork or patterned fabrics can also be quilted for added warmth and a rich looking texture.

There is a revival of crocheted and knitted bedspreads, which look stunning with most styles. Crisp, white cotton yarn is easy to work in sections and to assemble and it washes well.

BEDHEADS

Junk shops are a marvellous bargain hunting ground for old utility-look bedheads of the thirties or forties. They are attractive when painted a brilliant glossy colour. Or you could pad and cover them with fabric. Even more exciting is looking for hidden promise in articles which were never intended to adorn a bed; single carved wooden backs to washstands (chiffonières), a set of small folding screens, an embroidered fire screen or an old garden gate, perhaps – all have potential as bedheads.

There is a vast choice of ready made bedhead ranges, from Chinese wicker and cane to Victorian-look button upholstered velvet. A well placed bedhead can temporarily disguise a bad patch of wall. Camouflage an ordinary bed by disguising it as a couch and hide those switches which control the bedroom gadgetry for lighting, heating and morning tea and coffee making in the bedhead. Shelf bed-

heads can store magazines, books, stereo equipment – even the bed itself in some cases; 'blanket box' bedheads can take a suitcase, extra bedding and they can also double as extra seating. A large wall hanging such as tapestry, carpet, rug or mirror can also do well. American and Italian designers build big-time bedheads and use them as room dividers in single room living arrangements by building in, for example, a complete office/study area behind the headboard.

Simplest of all is a painted wall mural or frieze framing the head of the bed. Pick a simple pattern, for example in stripes or for a child's bed paint a night sky of stars and planets in fluorescent paint.

Many new beds have their own detachable headboards, sometimes dull affairs. Don't throw them away! Treat them to a more glamorous cover-up on the lines suggested here. Add a matching bedspread and you have bespoke bedtime luxury for a very small outlay. Incidentally, all of these bedheads are comfortable and easy-to-clean. You could also use this cover-up method for existing, unexciting wooden headboards or on a rough piece of blockboard screwed to the back of the bed.

BELOW *A less exuberant idea for a bedhead but equally attractive. It forms a natural focal point for the bedroom and is aided by the large cushions. The delicate touch is emphasized by the cushion's deep-frilled border.*

CUSHIONS

Cushions add colour as well as comfort to a room. As they are smaller than most other soft furnishings, they can be used to introduce vivid splashes of colour – just a touch of your own personality to give a room originality without dominating.

A mere 50cm of fabric are required to cover a pad up to 40cm square (or 70cm with self-piping), so that remnant counters and sales can be a fruitful hunting ground. Make sure, however, to buy enough for any patterns to be centred.

Conventional square pads, ready for covering, are available in preshaped foam, or filled with feathers or foam chips. These are in standard sizes rising by 5cm to a maximum of 46cm. Large floor cushions can be bought to order from larger stores or from foam merchants. Box, bolster and round pad shapes are also available. Alternatively you can make cushion pads in your own choice of shapes and sizes.

Rectangles, triangles, rounds, ovals, hexagons – where a cushion will be placed dictates its size and shape. Cushions should be in proportion to the furniture on which they are used. They should, for example, fit cosily into the corner of an armchair; they would look lost on an enormous settee. Group several smaller cushions together for a larger scale effect; take care to look at them as a whole, co-ordinating fabrics and styles.

For all cushions except seat cushions (which get harder wear, so need covering with furnishing fabric) almost any material is suitable. The fabric may suggest the cushion shape. Centre a group of flowers in a flowery chintz, like a bouquet, and cut a circular cover, or one with softly rounded corners; or use a rectangular pad or a bolster for stripes. Generally, soft, pretty prints look best on a squashy pillow, while severe geometrics suit firmer pads.

Cushions can be formal, e.g. in velvet or silk

BELOW *A group of cushions on a settee or window seat allow you to mix different patterns to great effect. If you are clever with a needle, you can also mix patterns for each individual cushion by using patchwork techniques.*

(either the real thing or less expensive man-made imitations) edged with piping or silk cord; but combine clever stitching with more unusual fabrics and trims, and the results can be striking. Cotton mattress ticking cut into various shapes with the grain or on the bias, can be pieced together differently in coordinating patterns. Plain furnishing cotton can be trimmed in endless ways with contrasting petersham ribbon. Make a pattern on denim, by adding a shape, top stitched on with contrasting thread, jeans-style. And why not improvize? An old silk blouse can be pieced together in an interesting way, backed with interlining, decorated with its original buttons, or with stitch detail; chamois leather looks delightful as random patchwork; and a plait of mending cottons makes a colourful yet delicate looking inset on a plain cover. Scope for creativity is limitless.

Design pictures for cushion fronts, cut out the individual shapes in coloured prints, and appliqué them on a plain background by machining over raw edges with a zig zag stitch. A set of appliqué cushions for a settee might incorporate one continuous picture across all the cushions.

The secret of good design is to work out complete colour and shape distribution on squared paper before starting to sew. Patchwork is no exception. Cushions are small items so that an intricate design need not be too time consuming.

Two layers of patches are needed for cathedral window patchwork – a plain background over which to offset shapes in prints. The choice of colours is what matters here – jewel-bright for the print, light and clear for the background to look like stained glass. Suffolk puffs have a delicate, lacy look – rounds of fabric are gathered in before they are flattened and joined to each other.

Tapestry cushions are traditional in formal designs, but acquire a bold new image by repeating rows of a simple shape such as a clover or maple leaf. Or design a patch of tapestry and repeat it over the whole cushion front in toning shades. Create texture with two contrasting colours, such as black and white, by working a chequerboard of squares in different stitches.

Use up wool scraps for a simple pattern of plain knitted squares, or knit a multi-coloured striped cover. Knitted and crochet cushions look warm and inviting. For example, remnants can be used up in other unusual ways: knit a narrow strip in stocking stitch, allow the sides to curl in to look tubular, then coil the strip and sew it to a fabric backing. Crocheted Afghan squares are easy and traditional; double crochet in bold colours has an up-to-date look of its own. Aran or Fair Isle sweater patterns can be adapted most effectively.

CHAIR COVERS

Making loose covers for chairs and settees requires professional know-how, time and patience.

There are, however, quick and clever ways to give old chairs a temporary facelift while they wait for a more permanent new look.

Throw a bright patchwork quilt or a rug of crocheted Afghan squares over a chesterfield so that one corner hangs over the seat at the centre front, with the rest spread across the curve of the back and arms. Make neat folds into the angles of the settee and tuck in the fabric round the seat. An old armchair with really bad springs can be covered casually with a sheepskin rug for added comfort as well as good looks.

As an alternative, cover seating with dark coloured sheeting, or even old curtain lining. Tuck and fold, and hold with hidden safety pins; add a splash of colour with a rich length of silk or an attractive fringed shawl draped over the back.

Ready made stretch covers are now available in such a profusion of shapes, colours and textures, that there is one for almost any easy-chair shape.

BELOW *There is no reason why cushions should always be square or rectangular in shape. Round ones, as here, are very pretty and can add an unusual charm to a room. Cushions are easy to make and the scope for inventive design almost unlimited.*

There are now really elegant varieties available in textured velvets which look as good as upholstery and have the advantage of being removable for cleaning. With the addition of scatter cushions in contrasting velvet designed to fit the angles of the chair, they can look tailor-made.

Upright chairs are easy to recover more permanently with a loose cover, or to reupholster. Easiest of all shapes to recover are chairs with drop-in seats.

137

HOW TO
Making a tablecloth

Ugly or even battered, but substantial tables can be given a new lease of decorative life with a pretty cloth. A well matched tablecloth complements fine furniture and gives added sparkle to a room.

TOOLS AND MATERIALS
Fabric to cover a tabletop and to
    overhang the sides
Thread

PREPARATION
Measure the table width if it is square or round; width and length if rectangular or oval. Work out the drop over edge from the tabletop; add double this amount, with a further 10cm for the hems, to each tabletop measurement to ascertain the width and length of cloth required. Cut the length of fabric to the larger measurement if there are two. Trim the width of the fabric to size, or make a square, centring the pattern. To widen a narrow fabric, add equal strips along each selvedge of the main piece with a second length. Match the pattern at the seams before cutting.

STEP-BY-STEP GUIDE
For a round table fold in two the prepared square along its length and width; mark and cut an arc inside the raw edges three or four layers as in the diagram using the length of one side as measurement from the corner between folds to the arc.

For an oval table cut a pattern of tabletop from a newspaper. Fold in two the prepared fabric rectangle along its length and width; fold the pattern in same way. Place the pattern on the fabric as in the diagram. Add 5cm hem allowance

to the drop measurement; by this same amount cut an arc outside that of the pattern from corner to corner inside the raw edges. Hand or machine hem.

To round off corners of square or rectangular cloths (or for the foot end of a throwover bedspread) measure the length of the drop from the tabletop (or bed) to the floor or the required height above the floor; add hem allowance. Mark a square at the corner as in the diagram, each side to be equal to final measurement. Now mark a curve inside the raw edges using the length of one side of the square as a measurement from the inner corner of the square to the curve.

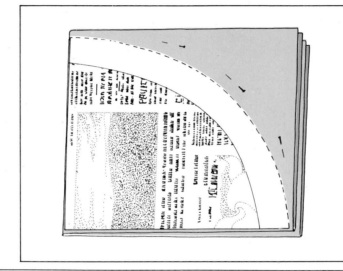

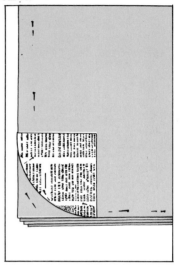

Making a fitted bedcover gathered sides

A fitted bedcover can give 'lift' to a room and is always pleasing to the eye. The following is a simple style to make.

TOOLS AND MATERIALS
Fabric to cover the bedtop and one
    end of the mattress, with more to
    go one and a half times round
    two sides and one end of the
    bed (for gathering), and to
    include hem and seam
    allowances
Thread

PREPARATION
Make up the bed without the pillows.

STEP-BY-STEP GUIDE
Measure the bedtop length and add 20cm to this to tuck round the mattress. Measure the bedtop width and add 3cm for the seams. Cut the fabric to the length measurement. If it is narrower than

the bedtop, cut a second length equal to the first. Add equal strips along the selvedge of the first piece from the second. Match the pattern at the seams before cutting. Trim to required width measurement.

If using prepared piping, tack

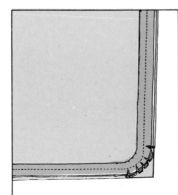

this to the right side of the top along the seamlines of the sides and foot end (cord facing inwards), starting 17.5cm from the head end.

To obtain the width of the bedspread sides, measure the drop from the bedtop to 2.5cm from the floor. Add 5cm to this measurement to allow for hem and seam. To obtain the length, take the measurements around sides of bed omitting measurement along head end. Double it and add 7cm for the hems. Cut strips of the fabric to width measurement and join end to end to obtain the length measurement.

Turn under a 3.5cm hem at each end of the joined strip. Tack, machine and press. Gather one

long side of the strip 1.5cm from the edge. With the wrong sides together, pin the gathered edge of the side strip to the side and foot edges of the top, starting and ending 17.5cm from the head end. Tack, machine 15cm from the raw edges and press.

Turn under a 3.5cm hem along the lower edge of the cover. Machine a small hem round the remaining raw edges at the head end.

If pillows are to be under the cover, you will need a gusset at the sides at the head end.

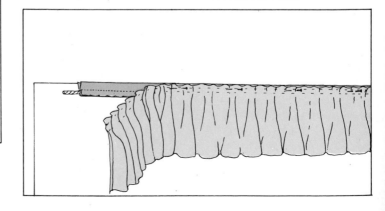

Making cushions

HOW TO MAKE A CUSHION PAD

The basic cushion pad is easy to make. It can be the foundation of many exciting and different kinds of cushions.

TOOLS AND MATERIALS

Cambric for the front and back of the pad (down-proof for feather filling)

Filling for a 40cm cushion: about 350 grams of down feathers or terylene wadding, or 200 grams of foam chips. For a firmer look, stuff tightly with kapok.

STEP-BY-STEP GUIDE

From cambric, cut two identical pieces to the required shape allowing 2cm more all round than the finished size outer cover. With the right side facing, stitch together 1.5cm from the raw edges, leaving a gap of 12cm to 15cm in the middle of one side. Trim the corners, turn

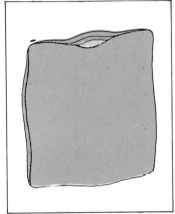

through the gap and insert the filling. To close the opening, push the filling out of way, fold in the raw edges and topstitch thickness together near the foldline.

HOW TO COVER A BOX-SHAPED CUSHION

Box-shaped cushions look tailored and stylish.

TOOLS AND MATERIALS

Pre-shrunk fabric for the top, underside and four sides of the cushion

Zip equal to the length of the back together with one side of cushion.

STEP-BY-STEP GUIDE

Centring the design of patterned fabric, cut two identical pieces to fit the top and underside, adding 1.5cm all round for the seams.

To work out the width of the side pieces, measure the cushion height and add 1.5cm to each of the top and bottom for seams. Cut

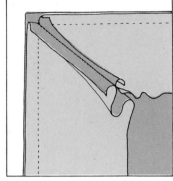

four strips to this width, one for each side, adding 1.5cm for the seams at each end each time. Match the front and back strips to the top.

If using prepared piping tack this to the right side of the top and underside along the seamline, the cord facing inwards.

With the right sides facing, pin, tack and stitch together the side strips end to end to make a tight frame for the cushion. Press the seams open.

Pin the top over the frame, with wrong sides out and raw edges flush, to form a lid; clip into the seams on the corners to get a sharp outline; tack, stitch and press allowances towards the middle of the top.

Place the zip on the underside; press the seam allowances to the wrong side along the back and

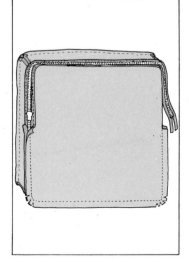

along half of each adjoining edge in a U shape; clip into the allowances at both ends of the crease and in the corners. Stitch the zip face down over the folded fabric on the wrong side, teeth over the crease line.

With the wrong sides out, place the underside over the remaining raw edges of the sides, as for top; pin, attaching the other half of the

zip to the sides. Open the zip slightly before tacking, stitch and turn right way out.

HOW TO COVER A BOLSTER

Bolsters are useful and can be exciting decoratively. Covering your own gives you the freedom to create the exact effect you desire.

To obtain a good, tight fit, allow a fraction more than cut seam allowance when machining.

TOOLS AND MATERIALS

Enough pre-shrunk fabric to go round the bolster, together with a little more for each end and extra for the seams

A zip about 10cm shorter than bolster

STEP-BY-STEP GUIDE

Wrap the patterned fabric round the bolster and decide which way the design is to run.

Cut a rectangular main piece the length of the bolster from end to end by its measurement round the middle, adding 1.5cm for seams all

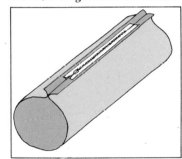

round. With the right sides facing, tack together the edges running down the length of the bolster into a tube. Stitch to a length of 6.5cm at either end of the tackline, press the seamline open and remove the tacking from the stitched sections.

Put the zip face down on the wrong side of the seam with its

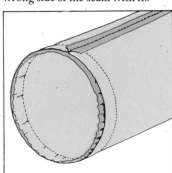

teeth over the tacked centre section. Tack in place, taking care not to pick up both layers of tube; turn right way out, open the zip fully and stitch, using a zipper foot.

Measure across the widest point at one end of the bolster and add

twice 1.5cm for the seams. Centring the design, if necessary, cut two squares of fabric with sides equal to this measurement. Round off the square using same method as for a round tablecloth (see page 138). If using prepared piping tack to the right side of the rounds along the seam-lines, the cord facing inwards.

With the right sides facing, pin one round to each end of the tube with the raw edges flush; tack, stitch and clip into the seams. Press the allowances towards the main fabric and turn right way out.

HOW TO MAKE SELF PIPING

It is sometimes more attractive to use self piping for soft furnishings.

TOOLS AND MATERIALS

Pre-shrunk matching or contrasting fabric from soft furnishing

Pre-shrunk piping cord

PREPARATION

To find the true fabric bias, pull a thread from selvedge to selvedge at one end of fabric, trim along this line, then fold over the trimmed end so that it is parallel with the selvedge. This foldline is the true bias.

STEP-BY-STEP GUIDE

Measure round the thickness of the cord; add 1.5cm to this. Cut the fabric in bias strips the width of

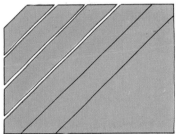

the final measurement. Join the strips end to end. Press the seams open. Place the piping down the middle of the joined strip on the wrong side, fold the fabric edge to edge round the cord and stitch close to the cord using a zipper/

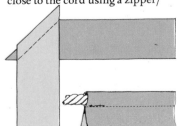

piping foot. Tack the prepared piping to the right side of the fabric along the seam-line with the raw edges flush, clipping into the allowance along corners and curves.

11. Decorative Extras

The walls, the floor, the ceiling, furniture, windows and doors: these are the basic components of any room, and have been discussed in previous chapters.

Now we come to all those personal and individual little touches which can be added to a room to make it well and truly yours – the decorative extras, if you like.

A PRIVATE PICTURE GALLERY

Today, everyone can be a gallery owner. All you need is a spare wall, sharp eyes and a magpie's hoarding instinct. Unlike a professional gallery, your choice can be all embracing. Anything frameworthy can take its place, from inexpensive posters, prints and postcards to stamps, labels and butterflies; there is no need to exclude genuine oil paintings, watercolours and drawings, too, if you have them! Do not be afraid of mixing them altogether for that is the idea – be as individual as you like. Whatever the result, a gallery of one's own is never dull. It provides an instant focal point in any room and, as you become a more experienced collector, you can change pictures round – and even give a chance of everyone in the family to have a go.

Tourist and travel agents can be fruitful sources for inexpensive posters, as are some of the larger food and drink manufacturers. Try writing to their publicity officers. Local cinemas, theatres, art galleries and museums sometimes have spare posters left over from exhibitions and these can be bought inexpensively. London Transport poster shops and most large department stores, art shops and museums have a section devoted to art postcards and posters. Photographic printers can enlarge your favourite black-and-white photographs to poster size to add a personal touch to any wall.

If you intend to take art collecting seriously, it is worth while visiting local galleries to look through their print portfolios. Small drawings and watercolours by well known artists are usually a good deal cheaper than an oil painting which would be wholly outside the limit of your pocket. Top cartoonists sometimes sell their work direct, so that it is worth while asking the publishers concerned.

Other items worth framing are antique labels, brass rubbings, embroideries, Victorian and Chinese paper cut-outs, stamps, maps and cigarette cards. You can buy these new but it is much more fun hunting for genuine examples in jumble sales and second-hand bookshops.

FRAMES

There are no hard-and-fast rules for framing, but if results are to please, some guidelines are necessary. If you are consulting a professional framer, you will still have to consider the background furnishings and wall covering or colour for the pictures. Some framers will obligingly cut the mount and mitre the frame moulding for a small charge and so take care of the hardest part. For people without the time or money to visit a framer there are some attractive kits available. They may be grouped into

four types: (i) slot together systems consisting of a mitred edging strip with glass and backing; (ii) box-frames of clear acrylic plastic taking pictures in international paper sizes; (iii) ready moulded frames (usually plastic) suitable for photographs and small pictures, such as postcards; (iv) metal framing clips, allowing a print to be sandwiched between glass and hardboard backing of the required size.

Other sources of frames are junk shops, jumble sales and rubbish skips (it really is amazing what one can get from these – but ask permission first). Do not be put off by a dreary print, broken glass or chipped moulding. Try to visualize the same frame restored – in a different colour perhaps. A glossy

red or white frame can add excitement and picking out the dominant colour of the picture can produce excellent results.

Chipped plaster moulding can be restored by taking a cast. Press a piece of plasticine over the sound part of the moulding. Mix some Polyfilla into a stiffish paste, fill the plasticine cast and leave to set hard. Remove the plasticine gently and give the plaster moulding a coat of all-purpose primer. When the primer is dry stick the moulding to the frame with a clear contact adhesive. Paint to match the rest of the frame.

You may be lucky and find a frame in an interesting wood or material better left unpainted, e.g. in bird's eye maple, tortoiseshell or marquetry

ABOVE *Create your own private picture gallery with anything that takes your fancy—postcards, prints, photographs, posters and the like. It is inexpensive and can look absolutely stunning.*

work. Some frames look so attractive in themselves that they are almost good enough to hang on their own without a picture inside!

A mount is a kind of inner frame which can set off fine art postcards, small prints, drawings, etc, by making them look bigger and more outstanding. Mounts look their best in stiff cards available in various colours and which can be covered with fabrics such as silk and velvet. Experiment by cutting windows in coloured paper and placing these over pictures to be framed. If it is difficult to make a colour choice try a neutral colour such as grey, beige or dark brown. Teamed with a plain gold or silver frame these combinations look elegant and will blend with almost any background. A limited range of ready-cut mounts can be bought at most art shops and their proportions adapted to suit individual requirements.

Alternatively, if your print or poster has seen better days, it can be made to look as good as new by professional dry mounting on to coloured card or thicker board. (Look in the Yellow Pages of the telephone directory for firms advertising this service.) Do not treat old or valuable prints in this manner: they are not intended to be removed from their backing and any attempt to do so will decrease their value.

Once you have acquired your pictures and frames think about the grouping and composition. The trick here is to be bold. Too often we see a single picture hanging in the middle of a wall with no supporting items. This is only effective if the picture is dramatic enough and in scale with the wall area. It pays to experiment. Get some squared paper and make a simple scale drawing of the wall on which you intend to hang your picture. If you work it out on paper first you may save a major replastering job later.

BELOW *Simple open shelving is the best way to display carefully collected sets of toys, tins, teapots or anything that appeals to you. This kind of display needs a lot of dusting, but the decorative effect is worth the effort.*

CLIP AND PIN-UP BOARDS

These are essential in a kitchen or at a desk. Why not try one in a bedroom or bathroom for beauty and slimming routines or in the hall for keeping track of family events, invitations, etc. There are no restrictions on size. If you have the space a whole wall can be used, covered with unsealed cork tiles or cork slabs. Alternatively, panels of primed fibreboard can be given a coat of emulsion paint or covered in felt, hessian or an inexpensive cotton print. If there is no wall space consider the sides of a desk, chest of drawers, wardrobe or the back of a door as a potential pin-up space.

Some very sophisticated pin-up boards cum screen arrangements can be bought from office and shopfitting furnishers but cheap alternatives can be made by re-covering old junk shop screens with fabric; or you can use artist's canvas stretchers, tacking fabric over them and hinging the frames together. In general, ready made clip and pin-up boards tend to be expensive and too small for any big-time organizing; D.I.Y. boards, on the other hand, can be tailored to suit individual requirements and are easily made up.

WALL HANGINGS

The earliest kind of wall hangings were probably fur and leather skins nailed over damp walls and draughty doorways. Later, more sophisticated cultures produced rich woven rugs and tapestries to

ABOVE *Wall hangings do not necessarily have to be tapestries. This collection of pretty beaded handbags makes an attractive feature on the wall.*

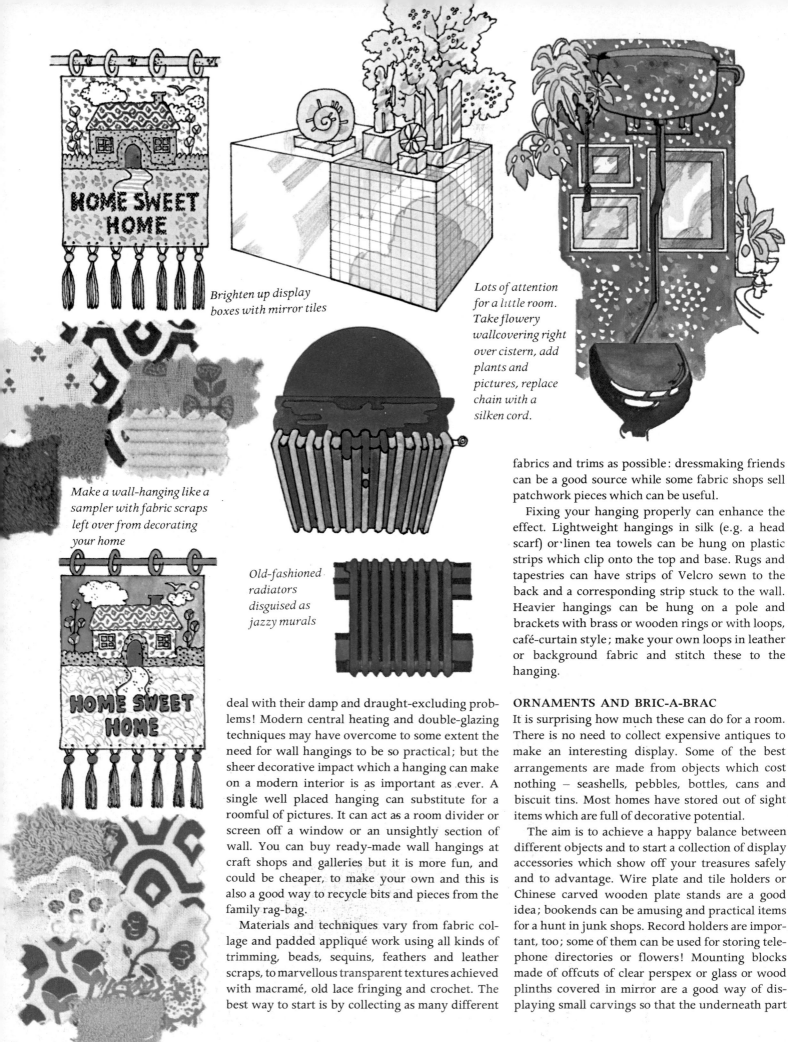

Brighten up display
boxes with mirror tiles

Lots of attention
for a little room.
Take flowery
wallcovering right
over cistern, add
plants and
pictures, replace
chain with a
silken cord.

Make a wall-hanging like a
sampler with fabric scraps
left over from decorating
your home

Old-fashioned
radiators
disguised as
jazzy murals

HOME SWEET HOME

HOME SWEET HOME

deal with their damp and draught-excluding problems! Modern central heating and double-glazing techniques may have overcome to some extent the need for wall hangings to be so practical; but the sheer decorative impact which a hanging can make on a modern interior is as important as ever. A single well placed hanging can substitute for a roomful of pictures. It can act as a room divider or screen off a window or an unsightly section of wall. You can buy ready-made wall hangings at craft shops and galleries but it is more fun, and could be cheaper, to make your own and this is also a good way to recycle bits and pieces from the family rag-bag.

Materials and techniques vary from fabric collage and padded appliqué work using all kinds of trimming, beads, sequins, feathers and leather scraps, to marvellous transparent textures achieved with macramé, old lace fringing and crochet. The best way to start is by collecting as many different

fabrics and trims as possible: dressmaking friends can be a good source while some fabric shops sell patchwork pieces which can be useful.

Fixing your hanging properly can enhance the effect. Lightweight hangings in silk (e.g. a head scarf) or linen tea towels can be hung on plastic strips which clip onto the top and base. Rugs and tapestries can have strips of Velcro sewn to the back and a corresponding strip stuck to the wall. Heavier hangings can be hung on a pole and brackets with brass or wooden rings or with loops, café-curtain style; make your own loops in leather or background fabric and stitch these to the hanging.

ORNAMENTS AND BRIC-A-BRAC

It is surprising how much these can do for a room. There is no need to collect expensive antiques to make an interesting display. Some of the best arrangements are made from objects which cost nothing – seashells, pebbles, bottles, cans and biscuit tins. Most homes have stored out of sight items which are full of decorative potential.

The aim is to achieve a happy balance between different objects and to start a collection of display accessories which show off your treasures safely and to advantage. Wire plate and tile holders or Chinese carved wooden plate stands are a good idea; bookends can be amusing and practical items for a hunt in junk shops. Record holders are important, too; some of them can be used for storing telephone directories or flowers! Mounting blocks made of offcuts of clear perspex or glass or wood plinths covered in mirror are a good way of displaying small carvings so that the underneath part can be seen. Shells, mineral crystals, sea urchins, snuffboxes, perfume bottles – anything tiny and intricate looks its best mounted this way.

But before starting to arrange anything there must be suitable shelves and tables. There is a bewildering variety of ready made ranges but, generally speaking, shelves fall into three categories – build-up box-type, adjustable wall-fixed track shelving, and free standing units. Some of these tend to be expensive but you can save money if you are willing to do some simple D.I.Y. The box shelf/table is a good starting point. Boxes can be built upwards or sideways, fit into small awkward spaces or convert into small tables useful at a bedside or armchair.

MAKING THE FUNCTIONAL LOOK DECORATIVE

This presents an exciting challenge for those saving up to renovate the interior of their present home but who find themselves faced with a regiment of unsightly fixtures and fittings. One inexpensive answer is to give a dramatic painted beauty treatment to all those depressing old pipes, radiators, cookers and lavatory cisterns. Sometimes results are so attractive that buying new replacements seems rather dull – and wasteful, too, when the article involved works efficiently! Old-fashioned kitchen scales, coffee grinders, mincers and sewing machines, for example, are among the most useful gadgets to have on display – they probably need no more than a good clean-up and a coat or two of shiny paint.

Most paint manufacturers, however, are reluctant to commit themselves on the painting of hot pipes or a cooker. Apart from one or two special brands the colour range is limited to black and white. Painted surfaces like these cannot be expected to last a lifetime. Six months is regarded as reasonable; up to two years, perhaps, if you are careful.

Refrigerators, lavatory cisterns and articles which do not get hot, can be covered over in a self-adhesive plastic or a wallpaper to match surrounding walls.

PLANTS AND FLOWERS

Fashions in pot plants come and go and some of the more exotic varieties need careful attention if they are to last. Lush specimens at horticultural shows and nurseries are grown by experts under special conditions; it is quite another matter when the same plants are in the home. Those not blessed with green fingers, or who have little or no time for tender loving plant care should acknowledge

A herb garden in a vegetable punnet: plunge the stalks in jamjars.

Anemones bloom in a tray-sized water garden, their stems fixed in 'oasis'.

A floodlit garden in the air: fill a painted pulley with bushy and hanging plants and train a spotlight on the display

Miniature Oriental garden in a bowl, complete with mirror-tile pool. Plant cactus in sandy soil.

Perforated paint-pots, tin trays, colanders hold plants happily; make a fringed macramé holder for a pottery bowl.

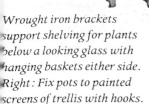

Wrought iron brackets support shelving for plants below a looking glass with hanging baskets either side. Right: Fix pots to painted screens of trellis with hooks.

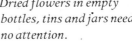

Above: Anything goes. Dried flowers in empty bottles, tins and jars need no attention.

the fact and turn their attention to hardy survivors. Top of this list come aspidistras, certain cacti, geraniums (best on sunny windowsills), *tradescantia* and *chlorophytum*; if these do not survive your next safest bets are dried flowers, grasses or plastic blooms! Some plastic plants look very convincing – palm trees, for example – and are much easier to look after!

If you want tropical luxury in the form of palms, African violets, orchids and Bonsai (dwarf) trees it is important that growing conditions are just right. This may mean turning down the central heating to cooler temperatures; or it may mean the reverse; it may also involve almost daily attention of some kind. Read carefully the instructions accompanying the plant.

Arranging pot plants gives lots of scope for display, from glass jar and bottle gardens to conventional window-boxes and jardinières. Alternatively, try one of the following arrangements.

● *Hanging garden* is a charming way of taking the Victorian wire basket a stage further. Have several different mixed kinds of leaves and flowers cascading down from different heights thus creating a mini forest of greenery. They look particularly spectacular in rooms with high ceilings, a hall, staircase or a landing.

Suggested plants for a hanging garden are chlorophytum, grasses, phyllocactus, tradescantia, ivy, saxifraga sarmentosa and geraniums. Less easy to grow, but worth the effort, are maiden hair and asparagus ferns, fuchsias and ivy-leaved geraniums.

Ferns like shade; geraniums like sun. Hang them where appropriate. Remember that hot air rises in rooms so that the temperature may have to be cooler if there is central heating. They will also require frequent watering; use an atomizer spray.

Holders and containers may include ready-made plastic-covered wire baskets from 46cm to 92cm diameter; string and bead macramé holders and pottery pots; old tin trays and colanders painted glossy green with holes pierced through sides for hanging. Old fashioned pulley clothes driers (some ironmongers' shops still sell them new; if not, hunt them out in junk shops), painted and hung from the ceiling can take larger displays; Perspex trellis painted green is attractive covered in hanging pots inside a room with sunny walls.

To hang up use brass chain, nylon cord or thin steel cable, with 'S' hooks. Hang the baskets and trays from brass ceiling hook plates which have been screwed and rawlplugged to the ceiling. Cup hooks can be used for small pots. Special plant hanger hooks with built-in pot holders can be screwed into wall-fixed trellis. Wrought iron brackets fixed to a wall or beside a mirror also look attractive.

● *Flower arranging.* Generally, simple arrangements are best – complicated urns and wired-up roses should be left to funerals and wedding receptions! Some of the most attractive containers are not purpose-made vases. Use your imagination – a forgotten china teapot, an old kettle with the lid missing, a chipped mug or a teacup can be the perfect shape for a posy. And why not try experimenting with trays, baskets and tin cans.

● *Floating islands.* Use a flat tray or dish as your centrepiece. Choose flattish flowerheads which have become a bit 'blown': anemones, marigolds and chrysanthemums will float easily enough, but heavier rose and tulip heads will need about 2.5cm of stalk stuck into damp oasis and blue-coloured gravel chips.

● *Herb or flower tub.* Arrange the herbs or flowers in thick clumps to look a bit wild. Use jamjars filled with water to hold the stalks and choose aromatic herbs, wild flowers or Sweet William to get the effect. A mushroom-type chip basket stained a colour looks good and is an excellent container.

● *Pop-art flowers.* Save those golden syrup, black treacle, mustard and Brasso tins as well as Marmite jars, Coke bottles and others. Do not remove the labels. Use them as amusing containers for displaying dried flowers. If using tins for fresh flowers, slip a small jam or paste jar inside and fill this with water.

● *Oriental garden.* Here is an old fashioned idea updated. Select a large bowl or tray and plant miniature rose trees, pepper plants and cacti (these last should be in a separate area from other plants because they need drier soil). Decorate with polished pebbles, moss, gravel and a bridge made of painted matchsticks – a lake can be made from a mirror tile sunk into the earth. Complete with small pagoda, birds, and a variety of figures.

HOW TO
Making picture frames

Picture frames have a decorative value in their own right. Professional framing is expensive, however. Making your own can be fun and will also save you money.

TOOLS AND MATERIALS
Mitre block (check that this will be able to cut frames at least 5cm wide)
Corner clamps
Sharp plane
Fine-toothed tenon saw
Bradawl for boring holes
Synthetic resin glue
Picture pins
Small hammer
Fine abrasive paper
Moulding
Backing card
Screw eyes (2)
$\frac{1}{2}$in (12.5mm) gold/silver box
Mounting card
Mount cutting knife
Metal rule
Picture wire for hanging
Piece of glass cut to size and with edges polished to make handling easier. Non-reflective picture glass 3mm thick is good for water-colours but will blur cross hatching and the fine lines of an engraving. It is also expensive.

STEP-BY-STEP GUIDE
Measure the four sides of the picture you wish to frame and mark out four corresponding lengths on the stepped or rebate side of the moulding, allowing at least 3mm on each length for trimmings. If the inside measurements were exact at this stage, the finished frame would be too small. Check that each of the four lengths is the correct size before cutting through.

Place each length on the

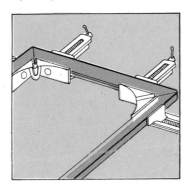

mitre block, rebate side uppermost and nearest to you. Saw carefully at 45 degrees taking care to see that the cut is as straight as possible. Plane over the sawn cuts until the exact length is achieved. Test each length by putting corner to corner.

Wrap a piece of tissue paper around each length before positioning in corner clamp. Cover each end with glue and stick corner to corner, i.e. making four right angles.

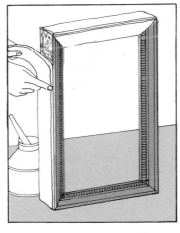

Cut straight into the mount card, and not from an existing edge, making a bevelled edge of 45 degrees. Use a metal ruler for the angle and practise on some old bits of card until you get the knack. Always cut along that edge of card area which will not be needed later. A mount will look better proportioned if its base is about one third wider than its top and sides.

Working from the frame back, fit in clean glass. Position the mount followed by the picture or print or postcard. Do not stick down if it is valuable; put a small amount of starch-based adhesive in each corner. Lay the backing card on top and lightly tap in the picture pins. Seal the gap all the way round with gummed brown paper.

Use a bradawl to make holes either side of the frame at the back, being careful to avoid splitting delicate wood. Set the screw-eyes in one-third of the length from the top of the frame. Check that these are level or the picture will not hang properly. Use picture wire or nylon binding; do *not* use string as this can rot. Alternatively fix wallplates if you want the picture to hang flush.

HOW TO MAKE A FABRIC FRAME

Fabric frames are a good way to treat old frames with interesting shapes or frames which are too damaged to repair.

TOOLS AND MATERIALS
Fabric remnants – cotton, velvet or silk
Wadding for padding out frames with extra deep mouldings
Clear fabric adhesive
Heavy-duty staple gun and staples or hammer and panel pins

STEP-BY-STEP GUIDE
Cut a layer of wadding and stick to the frame where necessary. Cut the fabric into strips the length of the frame side (or one length in the case of round or oval frames). Fold under at the corners and stick down with a bit of glue to form a mitred edge where appropriate. Tack or staple the fabric to the back of the frame. Repeat for the other sides matching any mitres edge to edge.

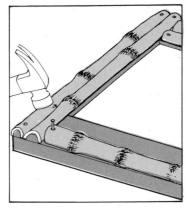

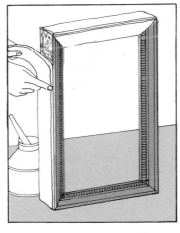

HOW TO MAKE A CHINESE FRAME

A Chinese frame is a means for brightening up old plain frames and is specially suitable for oriental subject matter.

TOOLS AND MATERIALS
Bamboo (garden cane)
Bradawl
Chisel
Hammer
Fine abrasive paper
Metal picture saw
Panel pins
Clear adhesive
Clamp

STEP-BY-STEP GUIDE
Remove any existing picture and glass from the old frame. Split the bamboo by tapping the thickest pieces sharply with hammer and

chisel. When a split appears, gently prise the two sides apart. Saw the bamboo to the lengths required and sand the edges. Make holes with a bradawl (about 5cm apart) and pin the bamboo to the frame. Or coat the bamboo and frame edges with adhesive and clamp in position until set.

HOW TO MAKE A FABRIC PICTURE

Fabric pictures are an inexpensive way to obtain a large picture, about 1.2m square.

TOOLS AND MATERIALS
Approximately one metre of bold printed furnishing cotton
Artist's canvas stretcher of approximately fabric size.
Heavy-duty staple gun and staples or hammer and panel pins

STEP-BY-STEP GUIDE
Line up the fabric in the frame and centre correctly. Cut the fabric pattern to the shape of the frame leaving about 5cm at each side. Working from the back of the frame, tap in four tacks in the centre of each side, turn the frame round and check that the fabric is still centred before finally tacking round the rest of the frame. Hand pleat or fold excess fabric at the corners.

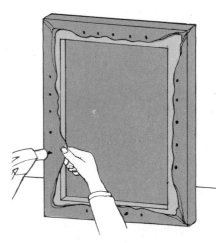

12. Outside the House

Do not neglect the outside of your house, as so many people seem to do. After all, the outside is what you see first when you come home. If the outside is looking attractive and well cared for, your house starts to welcome you and makes you feel at home as soon as you turn the corner or reach the end of your street. Your guests too receive the same favourable impression, and you have the added satisfaction that your house gives pleasure to a great many other passers-by, although you will probably never know them! If you are lucky enough to have a garden, you can enjoy the exterior of your house even more as you sit or work outside during warm weather.

Apart from this visual consideration, there is a second very important reason for caring for the outside of your home. Without regular exterior maintenance faults will develop such as leaks in roofs and damp penetrating through walls, which will in turn affect the function, durability and appearance of your interior furnishings. Indeed, maintenance and repair is the first major part of the job of caring for the outside of your home, before you begin the more exciting aspects of adding colour and extra decorative features. An inadequately maintained exterior not only causes deterioration to the fabric of the building, but also looks unsightly and unkempt, with patches of damp and mould, crumbling and cracked areas, or missing bricks and slates.

So your first job is to give your house a thorough maintenance check. Give it a long hard look from front and back, crossing the street if necessary to get a good view of areas such as the roof. Then examine specific parts more closely in detail, using a firmly-secured ladder where necessary. Call in professional help from a surveyor or builder for important, inaccessible areas such as roofs. Here are some of the main points to look for:

● *The roof*. Loose or missing tiles or slates must be repaired or replaced. If you have to replace missing tiles and cannot find those of a similar pattern or material, take them off the back of the roof and lay them in front. Crumbling brickwork on chimneys should be rebuilt; not only will it look unsightly, but it could be very dangerous. Repairs should also be made, if necessary, to the concrete flaunching into which chimneys are set. You will find flashings sealing the gaps where your roof meets another surface, for example around chimney stacks, dormer windows, skylights, over bay windows, or around vent pipes. Flashings may originally be made from felt, lead, mortar, zinc or an asbestos/bitumen compound; if torn or cracked they will look ugly, and could be letting in damp, so have them repaired where necessary. Crumbling mortar fillets must be hacked off and renewed. If you are having your roof completely re-tiled, think carefully before you replace it with a colour that is very different from the original, as it may not tone well with the rest of the exterior.

● *Gutters*. Gutters in good repair are vital to the well-being of your house. Ugly and destructive patches of wet and dry rot are so often started by faulty guttering. It is a good idea to flush gutters through with a hose from time to time to clean them, placing a bowl at the base of the downpipes to catch any dislodged debris. Small leaks may occur at joints between sections, or through cracking of the guttering itself. You can use a waterproof repair tape, or a non-hardening mastic for repairs. Damaged lengths should either be replaced completely, or they can be repaired in part with a glass fibre kit. If necessary, adjust the slope of your gutters so that the water runs away properly. Check bracket fixings, and have any rotten fascia boards replaced in part, or completely if there is a lot of decay. You may find it convenient to replace old cast-iron guttering with newer plastic types which need little subsequent maintenance.

● *Brickwork*. All loose pointing must eventually be raked out and redone. Porous walls which allow damp to come through into the inside of the house can be treated with a clear silicone water repellent, which must be applied during a spell of fine weather. Keep air bricks clear.

● *Rendering and pebbledash*. Repair cracks and missing patches as soon as you can, as water can collect behind and cause damp patches on inside walls. Cut back really big holes until sound rendering is reached. The holes can then be filled with mortar which should be applied in two layers. For pebbledash, pebbles can be mixed with the second layer. Smaller cracks can be repaired with a proprietary exterior filler. Hairline cracks can be disguised by a stone or masonry paint containing small particles of crushed rock, but obviously you will then have to paint the whole area to avoid a patchy effect. Before painting, always remove any mould or algae. Wash down the whole area with a solution of one part ordinary domestic bleach to four parts water. Repeat 24 hours later. Allow to dry for 48 hours, and then rinse with clear water. Previously painted brickwork and pebbledash should be carefully brushed down before repainting, and flaking or powdery areas should be treated to a proprietary stabilizing solution, available from your builders' merchants. Many paint firms offer free advice for exterior painting problems; it could be worth writing to their

Roof

Flashing

Wood cladding

Outside doors

Window frames

Chimneys

Gutters

Rendering

Air bricks

customer advice service with any particularly tricky problem. Serious problems such as rising damp will require the attention of a specialist firm.

● *Wall tiles*. You will find that these are nailed to battens which in turn are nailed to the wall. As loose tiles can allow damp to enter, give each tile a tug to see that it is firmly fixed. It is better to repair tiles at this stage, than to wait until they drop off, possibly causing damage and becoming lost. Tiling will have to be stripped back until the defective tiles are reached; these must be re-fixed, replacing rotten battening if necessary.

● *Wood cladding*. Rotten sections must be replaced. Old paint must be scraped off, using paint scraper and stripper. New paint (and this applies to all exterior woodwork) should consist of a minimum of primer, undercoat, and two top coats. Remove old varnish and if necessary restore the colour of original wood with proprietary wood restorer, before renewing varnish. New types of white plastic cladding look like white painted boards, but may be out of place on older buildings.

● *Windows and doors*. All gaps between framework and walls must be filled and sealed to protect against damp, and to improve the general appearance of your house. Non-hardening mastic can be used for narrow gaps, and this type of filler, which is usually an ugly grey, can be painted over. Wide gaps will require an initial plugging of a material such as rolled up rags, or a piece of rope. Areas of defective putty around window frames must be replaced, along with rotten sections of sills and frames. Bare timber sills and thresholds should be oiled. Cracked stone sills should be repaired and painted. Metal windows should be checked and treated for rust. All these faults not only look ugly, but unless remedied will cause expensive damage to your house.

Once you have tackled all these vital if unexciting jobs, you can turn your attention to more interesting aspects of exterior decoration. You can express your personality with an imaginative colour scheme and you can change or add various kinds of decorative features as suggested below.

COLOUR SCHEMES

The easiest way to select a colour scheme is to take a black and white photograph of the front view of your house. Have it enlarged to 200mm by 250mm. Using thin paper make several tracings of the outlines and main features of your house. Try out a number of colour schemes with poster colours and felt pens. Remember that your final colour choice will be affected by at least three things – the surrounding landscape, the houses next door and the architectural style of your own house. Some colours suit certain periods better than others. Do not forget that blinds and curtain linings show up more in newly painted houses; coloured linings can look very smart if they blend suitably.

Obtaining inspiration at the start can be a problem. You might borrow a colour scheme which you have admired on another house. Or take a look at your local pub: many of the older Georgian buildings have recently been painted in beautiful colour combinations and are worth copying. Try and curb the desire to paint eye-catching motifs. They seldom look good; it is advisable to leave this sort of thing to boutiques and gable end artists. In a small tightly knit community a drastic colour change might be upsetting for more tradition-bound members. Sometimes a house is known more by its colour than by its number or its name; in rare cases the local authority has been asked to intervene! Generally speaking the colour choice which you feel to be the most comfortable is probably the right choice for you. And remember that it is easier to change a small area of bright colour on the doors and windows than it is to repaint the walls. If your house is semi-detached it is a good idea to discuss your colour scheme with your neighbour as this type of house looks good treated as one of a pair.

In dirty town atmospheres white and pastel walls become grubby very quickly and may need frequent repainting if they are to stay looking smart. They retain their fresh looks for longer periods if painted in one of the deeper shades of grey, stone, olive green or terracotta with white kept for the window surrounds and woodwork.

Door and window frames are more easily painted in new colours and these can look very attractive. Again, experiment on black and white photo prints or make a sketch as before. If you are devoid of ideas gloss paintwork in a shade lighter or darker than the walls can be pleasing. If pipes are in good, i.e. rust-free, condition, camouflage them by painting in the same colour as the wall; rusty pipes should be treated with rust-remover, primed and painted with gloss paint.

WINDOWS

There are many firms which advertise a service for window replacement. Their aluminium-framed products can be double-glazed, if you wish, and

150

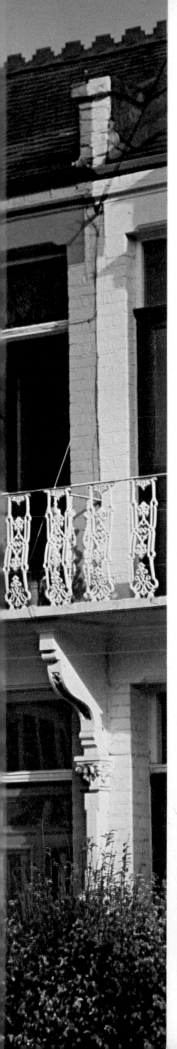

probably will never need painting. Correctly installed, these newer types of windows will eliminate draughts from faulty ill-fitting old window frames. However, take heed, for windows have been called 'the eyes of a house', and if you change them, the whole character of your exterior will undoubtedly be altered, possibly for the worse. For older houses, it is still possible to buy replacement windows which have the same appearance as the originals. Many houses have been ruined because their leaded lights were changed to Georgian styles or their Georgian sashes replaced with Victorian sheet glass or modern picture windows. In new houses, built in the last thirty years, it is likely that any window changes have been an improvement particularly where two of the back windows have been converted into patio sliding or opening doors.

DOORS AND DOOR FURNITURE
According to estate agents, many houses sell by their front doors alone! Along with windows, front doors are the most frequently changed item. A modern door fitted with a large panel of obscured glass may let in more light, but care must be taken to see that the design does not conflict with the style of the house. You will find that there is a wide choice available in new reproduction doors. Many original doors can be smartened satisfactorily simply by repainting very carefully, taking care to strip off all defective areas of paint, and to fill any uneven areas to give a smooth surface before proceeding to primer and undercoat, followed by top coat in a suitable colour. You will find a wide choice of 'door furniture' (numerals, knockers, letter boxes and so on) in hardware shops, with an even greater selection at specialist shops called architectural ironmongers. You can choose from shiny brass, silver-coloured chrome or anodized aluminium, or black cast-iron. Save up for a matching set, if you can. Alternatively, the very skilful can paint their own numerals directly onto the door, making sure that they are clear and easy to read.

FAR LEFT *Bright colours liven up this house.*

LEFT *A strong, plain colour makes an attractive feature of this door.*

TOP AND ABOVE *Brass door furniture can look stunning.*

EXTRA TOUCHES

If you have a town terrace house, ask the council to replace any street trees which have been cut down. Bare walls and unsightly details – a garage, a garden shed or a dustbin cupboard – can all be camouflaged with quick-growing creepers such as Russian vine on garden trellis or fast-growing cypress trees. A screen of these gives complete privacy if you are overlooked.

Patios and pergolas can be made exotic with trailing greenery. Clematis, vines, passion flowers, can all be trained in a column and over various structures. Window-boxes in wood or plastic can be painted or stained to match a fence or a window frame – or the walls. Concrete and plastic garden tubs look best on modern patios. Aim for plastic mobile garden tubs which you can not only move from one spot to another but take away when you move house.

Wooden tubs and reproduction antique urns blend better with old period houses but earthenware pots for growing parsley, strawberries and herbs look attractive anywhere. Many successful

garden containers can be made cheaply with old chipped or cracked casseroles or paté bowls (local delicatessens sometimes sell these). Chimney stacks can be fitted with plastic flowerpots. Consider stepped gardens with concrete blocks edging the borders so that there is easy access to plants.

The bugbear of basement living is the lack of sun and garden space but there are some plants like ferns, mosses and lily-of-the-valley which thrive there. Do some homework on the subject; more plants than you think can grow in a basement. If a lawn is out of the question why not roll out a green carpet? Plastic turf can look most convincing and is certainly less trouble to keep up.

Accessories such as birdbaths, sundials, swings and climbing frames, outdoor lighting and furniture help to liven up the garden but always consider their colour before making a final choice, remembering that these items must blend with the rest of the exterior. One or two well placed spotlamps can light up a front door, garden display or barbecue/patio area far more effectively than half a dozen wall-fixed lanterns.

ABOVE *What may have been a dingy patio is given life by the use of coloured tiles and shrubs in pots and tubs.*

RIGHT *This more traditional patio makes use of paving stones. The paved area is nicely set off by the surrounding greenery.*

153

RESTORATION

If you own an older type of house, restoring the exterior to what it originally looked like could prove an absorbing and rewarding spare-time activity. If you are prepared to do your own painting and general restoration, there is nothing to stop you doing some homework on the history of your house and so achieve the desired result.

The first step is to visit the local public library. Look under the historical section for building records, and try to trace the date of construction and the name of the architect or builder. If this is fruitless try the local planning authority: there is usually at least one person (or department) to give advice on local architectural matters of this nature. If your house was built recently, say in the past 25 years, the architect, the builder and the local planning authority will all have copies of any drawings.

For those about to embark on alterations of a more structural character, it is wiser to consult an architect or a builder.

Architects are not allowed to advertise, but you can approach the Royal Institute of British Architects, 66 Portland Place, London, W1 for the names of architects in your area, or you can try the Yellow Pages in the telephone directory. Ask whether he or she is interested in advising you over the restoration of your house. Tell him how much you are prepared to spend and make it clear if there is a limit in money or in time. You may have to persevere with your enquiries as most architectural practices are usually involved with large commercial projects and may not be able to undertake a small one-off engagement. Keep trying; if you are lucky you may discover someone sympathetic to restoration work of the kind you want. Fees vary greatly according to the time and work involved. For a single visit and some on the spot thumbnail sketches (or annotated photo prints) and giving advice on colour schemes, building materials, design faults needing correction, window bars needing replacement, the resiting of the television aerial, pipes and cables and general landscape problems the fee should not be too costly. It must be emphasized, however, that if more serious structural faults are involved these must take priority over redecoration.

Again, to find a builder, ask friends to recommend one, look in Yellow Pages or make a note of a building firm's board next time you are passing a house where you like the look of the restoration work being undertaken. Regional branches of the National Federation of Building Trades Employers and the Federation of Master Builders can sometimes recommend local builders and carpenters who specialize in restoration and build-on projects. There are also a few specialist conversion firms which can offer an all-in package deal (including architect's drawings and planning permission) and are skilled at blending old and new.

ABOVE *Two terraced houses of the same age, but notice the difference careful restoration has made.*

One of the main arguments put forward against the restoration and preservation of the character of an old house is the cost involved. Certainly it is cheaper and possibly less trouble to obtain factory made equivalents of items such as bricks, railings, window frames and tiles. But the bonus of the hand-made bespoke article is that not only does it increase the cash and historic value of your home, you can also learn about some fascinating crafts and techniques. Who knows? – you may later wish to take up some of them yourself! You can actually save money on replacement if you hunt round demolition yards for authentic windows, doors, roof tiles and mouldings. There are lots of houses being demolished; find out where the materials go. Ask enough questions and you are sure to find at least one source of supply.

Another helpful organization to advise on specialists in crafts such as thatching, stone masonry and wood carving is the Council for Small Industries in Rural Areas (CoSIRA). It has branches in most parts of the country (excluding Wales and Scotland).

Index

Acknowledgments

The publishers would like to thank the following individuals and
organisations for their kind permission to reproduce the photographs
in this book:

Behr Produktion 15 below, 46–47, 58–59 above; Berger 10, 22, 24
below right, 130; Michael Boys 63; Tony Byers 40 below; Camera
Press Ltd. 4–5; R. Clifford 16, 28 below, 55 left; Michael Crockett
54, 74–75, 106; The Designers Guild 28 above, 136; Electricity Council
40 above; Leo Ferrante 18 above, 29 above, 32–33 above, 88, 92, 95;
Melvin Grey 83; Clive Helm 44–45; International Magazine Service
(Uggla) 126–127; Sam Lambert 87; Marie-Claire 134; Bill Mason 56
centre, 110; Bob Matheson 43; Bill McLaughlin 11, 24 above left,
56 above, 66 right and left, 74, 76–77 below, 94, 103 above, 111, 117,
133, 146, 150–151, 151 left, above right and below right; Brian Morris
49 above, 56 below, 128 below; Nairn Information Bureau 57 left;
The Picture Library 52, 119, (Michael Joseph) 61, (R. Stowell) 29
below; Spike Powell 78; John Rigby 154; Sanderson Wallpapers &
Fabrics 75, 114; Lee Story 6–7, 30–31 below, 34–35 above, 36, 37,
41, 81, 102–103, 104–105, 147; Jessica Strang 51 above, 62 below,
143, 152, 153; Sungravure 93, 107, 120; Syndication International Ltd.
15 above, 18 below, 26 above, centre and below, 32–33 below,
52–53, 55 right, 76–77 above, 77 right, 82, 104, 121, 142; Elizabeth
Whiting 12 above and below, 14, 17, 19 above and below, 20, 23, 24
above right and below left, 25 above and below, 27, 30–31 above,
34–35 below, 39 above, 47, 48 centre, 51 below, 58–59 below, 60, 64,
65, 67, 68, 69, 84, 90–91, 96, 101, 109, 112–113, 118–119, 123, 128
above, 135, 137, (Tim Street-Porter) 48 below, 116–117, (Tubby) 48
above, 62 above; ZEFA 122, (Jahreszeiten Verlag) 39 below.

The publishers are grateful to the following for the loan of items used
in photography: cork flooring: Wicanders; Cushions: Designer's
Guild; Furniture: Conran; Habitat; Neal Street Shop; Ryman Interiors;
Lighting: Christopher Wray's Lighting Emporium; The London
Lighting Co. Tiles: Tilemart.

Text by:
Barbara Chandler: 21–35, 44–49, 55–63, 66–71, 81–84, 89–96,
101–108, 122–123, 126–131

Tony Byers: 36–41; Carolyn Chapman: 140–154; Emmy Hettener:
109–121, 124–125, 132–139; Jose Manser: 8–20, 42–43, 50–54,
64–65; Doug Marshall: 72–80, 85–88, 97–100.